Reading ACROSS Cultures

TEACHING LITERATURE IN A DIVERSE SOCIETY

EDITED BY

Theresa Rogers and Anna O. Soter

Foreword by Rudine Sims Bishop

Teachers College
Columbia University
New York and London

National Council of
Teachers of English
Urbana, Illinois

Published simultaneously by Teachers College Press, 1234 Amsterdam Avenue, New York, NY 10027 and the National Council of Teachers of English

Library of Congress Cataloging-in-Publication Data

Reading across cultures : teaching literature in a diverse society /
    edited by Theresa Rogers and Anna O. Soter.
        p.   cm.—(Language and literacy series)
    Includes bibliographical references and indexes.
    ISBN 0-8077-3552-3 (cloth : alk. paper).—ISBN 0-8077-3551-5
(pbk. : alk. paper)
        1. Literature—Study and teaching—United States.   2. Pluralism
(Social sciences) in literature—United States.   I. Rogers,
Theresa.   II. Soter, Anna O., 1946-   .   III. Series: Language and
literacy series (New York, N.Y.)
    LB1576.R396   1997
    808'.0071—dc20   96-32594

ISBN 0–8077–3551–5 (paper)
ISBN 0–8077–3552–3 (cloth)
NCTE Stock No. 50284

Printed on acid-free paper
Manufactured in the United States of America

04 03 02 01 00 99 98 97   8 7 6 5 4 3 2 1

(Continued)

Contents

PART II
Authors, Teachers, and Texts

Foreword

To sit and dream, to sit and read,
To sit and learn about the world
Outside our world of here and now—
Our problem world—
To dream of vast horizons of the soul
Through dreams made whole,
All you who are dreamers too,
Help me to make
Our world anew.
I reach out my dreams to you.
—Langston Hughes, "To You"

MUCH OF THE PROFESSIONAL writing on the teaching of literature in elementary and secondary schools has, in recent years, focused on reader-response theory and on multiculturalism in literature for children and young adults. Reader-response theory has provided the foundation for instructional approaches that emphasize the role of readers in constructing meanings and interpretations of texts, while multiculturalism has called for an expanded repertoire of authentic literary works to reflect the cultural diversity that characterizes American and global society. READING ACROSS CULTURES stands at the confluence of reader-response theory and multicultural literature or cultural studies, moving both in a new direction.

The professional writing on the role of multicultural literature in classrooms has primarily focused on the need to make visible underrepresented groups and to counter negative images and stereotypes. The main educational benefit of these strategies for readers who are members of such groups has been presumed to be that such literature would, by legitimating their images, their heritage, and their cultural experiences, provide opportunities for building self-esteem. This would in turn lead to improved scholastic achievement, particularly in regard to written literacy. For readers who are members of dominant groups, the assumption has been that becoming acquainted with and finding their own connections to literature about people from nondominant groups would help them to value all peoples, accept differences as a natural aspect of human societies, and even celebrate cultural pluralism as a desirable feature of the world in which they live. Less attention has been paid to the specific kinds of instructional strategies that might accomplish these ends, to the effects on response of the sociocultural identities that readers assume, and to the influence on those responses of the social and cultural environments in which readings take place.

READING ACROSS CULTURES helps to fill a gap by presenting stories of actual classrooms and the ways that teachers and students in those classrooms, from third grade to college, make and take meanings from a variety of texts. In so doing it takes us well beyond being satisfied with merely exposing readers to a variety of texts. It reminds us that the goal of multicultural education, and the role of literature within that context, is ultimately to help "to make our world anew," to transform society into one in which social justice and equity prevail, and that reaching that goal will require schooling in which teachers and students are able to confront and critique some of the thorny issues and -isms (such as racism and sexism) that are at the root of past and continuing inequities. READING ACROSS CULTURES shows how literature, through the power of its artistry, can be a catalyst for engaging students in critical discussions and for eliciting multiple perspectives and multiple voices in pursuit of understanding. It also reminds us that among those multiple voices are voices of resistance. Real change will not, therefore, be easy, nor will it come solely as a result of reading and responding to literature, which is, after all, an art form, not an instrument of indoctrination. Nor can literature, even with all its potential artistic power, be expected to carry the major responsibility for transforming the world.

In the classrooms portrayed in the first part of this volume, emphasis is mainly on the readers, the teachers, and the texts. They are not, however, the only players in the game of reading and interpreting literature, particularly cross-cultural texts. One of the main issues in the criticism of so-called multicultural literature, especially literature for children and young adults, has been the extent to which an author's sociocultural background influences or interferes with the ability to create literature about characters who are members of a different social group, particularly when the author is a member of a dominant group writing about those who are not. In READING ACROSS CULTURES the author is included in the conversation, as is the critic concerned with patterns in the representations of social groups or with critical interpretations of literature across cultures and the teacher educator aware that his or her instructional strategies will have an effect across generations of readers. In short, Theresa Rogers and Anna Soter and the other authors in this collection take on the complexities of reading, writing, interpreting, and critiquing literature in the context of both culturally diverse and more nearly monocultural classrooms as well as the pluralistic larger society. In so doing they clarify issues and indicate some possible steps toward resolution of some of those issues.

Teachers, teacher educators, and researchers with an interest in cultural studies, multicultural literature, and reader-response theory will find that READING ACROSS CULTURES can be a guide through some of the swiftly flowing waters of contemporary literary theory and criticism. It does not simplify the issues, because they cannot be simplified, but with its own set of multiple perspectives and diverse voices, it helps to clarify our vision and point the way forward toward a better understanding of the role that reading literature can (and cannot) play in helping to transform schools and society, the ways that reading, writing, discussing, teaching, and critiquing literature can help "to make our world anew."

Rudine Sims Bishop
Ohio State University

Acknowledgments

WE ARE INDEBTED to many people for helping us to develop this book from the seed of an idea to published form. We would like to thank the chapter authors for keeping faith and for contributing such fine work within some very tight deadlines, especially toward the end. We are also grateful to Rudine Sims Bishop for agreeing to open this book with her graceful prose and thoughtful insights into the issues raised. We also would like to thank Carol Collins, Sarah Biondello, Karen Osborne, and Lyn Grossman at Teachers College Press for all their helpful advice and careful editing along the way, as well as the anonymous reviewers who have helped to make this a more coherent volume. Finally, a special thanks to our much-loved husbands and sons (Dan, Rob, Ben, Shaun, and Christopher) for their patience and support during this long process.

Introduction

THERESA ROGERS AND ANNA O. SOTER

IF WE THINK of literary criticism and the teaching of literature as having
its own narrative, we might say that there has been a turn in that story
toward the social, cultural, and political contexts of literary creation and
reception. This narrative, which is more recursive than linear in nature,
has taken us from the author/audience relationship (e.g., Aristotle), to
the authors themselves (e.g., the romantics), to the text and to language
itself (e.g., structuralists and New Critics), and back to readers and contexts, as well as to the impossibility of intention and determinacy of
meaning (poststructuralism, including reader-response theory). It is a
narrative that requires an "ever necessary retelling" (Jauss, 1982) as new
readers with new expectations and in new contexts approach a text (Rabinowitz, 1989).

This recent narrative turn, most notably for elementary and secondary classrooms, emphasizes both the need for multicultural literature and
(paradoxically) the limitations of reader-response theories (as they are
currently constituted) to speak to the actual responses of diverse readers.
Reader-response theory has been the first major influence on the teaching
of literature in schools since New Criticism, although new critical or traditional approaches still hold sway in many, and perhaps most, classrooms. However, as reader-response criticism begins to make itself felt in
schools, it has already been through years of scrutiny and criticism, both
as a theory and in terms of its pedagogical value.

As a theoretical perspective, reader-response criticism has not adequately addressed either the role of the author and the author's social
and cultural influences (cf. Rabinowitz, 1987) or the relationship between
literary and other cultural texts (cf. Ryan, 1989; Willinsky, 1991). As instructional practices, response-oriented approaches often fail to encom-

pass the social complexity of classroom communities with students of varying backgrounds, abilities, and experiences (cf. Eagleton, 1983) and the possibilities for critical inquiry into literacy practices themselves, as well as the discourses surrounding those practices (cf. Luke & Baker, 1991).

Cultural studies, on the other hand, offer some new perspectives on literary response for teachers. As Berlin and Vivion (1992) argue, "English studies can no longer treat literary texts as purely aesthetic documents transcending the realms of the political and historical, and rhetorical texts as mere transcripts of empirical and rational truths" (p. vii). This narrative turn toward cultural response helps us to see that the literary canon itself is a social construction (cf. Tompkins, 1985), that literary texts are complex intertextual weavings that refer to other literary and nonliterary texts (Bakhtin, 1986; Barthes, 1977), and that authors themselves, as well as readers, are at least partly constructed by their own social, political, and cultural contexts.

Many of us who have contributed to this volume were initially influenced by reader-response or audience-oriented critical perspectives that have since been informed by one or more areas of cultural studies, such as critical pedagogy, feminist studies, Black studies, postcolonial criticism, and Marxian criticism. At the same time, we are cautious about seeing literature as purely political documents. Rather, it is the power of literature as artistic as well as cultural texts that persuades us and our students to be moved enough to look deeply at both the aesthetic and cultural contributions they make and to look outward from the works to their social meanings. As Parini (1995) recently argued, "knowing how much or how little emphasis to put on ideology in interpretation strikes me as the beginning of wisdom" (p. A52). Since we are educators rather than critics, we are constantly mindful of the very real consequences of our theoretical and practical approaches to teaching, and so we must weigh any extreme positions against the strengths and needs of the students we teach.

The idea of cultural response as a theoretical frame also raises many other important questions and issues when teaching literature to children and young adults: What do we mean by culture? Why and how do we teach literature from a cultural (and multicultural) perspective? What is the nature of response in actual interpretive communities? Why, and in what ways, do readers resist cultural texts and readings? What is the role of the author in creating literature and how is the author configured in cultural readings? These issues are themes that run through this volume and are answered in various ways across various contexts: the first half of the book focuses on actual classroom stories of reading from grade 3 through college, and the second half on the role of the literature itself, on authors, and on teachers, when we read literature within and across cultures.

In the early chapters of this book, "culture" often refers to race and to ethnicity, as well as to related issues of class and gender, as they are raised in classroom conversations. Since these are stories of American— mostly urban—classrooms, race is often seen in terms of African American or Latino/a as opposed to white, or European American—cultures that Sims Bishop (cf. Cai & Sims Bishop, 1994) has referred to as "parallel." In the second half of the book the notion of the cultural "other" is also extended to religion (e.g., Jewish), to homosexuality in a heterosexist society, and to cultures beyond our borders.

While these are the very real concerns of the teachers and students represented in these pages, we also recognize that some may see this as a theoretically limited definition of "other," particularly in contrast to recent postmodern critiques that plead for an even more inclusive and complex notion of multiculturalism (cf. Keating, 1995; Schwartz, 1995). These critiques point out that the idea of race, gender, and class, of culture, and of the "other" are themselves, to some degree, socially constructed and must be contested in an effort to create curricula that "move against and beyond" traditional boundaries (hooks, 1994) and reach toward social critique and social change.

Many of the chapters in this book do, either implicitly or explicitly, address the role of social questioning and critique in the context of literature teaching, as well as the goals of providing more inclusive communities for our students. Until now, there has been more rhetoric about these goals than stories of how inclusion is, or might be, effected. The stories told here provide ways to understand what issues arise when real students resist, "talk back to," or engage with literature and each other; the stories also create some road maps for teachers who struggle with these issues on a daily basis.

For instance, literature classrooms in which teachers face resistance (several examples of which can be found in these pages) are not the bounded, consensus-building communities imagined by some reader-response critics (e.g., Fish, 1980). Readers resist texts and readings, as well as real and implied authors, because of their cultural memberships and various identity positions: as female, as African American, as homosexual, as white students who resist challenges to their own privilege, or as Americans who cannot grasp the cultural meanings and values in stories of other countries. These communities, then, become sites of struggle

(Eagleton, 1983) that we must navigate with a deeper understanding of culture and of difference, and of the way we create, and the consequences of, our cultural interpretive practices.

PART I: CLASSROOM STORIES

Chapter 1, "Negotiating the Meaning of Difference: Talking Back to Multicultural Literature," by Patricia E. Enciso, describes a fourth- and fifth-grade classroom in which the students "talked back" to the novel *Maniac McGee*, by Jerry Spinelli, as they constructed their own social positions for themselves and others. Enciso argues that cultural metaphors, mappings, and dehistoricizing strategies in the novel challenged the students to renegotiate the meaning of difference in the text and among themselves. Enciso also points out that allowing these cultural conversations into our literature classrooms provides a space for all children to negotiate difference, not just those children whose cultural references and perspectives are already understood and valued.

In Chapter 2, "Re-Visioning Reading and Teaching Literature Through the Lens of Narrative Theory," William McGinley and colleagues, providing examples from two very different upper elementary classrooms, remind us that stories are a means to personal and social explorations and reflections—that they provide life-informing and life-transforming possibilities. Drawing on narrative theory, they argue that stories endow experience with meaning, provide culturally shaped ways of organizing that experience, and reflect prevailing theories about the "possible lives" and "possible selves" in our culture. They also point out that we still know very little about how children actually draw on these life-informing possibilities of narrative—or of the nature of the personal and social understandings that children acquire as they transact with stories in classrooms.

In Chapter 3, "Students' Resistance to Engagement with Multicultural Literature," Richard Beach explores the many forms of resistance that students adopt when their values are challenged—stances that reflect their own privileged perspectives as well as resentment toward alternative versions of reality presented in multicultural literature. In a study of high school students' responses in a variety of settings, Beach found that some students in largely white suburban high schools adopted stances of white privilege that reflected an individual ideological perspective on portrayals of racism in American literature. In contrast, students who were more engaged with multicultural literature were more likely to perceive racism as an institutional phenomenon—a stance that was based on personal experiences.

In Chapter 4, "No Imagined Peaceful Place: A Story of Community, Texts, and Cultural Conversations in One Urban High School English Classroom," Theresa Rogers describes a classroom in which the teacher struggled to create a community in which many, sometimes competing, voices could be heard. By looking at the role of community, intertextuality, and cultural conversations in this classroom, she illustrates the ways in which one teacher moved away from a focus on authoritative interpretations of canonical texts toward inquiry into a wide range of texts as personal, social, cultural, and historically placed constructions. Rogers argues that this approach to teaching literature is not sanctioned by the larger cultural norms of high schools in the United States, since few teachers see issues of race, class, and gender, or literacy practices themselves, as open to critical inquiry in the classroom.

In Chapter 5, "Multiplicity and Difference in Literary Inquiry: Toward a Conceptual Framework for Reader-Centered Cultural Criticism," Mary Beth Hines draws on various approaches to teaching literature at the middle, high school, and college levels to explore a framework for a reader-centered cultural criticism. Noting that we have failed to create communities, or "homespaces," for nonmainstream and oppositional students in schools in general, as well as English classrooms in particular, she suggests that we develop conceptual frameworks for literary inquiry that invite students to read "selves, texts, and worlds" in communities that foster multiplicity of meaning, and an interrogation of difference and diversity.

PART II: AUTHORS, TEACHERS, AND TEXTS

The second half of the book focuses on issues related to the teachers, authors, and literature that are at the center of the struggle to create new ways of reading within and across cultures in elementary, secondary, and college classrooms. One issue that is raised is the role of the author in a time when the focus has shifted toward a critical view of literature in our schools. There is a tension in how we understand the role of the author in this new context that was not present when canonical literature was at the center of the curriculum; that is, when we introduce literature that is meant to "authentically" represent the "other" (or ourselves as the other), the role of the author is rescrutinized. We face a tension between the author as creative individual responsible to craft or muse, and the author as having a social responsibility, as described by the African writer Chinua Achebe:

> The writer cannot be excused from the task of re-education and regeneration that must be done. In fact he should march right in front. . . . I for one would not want to be excused. I would be quite satisfied if my novels . . . did no more than teach my readers that their past—with all its imperfections—was no one long night of savagery from which the first Europeans acting on God's behalf delivered them.

Achebe refers to his writings as perhaps "applied" as opposed to "pure," indicating a role for literature as educative as well as aesthetic. When dealing with literature from other cultures, then, teachers are faced with aesthetic as well as cultural differences: Can we use the same literary critical practices with literature that is not only from a different cultural but also from a different aesthetic tradition?

Finally, as several of the chapters in this volume illustrate, the role of teachers is also an issue when dealing with cultural as well as aesthetic readings of literature. Teachers may need to reconceptualize their own understandings of literature as historically and culturally placed and literature classrooms as "cultural sites"—places of interrogation, struggle, and social questioning and critique.

Behind all of our discussions of what we would like to see happen with respect to the teaching of literature from a multicultural perspective is the issue of how teachers are educated to read and teach from such a perspective. In Chapter 6, "Exploring Multicultural Literature as Cultural Production," Arlette Ingram Willis addresses this issue directly as she adopts the frame of critical literacy for "improving the current generic approaches to literacy training of preservice teachers." Through "sagacious use of multicultural literature," Willis argues, we can enable preservice teachers to become critical thinkers about the "choices they make when teaching literacy." Using herself and her own teaching as a model, Willis shows how we can position ourselves, identify who we are relative to our goals in our teaching of literature, and, through articulating our own values, become correspondingly aware of the values that permeate all literacy instruction.

In Chapter 7, "Reflections on Cultural Diversity in Literature and in the Classroom," Laura E. Desai points out that when looking at the role of culture in a reader's response, we must first consider the multiple communities that frame our social, cultural, and political context, and then we can begin to consider the role that a teacher and the classroom play in this process. She attempts to answer two questions: How can responses be ethically negotiated among the multiplicity of voices in a classroom community? How is the teacher to bridge these voices? Based on her experiences in an urban fourth-grade classroom, Desai shares her conversations with the teacher about dealing with uncomfortable issues raised by the multicultural literature and describes their collaborative search for an "ethics of response in a society framed by multiple communities."

In Chapter 8, "Out of the Closet and onto the Bookshelves: Images of Gays and Lesbians in Young Adult Literature," Mari M. McLean extends the notion of "other" to those who, as she observes, are "conspicuously absent" in multicultural educational materials. Arguing that gays and lesbians are ignored in the selection of groups represented by the descriptive use of the term "multicultural," McLean presents a case for widening that term by drawing on Boas's definition of culture. She also argues that, like members of other cultural groups, members of the gay and lesbian community can identify a history, cultural artifacts, and notable individuals who have made significant contributions. McLean suggests that as young adults begin to define themselves in terms of personal and social identity, positive images in gay and lesbian literature can provide "mirrors" for the "minority youth's culture and experience." She focuses on the need of many adolescents for acceptance by their peers, and specifically on the challenges that gay and lesbian young adults face as they seek validation of their experiences and perspectives.

The question of who should write multicultural books for children is at the center of Chapter 9, "Reader-Response Theory and the Politics of Multicultural Literature." Mingshui Cai argues that embedded in this question are many complicated issues that range from whether or not outsiders can write authentically about the attitudes and experiences of those in another culture; to the role of the author's own cultural identity in his or her aesthetic creation; to relationships between imagination and experience; to authors' social responsibilities; to tensions between author/reader relationships; and to tensions between principles of aesthetic freedom and reader responsibilities. Using real author/implied author relationships as a frame for discussing the foregoing issues, Cai illustrates how complex and politically and aesthetically sensitive these issues are.

In Chapter 10, "Reading Literature of Other Cultures: Some Issues in Critical Interpretation," Anna O. Soter acknowledges that literature has always had the power to move us, to reach us through its natural connection with the worlds of our imagination. At the same time, she presents us with challenges teachers face when students resist literature that represents other cultures that, in turn, represent other value systems. As students respond to content that, at times, presents aesthetic, ethical, and moral values that may be repugnant to them, Soter examines how teachers can use initial connections as the ground for subsequent interpretive criticism and aesthetic appreciation. To do this teachers can create "spaces" that allow student readers to become accustomed to the nuances and rhythms of these different aesthetic models so that they can move from "aesthetic restriction" to "aesthetic distance." The greatest challenge, she suggests, is that when using literature representative of other cultures, "the teacher, as often as his or her students, must be prepared to not know, to learn how to experience the unknown afresh."

With this book, we hope to move beyond simple assumptions about the value of multicultural literature and the ways readers respond to that literature. READING ACROSS CULTURES involves exploring who we are, participating in the lives of others, negotiating social relationships, and critiquing our cultural assumptions about difference. This process does not occur without struggle and resistance, and there are no operating instructions for teachers who choose to create classroom communities with spaces for sustained dialogue about literature and culture. Instead, we offer you these stories and insights from a range of students, teachers, and classrooms in order to continue the conversation about literature, culture, and teaching.

REFERENCES

Bakhtin, M. M. (1986). *Speech genres and other late essays* (V. W. McGee, Trans.). Austin: University of Texas Press.

Barthes, R. (1977). *Image-Music-Text* (S. Heath, Trans.). New York: Hill & Wang.

Berlin, J. A., & Vivion, M. J. (1992). *Cultural studies in the English classroom.* Portsmouth, NH: Boynton/Cook, Heinemann.

Cai, M., & Sims Bishop, R. (1994). Multicultural literature for children: Towards a clarification of the concept. In A. H. Dyson & C. Genishi (Eds.), *The need for story: Cultural diversity in classroom and community* (pp. 57–71). Urbana, IL: National Council of Teachers of English.

Eagleton, T. (1983). *Literary theory: An introduction.* Minneapolis: University of Minnesota Press.

Fish, S. (1980). *Is there a text in this class: The authority of interpretive communities.* Cambridge, MA: Harvard University Press.

Jauss, H. -R. (1982). *Toward an aesthetic of reception.* Minneapolis: University of Minnesota Press.

hooks, b. (1994). *Teaching to transgress: Education and the practice of freedom.* New York: Routledge.

Keating, A. (1995). Interrogating "whiteness": (De)constructing "race." *College English, 57,* 901–918.

Luke, A., & Baker, C. (1991). Toward a critical sociology of reading pedagogy: An introduction. In C. Baker & A. Luke (Eds.), *Toward a critical sociology of reading pedagogy* (pp. xi–xxi). Philadelphia: Johns Benjamin.

Parini, J. (1995, November 17). Point of view. *Chronicle of Higher Education*, p. A52.

Rabinowitz, P. (1987). *Before reading: Narrative conventions and the politics of interpretation*. Ithaca, NY: Cornell University Press.

Rabinowitz, P. (1989). Whirl without end: Audience-oriented criticism. In G. D. Atkins & L. Morrow (Eds.), *Contemporary literary theory* (pp. 81–100). Amherst: University of Massachusetts Press.

Ryan, M. (1989). Political criticism. In G. D. Atkins & L. Morrow (Eds.), *Contemporary literary theory* (pp. 200–213). Amherst: University of Massachusetts Press.

Schwartz, E. (1995). Crossing borders/Shifting paradigms: Multiculturalism and children's literature. *Harvard Educational Review, 65*(4), 634–650.

Tompkins, J. (1985). *Sensational designs: The cultural work of American fiction, 1790–1860*. New York: Oxford University Press.

Willinsky, J. (1991). *The triumph of literature/The fate of literacy: English in the secondary school curriculum*. New York: Teachers College Press.

PART I

Classroom Stories

CHAPTER 1

Negotiating the Meaning of Difference

Talking Back to Multicultural Literature

PATRICIA E. ENCISO

Talking back meant speaking as an equal to an authority figure. It meant daring to disagree and sometimes it just meant having an opinion.

—*bell hooks*, Talking Back

IN HER REFLECTIONS on her experiences as a child among adults in her southern black community, bell hooks states that "to speak . . . when one was not spoken to was a courageous act—an act of risking and daring" (p. 5). She is concerned with the silencing that marked her childhood and the struggles she has engaged in to be heard as an African American feminist and activist. Her purposes for understanding what it means to speak one's mind in the face of domination may seem far removed from the conversations children and teachers have about literature. However, like hooks, children encounter versions of the world in literature that are new or in conflict with constructions of themselves and others. They must, as Dyson suggests (1993a, 1993b), act as social negotiators with this new material, creating meaning about themselves and others while drawing on other cultural materials (equally infused with meaning) from home, peers, school, and other public spheres.

As children read about racial, ethnic, and class differences in literature, they encounter metaphors of and meanings about difference; these new metaphors and meanings must be negotiated by children as they struggle to understand how they will see themselves, their peers, and their teacher in light of the literature's new possibilities. As Dyson (1993a) outlines:

Although the teacher governs the official school world, in which children must be students, the children are also members of an unofficial peer world, formed in response to the constraints and regulations of the official world, and they are members as well of their sociocultural communities, which may reform in the classroom amidst networks of peers [citations omitted]. (p. 5)

In multiple social arenas within the classroom, children "talk back" to the materials presented to them as they simultaneously create social positions and definitions for themselves and others. This dynamic operates as much around any classroom assignment as it does around reading and responding to multicultural literature. However, multicultural literature raises questions about how we construct differences and how we have enacted and continue to enact social practices related to difference. In this chapter, I describe and analyze constructions of difference in a current, popular piece of multicultural literature,[1] *Maniac Magee* (Spinelli, 1990). I also describe the ways a group of fourth- and fifth-grade children negotiated authoritative constructions and meanings of difference— about themselves, their peers, and myself—while they read and responded to this story. As we read and discussed *Maniac Magee*, it was apparent that popular culture was often their primary vehicle for claiming and explaining differences about themselves and others. Thus I will consider ways in which popular culture was used to both control and "talk back" to multiple constructions of difference within the intersecting spheres of the children's definitions of themselves and one another in and out of the classroom.

RUNNING INTO DIFFERENCES IN *MANIAC MAGEE*

The opening chapter of *Maniac Magee* offers a cryptic, puzzling introduction to the legend that has grown up around a young boy after his year of running in and out of the segregated town of Two Mills End. The narrative soon turns to a recounting of the events that have formed his legendary status. Jeffrey Lionel Magee, a 12-year-old Anglo boy, has run away from his foster home into the East and West sides of Two Mills End, performing one fantastic feat after another. He appears to be an indomitable, open-hearted sort of kid, whose fame has spread along with his new name, "Maniac."

Maniac Magee's new world is racially divided, although Maniac himself is indifferent to these divisions during the first part of the story when he runs at will from one end of town to the other. The East and West sides of Two Mills End are peopled with characters who are kind and generous, playful and spirited, hardworking and hopeful. Some are also angry and bigoted, in particular Mars Bar, the African American male whose cool pose and tough demeanor set him up as Maniac's antagonist. Also in conflict with Maniac is John McNab, the leader of a white suprem-acist group called the Cobras, who lives with his raunchy father in a home dedicated to winning the race war. More commonly, Maniac finds people, black and white, who recognize racial differences but who just get on with life and who seem to be silent or ignorant about how and why racial prejudices are developed, enacted, and upheld. Regardless of all indicators of racial segregation, indifference, or intolerance, Jeffrey Lionel "Maniac" Magee steadfastly ignores the communities' accepted norms of attitude and interaction. Spinelli (1990) writes, "Maniac Magee was blind. Sort of. . . . He could see things, but he couldn't see what they meant" (p. 57).

Through Maniac's actions and the narrator's perspective, readers learn that prejudice takes many forms and has seeds that may be planted and fertilized or uprooted and replaced. Maniac's innocence and open-ness to all people instruct us that racial divisions may be reconciled through mutual understanding. Indeed, in the narrator's view, Maniac's transparent vision and purity of intention not only fosters but also achieves racial harmony:

"And sometimes the girl holding one end of the rope is from the West side of Hector [Street], and the girl on the other end is from the East side; and if you're looking for Maniac Magee's legacy, or monument, that's as good as any" (p. 2).

This story, which addresses and reconciles racial differences, was read and discussed by 16 fourth and fifth graders and myself—all of us bringing our own racial, ethnic, gender, class, political, intellectual, and linguistic differences to our reading. We met, in two groups, several days a week for four weeks at the end of the 1992 schoolyear. The groups were heterogeneously mixed, based on the teacher's determination of diversity of ability, gender, ethnicity, and race. My intention with the children was to find out how they made sense of the themes, characters, and plot of the story. Although we had our personal histories and perceptions of dif-ference from which to build interpretations and voice opinions, we had to place these in relation to one another, the authority of the book, the author, and the meanings of difference inscribed in the story (Belsey, 1980). In other words, the official world of the classroom and its materials had to be socially negotiated through the children's unofficial peer world as we not only read the story but also positioned ourselves and one an-other in relation to it. We had to find ways to "talk back," to make a place for ourselves alongside or apart from Maniac Magee and company.

From the beginning of our meetings, the official world of schooling was cause for "talking back." The book itself held authority for the children insofar as it was selected by me, an outsider/adult, and was the focus of our discussions and activities. We did not engage in an open discussion about my choice of this book, nor did we talk at any length about my role in their classroom. Thus the representations of race relations in the literature could be seen by the children to represent my perspectives. My authority as an adult, then, was interwoven with my choice of our reading material. To talk back to the book would be, in many respects, to talk back to me.

The authority of the book and my association with it was further elevated by the Newbery gold emblem on the front cover. Implied in the award and in its selection as a classroom set is the teacher's recognition of a "good book" that is deemed useful and of interest to children. Cathy, who enjoyed reading but who was often excluded by other girls during group writing and reading activities, questioned teachers' ways of elevating books and reading: "How come most teachers, most adults like it when kids read? It's like if someone says they like to read they say, 'Oh. You're such a good little girl or boy'?" Through her question she has talked back to a hidden curriculum of values and valuing that carries a suspect reward for compliance with the adult world's view of literacy for children (Stuckey, 1991).

A third layer of authority is related to the book as an art form that uses metaphor, characterization, setting, narrative perspective, and genre to construct representations and meanings of difference. Belsey (1980) and others have argued, from Althusserian theory, that literature is, in fact, an "ideological apparatus" (Belsey, 1980, p. 56), meaning that it is "a *system* of representations (discourses, images, myths) concerning the real relations in which people live" (p. 57). This does not mean that literature is simply propaganda or that it is opaque to any critical analysis of those representations. However, the majority of children's literature constructs characters as "consistent subjects who are the origin of meaning, knowledge and action" (p. 67); that is, the characters appear to be "free agents," speaking and acting for themselves, outside of the complex sociopolitical contexts in which they were imagined. Thus it is difficult to recognize the ways language operates as an ideological and identifying force in the making of "their" meaning. Belsey suggests that this literature, "classic realist fiction," of which *Maniac Magee* is representative, places the reader as a participant in the story, "unfettered" by an awareness of the power of language to form ideologies and representations about "others" that are part of the story and part of the reader's life.

While these metaphors and meanings are not necessarily consciously constructed by authors, they are drawn from the author's experience of living as a racialized person in a racialized society. Spinelli (1991) wrote, in his Newbery acceptance speech, of Niki Hollie, a black childhood friend who had been raised in an orphanage and who, like Maniac, became a tireless runner. Unlike Maniac, however, the impetus for Hollie's running was an incident at the local swimming pool, from which he had been shut out because of his race. Spinelli writes that Hollie's story was "the first patch in the quiltwork that became *Maniac Magee*" (p. 430).[2] He recalls that in contrast, for him, "There were the summer afternoons on the Elmwood Park basketball court, myself the only white skin among fifteen or twenty blacks. I remember a small, quiet feeling of gratitude, of pride of admittance. There was no turnstile for me" (p. 430). Thus Spinelli is situated as a European American writer in a racialized society.

Toni Morrison, writing about nineteenth-century authors and their work, makes a point which is pertinent to today's writers for children. She explains in *Playing in the Dark: Whiteness and the Literary Imagination* (1992):

> Responding to culture—clarifying, explicating, valorizing, translating, transforming, criticizing—is what artists everywhere do. Whatever their personal and formally political responses to the inherent contradiction of a free republic deeply committed to slavery, nineteenth century writers were mindful of the presence of black people. (pp. 49–50)

Spinelli is not bound to the kind of selective discourse about African Americans that belied white writers' views and opinions more than 100 years ago. He is, however, part of a culture that continues to create and sustain codes and meanings that become linguistic shortcuts for representing and, in turn, interpreting racial differences. Morrison outlines a number of these linguistic moves in her analysis of white writers' use of what she refers to as "the Africanist presence" in American literature. Among these codes are two, in particular, that are significant to this study because of their power to foreclose dialogue among characters: the *dehumanizing metaphor* and the *dehistoricizing allegory*. These foreclosures, I will argue, became the subject of the students' efforts to position themselves in relation to the hegemonic representations of difference found in the voices of the author/narrator and characters, and in the ideologies about difference expressed by their classmates. Talking back meant challenging these foreclosures and creating and negotiating transformative definitions of difference that could sustain further dialogue.

In the rest of this chapter, I first consider the linguistic strategies that construct the Africanist character through *metaphor*; in relation to this literary construct of difference, I describe and analyze the ways children negotiated the meaning of difference in the text and among themselves. Then I turn to the linguistic strategy, which Morrison calls the *dehistorizing allegory,* whereby "history, as a process of becoming, is excluded from the literary encounter" (p. 68). In this study, Morrison's term refers to Spinelli's use of a timeless, larger-than-life, legend genre to situate and amend race relations. Again, I relate this authorial choice to children's interpretations and social negotiations of difference.

MEETING MARS BAR AND MANIAC: CONSTRUCTING DIFFERENCE THROUGH METAPHOR AND MAPPING

Morrison refers to the ways social and historical differences—such as those created through racial categories—can be transformed, through metaphor, into universal differences such as the differences between humans and nonhumans (p. 69). Africanist characters may become pseudo-human, for example, and their speech may be equated with animal sounds so that the possibility of dialogue is obliterated. As I read Morrison's analysis, it is not only the strategy of universalizing that is critical; it is the linguistic possibility that is used by writers to preempt black speech so that the protagonist, an Anglo character, can encounter the racialized world without directly questioning or discussing its implications for and with black characters.

This construction of difference through a "universalized difference" is evident in *Maniac Magee.* Although Spinelli's black characters are not entirely speechless, nor unintelligent, their speech is often interrupted or stylized in ways that reproduce both literary traditions and popular cultural stereotypes.

Mars Bar, Spinelli's black male counterpart to Maniac, is characterized by his intimidating presence. He is larger than life, as is Maniac, but his only unquestioned "move" (as opposed to Maniac's innumerable athletic and social accomplishments) is his ability to stop traffic with his glare and swaggering, threatening walk. Spinelli describes him as mean and essentially lacking in insight or self-control. Already, these codes for Mars Bar's character are, metaphorically, akin to the protective territorial moves made by animals. When these images are set in motion in relation to the character of Maniac, Mars Bar becomes even more a metaphor and a reinvention of popular, media-constructed images of black dangerous, inarticulate males.

In an early episode in which Maniac first meets Mars Bar in the East End, Maniac asks directions. Instead of giving an answer, Mars Bar cyni-

cally offers Maniac a bite of his trademark candy bar. To everyone's as-
tonishment, Maniac accepts the offer. Spinelli writes:

> Maniac shrugged, took the Mars Bar, bit off a chunk, and handed it back.
> "Thanks."
>   Dead silence along the street. The kid had done the unthinkable, he had
> chomped on one of Mars's own bars. Not only that, but white kids just didn't
> put their mouths where black kids had had theirs, be it soda bottles, spoons
> or candy bars. And the kid hadn't even gone for the unused end; he had
> chomped right over Mars Bar's own bite marks.
>   Mars Bar was confused. Who was this kid? What was this kid?
>   As usual, when Mars Bar got confused, he got mad. He thumped Maniac
> in the chest. "You think you bad or somethin'?"
>   Maniac, who was now twice as confused as Mars Bar, blinked. "Huh?"
> . . .
>   Mars Bar jammed his arms downward, stuck out his chin, sneered. "Am
> I bad?" . . .
>   "I don't know. One minute you're yelling at me, the next minute you're
> giving me a bite of your candy bar."
>   The chin jutted out more. "Tell me I'm bad."
>   Maniac didn't answer. Flies stopped buzzing.
>   "I said, tell me I'm bad."
>   Maniac blinked, shrugged, sighed. "It's none of my business. If you're
> bad, let your mother or father tell you." (p. 35)

Maniac's polite befuddlement is counterpointed by Mars Bar's angry
confusion. Neither character is able to understand the other's perspective,
but Maniac's blindness is definitely less threatening than Mars Bar's confusion and anger. In this public street scene, they speak past one another
while the narrator provides the subtext for their actions and reactions. It
is the narrator/author, then, who speaks for Mars Bar and his community.
Mars Bar is not humanized—able to tell his own story—until the end of
the book, when we hear his reflective voice in dialogue with Maniac
about fear and family.

The characterizations of Maniac and Mars Bar can be found in earlier
books about black and white relations, particularly in the books Sims
(1982) has described as emphasizing "social conscience," such as *Iggie's
House* (Blume, 1970), that were written primarily during the late 1960s
and early 1970s. These are stories, written by white authors, about the
problem of segregation and the white protagonists' roles in understanding and rectifying the situation. Black characters certainly have a part in
these books but are typically not self-determining. Rather, they are the
beneficiaries of the efforts of white characters, like Maniac, who want to
change society.

Mars Bar's character can also be found, as has been mentioned, in the popular mainstream press and throughout American literature. He is found in news stories about violence in America, in stories of school failure, and in fabricated stories of murder. In the context of our reading of *Maniac Magee*, the children and I had repeatedly seen (at home) the video footage of Rodney King's arrest and subsequent beating as it was broadcast on the evening news. More recently, a white woman in South Carolina—Susan Smith—had blamed a black man for kidnapping the children she had murdered. The local police and the national and international news media accepted and pursued her story as if it were true. In both of these media events, the black male's behavior was portrayed and interpreted as predatory, out of control, and inhuman.

Maniac also has counterparts in popular media. He is made to be "out-of-this-world," as if he were an E.T., unfamiliar with and utterly innocent of the social constructions of racial difference that permeate everyone else's lives. He does not, then, have to understand his own whiteness or his own implication in the history or future of a racist society. Morrison's (1992) analysis of whiteness in American literature explores the paradox of creating a "new" self, an "innocent" self in relation to "the presence of the racial other" (p. 46). Innocent whiteness deployed in relation to the Africanist character, she argues, is one "strategic use of black characters to define the goals and enhance the qualities of white characters" (p. 52). In my view, the placement and meaning of racial difference in *Maniac Magee* makes possible a divided, ahistorical setting through which Maniac can explore the meaning of race and home, while it simultaneously creates a setting of personal and historical silence for Mars Bar.

As a European American child, Maniac can maintain his innocence as he makes forays into opposing neighborhoods and homes. However, he senses "in some vague way" that the white children, brothers to John McNab, were "spoiling, rotting from the outside in, like a pair of peaches in the sun" (p. 155). His belief is that he must take action to save the children: "Soon, unless he, unless somebody did something, the rot would reach the pit" (p. 155). But by the time Maniac reaches this realization he has already humiliated Mars Bar during a footrace and will humiliate him again when he tricks him, in the hopes of attaining racial harmony, into meeting the McNabs at their white supremacist fortress. Maniac's innocence is understandable, given that he is a child, but it is also a pretext throughout the story for his view of difference, for his misinterpretations of volatile situations, for his "recovery" by the black community. As will be shown, the children with whom I worked regarded Maniac's utter innocence as implausible but within the realm of explanation. In other words, innocence in a racist society does not really make sense, but the pairing of innocence and racism *can be made reasonable* when the alternative discourse—questioning the construction of social and racial categories and their accompanying privileges—is both difficult and disorienting.

Maniac Magee's stature and innocence are further heightened by his legendary status. This construction allows him to be seen (and rationalized) as better than anyone at any sport or game. He unties the knot at Cobbles Corner that had rested, undefeated, for years in the East End's [read African Americans'] favorite drugstore. He even outplays "Hands Down," the glory of the East End's football team. Maniac's legendary persona is new and exciting to readers. However, his ability to be a better insider than the insiders is not unusual in popular, Hollywood portrayals of cross-cultural encounters. In *Dances with Wolves*, for example, Kevin Costner portrays a white soldier who learns the ways of the Lakota people and eventually leads them into battle. The portrayals of white outsiders' moves toward the inside appear to be sympathetic to the lifestyles and sensibilities of the "other." However, such sympathies can also be read as an appropriation of the "other" that inevitably limits and diminishes the self-determining potential of a people. Indeed, in the story of Maniac Magee, this sense of distrust and outrage at being "bettered" is expressed through graffiti and the destruction of precious books by some anonymous members of the East End's black community. It is implied that Mars Bar had a hand in this sign of rejection of Maniac.

Clearly, Mars Bar and Maniac are more than the unique constructions of one author's imagination. They represent the linguistic choices of an author who is situated in a racialized society. The characters' differences in *Maniac Magee* are created through metaphors that construct a humanitarian, heroic white child who is innocent of color and social meanings of race, in contrast to a threatening, status-driven young black man who is situated in a black community, where he is a leader, yet neither self-determining nor accomplished in relation to the white outsider. Such differences create a dualistic, essentialized view of whiteness and blackness, suggesting that black males are "naturally" angry and white males are "naturally" in search of a resolution of racial disharmony. (Mars Bar never expresses a desire for harmony.) As essentialized characters, Maniac and, particularly, Mars Bar are unable to realize the complex selves they might be in a multitude of social settings.

Readers are, likewise, situated in a society that persistently invents and naturalizes dichotomous racial relations. Thus, while reading *Maniac Magee,* young readers may also construct (or reconstruct) meanings of difference, already informed by popular and personal experiences, that will define themselves and others.

As Britzman, Santiago-Valles, Jiménez-Munoz, and Lamash (1993) argue, it is an ongoing project among individuals (teachers, children, parents, school board members, etc.) to "set themselves off from the 'others' that they must then simultaneously and imaginatively construct [citing Anderson, 1983]" (p. 193). In the process of imagining and then claiming these differences as "real," we are also in danger of constructing an ideology or a view of our relationships with one another that reproduces long-standing hierarchies and inequities. In the following section, I describe the ways the children and I borrowed from cultural referents to define others and "make real" the metaphors of difference represented by Maniac and Mars Bar.

CULTURAL MAPPING: PLACING THE MEANING OF DIFFERENCE

The differences between Maniac and Mars Bar, as portrayed in literature and the media, are not new. They are constructed out of the language and society that construct differences in the first place. The question for response to literature studies, however, has to do not only with the social, political, and cultural context in which literature is produced but also the complex, intertextual, identity, and power relations that are part of the reader's interpretation of the literature. I have found the concept of cultural mapping (Britzman, Santiago-Valles, Jiménez-Munoz, & Lamash, 1991; Hall, Critcher, Jefferson, Clarke, & Roberts, 1978) to be useful in analyzing the ways children made Maniac Magee and Mars Bar familiar and, in turn, illustrative of their meanings of difference.

Hall and colleagues (1978) have argued that our interpretations of social experiences are based on cultural maps that provide the framework for constructing the meaning of new events. They state:

> An event only "makes sense" if it can be located within a range of known social and cultural identifications. . . . This bringing of events within the realm of meanings means, in essence, referring unusual and unexpected events to the "maps of meaning" which already form the basis of our cultural knowledge, into which the social world is *already* mapped. (pp. 54–55, quoted in Britzman et al., 1991, p. 90).

Related to Hall and colleagues' concept, Belsey (1980) refers to advertisements and our reading of the signifiers of identity such as names, clothing, hairstyle, and speech patterns that construct a meaning, or "signified." She describes the relationship between the familiar ground we use to make interpretations, the construction of that ground by readers and authors, and the ways such signifiers become apparent in the kinds of characterizations I have just described. She states:

> These advertisements are a source of information about ideology, about semiotics, about the cultural and photographic codes of our society, and to that extent—and only to that extent—they tell us about the world. And yet they possess all the technical properties of realism. Literary realism works in very much the same kind of way. Like the advertisements, it constructs its signifieds out of juxtapositions of signifiers which are intelligible not as direct reflections of an unmediated reality but because we are familiar with the signifying systems from which they are drawn—linguistic, literary, semiotic. This process is apparent in, for instance, the construction of character in the novel. (p. 49–50)

Authors, students, and teachers "[refer] unusual and unexpected events to the 'maps of meaning' which already form the basis of [their] cultural knowledge" (Hall et al., 1978, pp. 54–55). Although we may not intentionally invoke maps of meaning that create racially based exclusions and inequities, we have learned ways to interpret signifiers that refer us to larger maps of meaning about ourselves and others. As will be shown, some of our maps unintentionally, but nevertheless successfully, foreclose more complex, alternative ways of describing and analyzing who we are in relation to others. In the following excerpt, the children and I try to "place" Mars Bar, using the textual signifiers constructed by the author and the maps of meaning we know that make the signifiers familiar and meaningful.

After reading the street scene episode described above, I attempted to engage one small group of children in a consideration of prejudice by comparing Mars Bar to John McNab, the white supremacist bully. However, their focus was on Mars Bar, the tough guy.

KEVIN: I think Mars Bar thinks he's so tough but he's really not 'cause he wasn't really tough 'cause the kids . . . he gave him that glare from his eye 'cause he was just like born or something with it. So he gives them that and they all . . .'cause they never ever took a chance at him. So they don't. He thinks he's tough, but he really isn't. He's just trying to cover it up.

PAT: OK. The people think he's tough, and he thinks he's tough, but actually there's more to him than that. What about McNab? Is he really tough?

THOMAS: (*From the background. He's standing to the side of the round table rather than sitting with us.*) Uh huh.

KEVIN: Yeah. He's the one that doesn't try covering up.

PAT: He doesn't try covering up. OK. Why would Mars Bar cover up, and McNab wouldn't?

MARK: 'Cause it's like some people act really strong when they aren't. And they take up as professionals.

    . . .

PAT: You were saying something too Shaun . . . about how TV shows work. . . . You were saying that you weren't surprised about Amanda stepping in.

SHAUN: 'Cause like. The star like gets beat up by the bully but really at the end someone, like a girl, has to come out an help him 'cause he can't fight for himself or something. So that's why that's what I see on a lot of TV shows.

PAT: Were you glad that Amanda stepped in?

SHAUN: No.

As we interpreted Mars Bar's and Maniac's responses to each other, we had to make sense of what they were doing by placing their actions within an already familiar framework. In this case, the children speculated that Mars Bar was born a tough guy and would become even tougher and "take up as a professional." Their interpretation could make sense to them, given negative mainstream news media images of black males and the pervasiveness of representations of black "professional" tough guys on television sitcoms and sports programs. The signifiers they read—such as "glare" and "jutting out his jaw"—related to the familiar maps of meaning that could explain Mars Bar's persona. We did not consider the fact that Mars Bar is a *constructed* character—constructed as a "universalized" dehumanized metaphor in contrast to the innocent, heroic whiteness of Maniac. By not foregrounding the constructed nature of the character and its multiple signifiers, we, as readers, became participants in the ideology of the text that sees difference in terms of dualisms, that is, either/or, good or bad, innocent or "streetwise," threatening or inexplicable.

The culturally familiar meanings of black and white, good and bad were played out by the children and by me, in part, because we did not understand, at the time, the possibility of examining these dualities in the first place. Britzman and colleagues (1993) suggest a pedagogy that works against such dualities:

[G]esturing toward [naming and examining] the constructed real—of the narratives, of the classroom dynamics, of the identities of every participant,

and of the . . . [s]tory—may [allow] students to perceive experience otherwise, in more ambivalent and contested ways. (p. 197)

Although I recognize their argument as powerful and potentially transformative, it was not a guide at the time I was teaching and learning with
the children about *Maniac Magee*.

From another view of pedagogy, it has been argued that the metaphors in *Maniac Magee* should be viewed as "imagined" and as literary
vehicles for a more compelling story about the nature of truth and the
perception of reality (Rosenthal, 1995). I found, however, that the children
were continually trying out their understanding of other cultural material
and the definitions of their own identities in relation to the story's signifiers of difference. Regardless of the "official," intended focus of our discussions, the story and its signifiers turned us toward ourselves, one
another, and our definitions of differences. The social, unofficial negotiations that surrounded our reading were marked, over and over again, by
efforts to situate ourselves in relation to the characters' and one anothers'
perceived identities.

"WHAT IF": CREATING AND EXPLAINING OURSELVES

The above excerpt illustrates the ways in which children referred to cultural maps of meaning to explain Mars Bar's actions and "nature." In the
following excerpt, the children interpret the signifiers within the story
while they simultaneously interpret themselves for one another. Even
though they cast themselves in the imagined realm of hypothetical situations in an attempt to remove themselves as participants in a racialized
society, it was impossible for them to talk about "the other" without also
talking about themselves.

We continued our discussion of the street scene episode but began to
speak—and not speak—about race as a basis for the characters' thoughts
and actions. In the moments when they speak of race, the children simultaneously attempt to say, in effect, "this is not me speaking." However,
their pointing to themselves as "not speaking" is, I believe, a code for
speaking about their racial differences in relation to the book and to
one another.

PAT: What about the part where Maniac eats Mars Bar's Mars Bar?
SHAUN: I'd never do that. That's sick, I think.
PAT: Thinking about somebody else's . . .

MONICA: Well, it's not that I wouldn't, it's . . . but . . . like . . . If I was in that situation, I would *not [eat the candy bar] because he was black or anything.* But just because . . .

MARK: Germs.

MONICA: Yeah.

PAT: So it doesn't matter about who is black or white or green or orange. You just wouldn't take a bite out of *somebody's* . . .

SHAUN: If he was orange or green, I would never take a bite. (*Laughter from others.*)

MARK: (*Sings*) "He's my brother. No matter if he's green or orange." [Tune from the song, "He Ain't Heavy, He's My Brother"] That would be strange. One time I had someone who had a green cat for a day. It was really green. It fell into green paint.

PAT: Oh, that's funny. So, uh, you probably would not have eaten the candy bar. Why do you think Maniac did?

MARK: Because /he's hungry!/ [slashes indicate overlapping speech]

MONICA: /Because he's hungry!/

MONICA: He's hungry and he doesn't know.

MARK: He probably thought, ah. It's just a . . .

MONICA: He thought he was being nice.

PAT: Yeah. He thought Mars Bar was being nice.

SHAUN: Man, I wouldn't have ever. Still, *even if a white person offered me a candy bar.* I'd say, first I take a bite, then you can. (*Laughter.*)

MONICA: I wouldn't have tooken a bite. Also, because you could tell he didn't want him to take the bite really. But he just said that.

PAT: But Maniac didn't understand that.

MONICA: Right. He didn't understand anything.

THOMAS: Mars Bar probably gets Mars Bar candy bars.

SHARON: He probably steals them.

All of us talked *around* race, even dismissed it as relevant—and thereby implied our recognition of its presence. As members of a racialized society, we began to implicitly situate ourselves within it—in the classroom, among peers, with this literature. Kirin Narayan (1993), writing about the multiple identities practiced and interpreted by anthropologists, states that "a person may have many strands of identification available, strands that may be tugged into the open or stuffed out of sight" (p. 673). The story of Maniac Magee tugged identities into the open, identities that had to do with race and belonging.

Monica referred race to the hypothetical world of "what if." As she picked up references to racial conflict from the episode, she situated herself as white, while imagining someone opposite her as black. But she claimed that race was not the real problem for her—germs were the problem. It is possible that the narration of white and black relations (e.g., "white kids just didn't put their mouths where black kids had had theirs") made it impossible for Monica and her peers to openly admit to the race relations in this scene. It was more tenable for them to overlook or laugh at this essentialized construction of difference than to see parallels in their own experiences.

My comment about "any color" unintentionally created an affirmation of their emerging perspective that color could be a laughable characteristic rather than a construction—worthy of dialogue—about human relations. Indeed, Mark followed my "multiple colors" reference with a transformation of a popular song and a brief story about his green cat. And then Shaun, who intended to pose the conflict between Mars Bar and Maniac as a matter of one tough guy meeting another, invoked Mark's and Monica's versions of race and germs to argue that not only would he not eat the candy bar because of germs, but he would not eat it even if the other guy was white (like himself).

The combination of these references points to the ways children not only made sense of a literary text but also constructed their own racial differences in relation to the text and one another. Although none of the children declared themselves as "white" or "black," they implied an allegiance with a naive white perspective, similar to Maniac's.

The conversation described above took place among a predominantly European American group of children. Only Thomas, who is African American and usually soft-spoken, offered one comment that upheld Mars Bar's humanity and the possibility that he and the others could imagine a positive relationship with him: "Mars Bar probably gets Mars Bar candy bars." However, his hypothesis was dismissed. Sharon ended any discussion by implying that Mars Bar had not earned his name (as Maniac had), he had stolen it. Thus she situated herself alongside Maniac while excluding the possibility of dialogue with Mars Bar or Thomas.

MEETING ONE ANOTHER: TRANSFORMING CULTURAL RESOURCES INTO SOCIAL ALLEGIANCES

The children's interpretations of *Maniac Magee* can be seen as the transformation of a cultural product into a cultural resource that enables them to explore and express their ideas about difference and their alignments with one another's definitions of difference in the specific setting of their classroom's social network. In *Understanding Popular Culture*, John Fiske (1990) examines the power relations and meaning relations between cultural products (such as the book, *Maniac Magee,* or the song Mark quoted), cultural resources, and social allegiances. According to Fiske, cultural resources, such as Mark's song reference, are the transformed products of a culture, used as the material through which we can express our own meanings of difference about ourselves and others.

Viewing the book as a cultural product, transformed into a cultural resource for the purpose of defining social relations, enables us to examine the following excerpt as more than a naive understanding of race relations. In Chapter 16 Maniac puzzles over the nature of skin color and the meaning of black and white. Maniac believes that we are all many colors—black and white are meaningless. In an impromptu discussion following our reading of that section, Monica, Shaun, and Cathy, who are European American, expressed their agreement with Maniac's view:

MONICA: 'Cause black and white are the total opposites, and we're not that much different.

CATHY: We're not white. *We're skin color.* We're not white.

MONICA: And there is no light brown here.

SHAUN: And there is no color white. There's a whole bunch of different colors of white.

PAT: Just like there are a whole bunch of different colors of brown.

CATHY: Actually, we're kind of red, too. Look at yourself.

PAT: Yeah. We are. Some people have a lot of red tone to their skin. OK. Uh. So you're saying there are different kinds of skin color, but people tend to call it one thing, and that separates us. And something Maniac has done is say . . . He begins to recognize that skin color matters. He slowly begins to recognize that.

MONICA: *No.* He doesn't know it matters. He knows that people *think* it matters.

PAT: Good point.

MONICA: But *he* might not think that it matters.

SHARON: He doesn't think that the color of your skin matters. But you should be friends.

The cultural product, a character, Maniac Magee, who is trying to understand why people are defined and divided on the basis of race, became a cultural resource for the children as they not only expressed their understanding of race but also implied their social alignments with one another. In the context of this discussion, denials of race also designated alignments with race. When the children proposed that white either does not exist or is part of a spectrum of colors, they also implied that definitions of difference are not dependent on a consideration of skin color. Ferdman (1990) argues that such a view is often held by children who are white or "mainstream" because the world they exist in "normalizes" white, thus making skin color irrelevant. Cathy stated as much when she said, "We're skin color."

This view of racelessness permeates American literature and classroom discourse. But as Morrison (1992) argues so eloquently:

> The world does not become raceless or will not become unracialized by assertion. The act of enforcing racelessness in literary discourse is itself a racial act. Pouring rhetorical acid on the fingers of a black hand may indeed destroy the prints, but not the hand. (p. 46)

The hands of Marisa and Richard are brown and black. In the context of rhetoric meant to erase differences, Marisa and Richard also had to examine and begin to specify their social alignments with the characters and their peers, but from the perspective of the "racialized other." When Richard joined the book discussions after a week's absence, he immediately identified with Mars Bar, but jokingly so.

MARISA: Uh. Is Mars Bar black?
PAT: Uh hmmm.
RICHARD: Me and Mars Bar are black.
ALAN: (*Laughs.*)
PAT: What are you thinking, Marisa?
MARISA: Who is chasing Maniac?
RICHARD: That's me!

His alignment with Mars Bar has to be seen in the context of the group. He was outspoken and playful about his African American heritage and was the only child who asserted race as a significant dimension of the story's meaning. Later, in our discussions, Richard aligned most strongly with a minor character, Mr. Beale, the African American father who was part of Maniac's East End foster family. Richard painted several pictures of the entire Beale family but spoke of the father as a strong male with self-respect and a sense of responsibility. Thomas also identified with a minor African American character named Hands Down, an inventive, winning football player who invites Maniac to play in the East End street games.

Marisa was much more circumspect about her alignments and the meaning of racial differences. As our discussions of the book began, it was clear to the group that racial segregation was part of the story. Without identifying herself explicitly, Marisa commented, "This is weird.

'Cause you know how like [they] talk about it and there's a black part and a white part. Where would like Mexicans or Chinese or *someone like that* [emphasis added] be? Could they be friends with either of them?" She also stated that she was tan and could, therefore, go to both sides of Two Mills End, like Maniac. Recognizing her ambivalence about speaking of herself as "different," I attempted to elevate the status of "brown skin" by speaking to her and the group of my Mexican American heritage. Marisa listened, but the conversation went no further. Implicit in Marisa's inquiries and racial identification is the sense that she is not white or black and is therefore uncertain how to claim an alternative definition or alignment in the context of this book or her peers' understanding of race and difference. Her negotiations of the meaning of difference had to be more delicate, it seemed, than Richard's.

GROUNDING THE LEGEND AND OURSELVES: TALKING BACK TO A DEHISTORICIZED NARRATIVE

Marisa and Richard seemed to be far more aware of the implications of racial identification than their classmates. What became difficult for them was positioning themselves when the terms for defining difference were essentializing and dichotomous. Both children held significant positions in the classroom network of friends. Richard was outspoken among his African American peers and playful and friendly with many other class members, but he often felt that his popular cultural referents and playful ways were dismissed or punished while other "white" children's referents and mannerisms were allowed (Enciso, 1994). Marisa saw herself as a member of the "smart" girls who were also mischievous but "good students." It was difficult for Marisa, in particular, to define herself as "other." The story of Maniac Magee created a dilemma for her: She was neither white nor male, though she was attracted to Maniac's heroics, and she was not black, like Mars Bar or Amanda Beale. She could not claim either identity, but the narrative assumed she could or must find a place for herself within that literary world. Richard found a place for himself within the story's world, but he recognized that alignments with Mars Bar would be problematic while alignments with Mr. Beale might seem insignificant to others. Their dilemma was related to the narrative's metaphors, to cultural referents related to those metaphors, and to the nature of language in social contexts that "fix" us in relation to one another.

Even when our statements about ourselves and others are made subtly, it is difficult to escape the culturally formed referents and ways of using language that construct differences. Our statements and cultural referents specify not only with what and whom we identify, but also with what and whom we *do not* identify. How do children talk back to such linguistic mazes?

The source for Marisa and Richard's challenge to the fixed descriptions of difference in *Maniac Magee* is found in their responses to the genre itself. They became aware of the timelessness and lack of historical context that accompanies a legend genre. They puzzled over the lack of signifiers that would have helped them understand both the existence of and resistance to segregation and prejudice.

Morrison (1992) has recognized the "dehistoricizing allegory" as a powerful linguistic strategy that allows American writers to "construct a history and context for whites by positing historylessness and contextlessness for blacks" (p. 53). As in *Maniac Magee*, we know where he has come from (his foster aunt and uncle and the death of his parents), we have a sense of why he is determined to reconcile differences (people should talk to each other), but we have no sense of this same viewpoint from the black characters in the story. They seem to regret the situation of segregation but do not speak of resistance, let alone of its economic and political impact on their lives. White characters, on the other hand, are either blind to racial differences or possess an animosity and separatist view that is derived only from deplorable parenting. No historical framework is provided for the division and attitudes existing in Two Mills End. We only know that Maniac has landed in the middle of it and wants things to change.

Such "dehistoricizing" allows for the remarks shared by Mark, an outspoken European American boy who often exaggerated and extended ideas for the sake of creating interest and humor. The history he creates is parodic and effectively diminishes the past dimensions and present influences of the civil rights movement in this country.

PAT: What do you think about the division between the East side and the West side? Is that something that you know?

MARK: Oh, sure.

PAT: In what way?

MARK: Well, not in these days . . . I mean.

MONICA: Well, like, if . . .

MARK: Before, you would have like, uh, separated bathrooms, fountains, chairs, tables . . .

MONICA: Schools.

MARK: Pencils.

THOMAS: Pencils?

MARK: Yeah!

MARK: Like seriously, they had separate brands or something so they
    wouldn't even know it.
MONICA, KEVIN, SHAUN: (*Laugh.*)
MARK: I remember one case where they, uh, ride on the bus or some-
    thing.
PAT: It was really. Yeah, it was very, very segregated before. So that
    could be what you know historically, but that's not something
    that you know now?
MARK: Like the blacks' territory and the whites crossing over. Get
    ready to ruuuummmble. (*Sings/talks words from* West Side Story.)

Mark fills the void of history with cultural references and social posi-
tionings that appear to align him with his classmates and me. Although
Mark does not intend to be dismissive or mean-spirited, he does succeed
in claiming a space for himself at the expense of his African American
classmate. Perhaps it is not the place of this book to explore social history.
However, in its absence, it is imperative that educators be alert to the
slippery ground created by the popular cultural and social alignments
that take its place.

One piece of history alluded to in the story did make a difference to
Marisa and Richard. A minor East End character declares his disdain for
Maniac's presence and in so doing implicates white people in the history
of segregation: "You got your own kind. It's how you wanted it. Let's keep
it that way" (p. 61). This brief reference to the past prompted an extended
dialogue among Marisa, Richard, and myself about our understanding of
ourselves in a racialized society. Joining our discussion was Alan, a European American boy who often teased other children but listened closely
to Richard.

I began our discussion by asking Marisa what might have happened
to the older East End black man that made him tell Maniac to leave the
East End. Marisa moves my questions about history to her present life,
to the context through which she views and must negotiate racial differences. Both Richard and I are surprised by her family relationships; they
are completely counter to the erasures and dualities that defined difference throughout our discussions of *Maniac Magee.* But her exploration of
difference encourages us to join her in naming ourselves as "racial [and
ethnic] other."

PAT: What might have happened to that old man? 'Cause he's older
    remember.

MARISA: He grew up when things were really prejudiced. Maybe he was a kid when his parents were slaves or something.

PAT: I'm not sure when this story happened but if it happened a long time ago, like even in the thirties, that's possible. But even his grandparents would have been enslaved and you'd be angry about that.

MARISA: I have some black relatives in my family.

RICHARD: Who? How?

MARISA: They're on my (inaudible) (*She continues talking about her little cousin who is often in her care and often up to some mischief*).

. . .

MARISA: I have some aunts and uncles who are black.

PAT: Uh hmm. A lot of people . . .

RICHARD: By marriage?

MARISA: Well my cousins . . .

RICHARD: By birth?

MARISA: And my (inaudible) I have a black cousin. And her dad's black.

RICHARD: Her [referring to Marisa] mom's Mexican. Right?

MARISA: White.

RICHARD: Uh. OK. I know. 'Cause your mom married a black Mexican right?

MARISA: (*Nods.*) So my dad's colored and not white.

PAT: Uh hmm. And my dad's Mexican American.

MARISA: It's like my mom has blonde hair and I have black hair like my dad.

PAT: Like my dad, too. His complexion is like a deep brown and he has very dark brown eyes and dark black hair.

MARISA: I have dark brown eyes.

PAT: Yeah. Most of my family has dark brown eyes. Just like his. But some of us are fair and some are darker skinned.

RICHARD: Not like me (*smiles*).

PAT: So we all think about our skin color. And we know that people notice our skin color. Right?

ALAN: Not mine.

RICHARD: /*Yeah, they do, boy!*/

MARISA: /*Yeah!*/

Where the story lacked historically and personally meaningful signifiers of difference, Marisa and Richard supplied their own. They expressed an implicit understanding that they did not land in the middle

of a racialized society; they saw themselves, instead, as an integral part
of our society's perceptions of difference. More importantly, they recognized that speaking of racial difference and its construction is crucial to
self-understanding and social transformation.

When Marisa moved the story of segregation to the present, she
"talked back" to a construction of difference that renders her invisible.
Her story is a pointed reminder that "multicultural literature" may not
be as representative of children's lives, desires, and relationships as it may
strive to be. Indeed, Britzman and colleagues (1993) argue that much of
what we present as "multicultural" to students presents old stories in
the guise of new configurations and settings. Furthermore, the literature
labeled "multicultural" creates the impression that it is somehow more
informed, more capable of embracing a complete understanding of differences. Rather than assume that any literature can possess such redemp-
tive qualities, it is more tenable to assume that difference is constructed
always, everywhere. Many constructions, however subtly imagined, will
adhere to long-held versions of racial hierarchies and essentialisms. The
power of the literature is not in its capacity to present a "truer" version
of differences (and resolutions of difference) but to open up dialogues
about the construction and negotiation of differences we observe and live.
Maniac Magee presents a possibility for such dialogue, but its foreclosure
of dialogue among the characters and across historical experiences makes
open negotiations a difficult, if not risky, maneuver for children.

Richard and Marisa, however, are prepared to "talk back." In a reflective dialogue following Marisa's story, Richard and Marisa explored a
hypothetical history of negotiations about difference and how it might
be possible to rework the language and practices of segregation. Richard
moves, then, to cultural referents that have guided his understanding of
race relations. His referents are part of a "cultural map" that places racial
hatred in the context of an ongoing struggle to transform it through a
liberatory theology and social action.

> MARISA (*to Richard*): Are you prejudice?
> RICHARD: Yep. I'm prejudice. No. I'm just kidding.
> ALAN: [*Laughs.*]
> RICHARD: Not on my life.
> . . .
> RICHARD: Why do you ask me this?
> PAT: How do you think it happens?
> RICHARD: Learn it from the older generation and pass it on—the neg-
> atives is all.

PAT: Do you think you have to be brave not to be prejudiced in this country?

RICHARD: It is prejudiced in this country.

. . .

PAT: How can *you* not be prejudiced?

MARISA: Well, you don't care what color your friends are. Like, say, your mom. Say like (inaudible). OK. Like . . . The great grandmother could have taught her daughter to be prejudiced and probably the last mother whatever had a kid and didn't teach her about prejudice and so they weren't prejudiced and . . .

RICHARD: Women can be prejudiced but the Ku Klux Klan wouldn't let women join them.

PAT: Hmm.

MARISA: And like, then that her child wouldn't grow up to be prejudiced and it would be easy for her child to make friends with all different colors of people. And then her mom would wonder why she [the mom] don't have much friends like her kids.

PAT: Hmm. So it's going to be hard for one generation and the next generation. . . . It will be a bit easier after that.

RICHARD: Did you ever see *The Little Boy King?* [About] Martin Luther King?

PAT: No.

RICHARD: You never saw it?

PAT: No. I bet it's a good movie.

RICHARD: I watch it just about every day.

PAT: Really?

RICHARD: I got the movie and the movie *Roots* and *Gandhi.*

PAT: Yeah. I saw *Gandhi.*

RICHARD: Four hours long. And, uh, what's it called? *The Ten Commandments.*

PAT: Uhm hmm.

RICHARD: I got that. I love that movie *The Ten Commandments.*

PAT: Do you think Amanda Beale's family knows about Martin Luther King?

RICHARD: Probably not.

PAT: Why?

MARISA: Probably so.

RICHARD: What year was this?

PAT: That's a good question. I don't know. What year do you think?

RICHARD: About 1930 something.

MARISA: Let's check the date.

Marisa lets us know, through her story and her ideal familial discourse, that difference is defined and shaped by the people you know and love. She implies that a younger generation of girls must defy older women's constructions of difference if we are ever to form friendships across racial lines. Her version of social change is similar to Maniac Magee's insofar as both assume that by reimagining ourselves in relation to others, we may be able to help others do the same. However, Marisa's ideal is grounded in a personal racialized history, not a race-free past. Similarly, Richard's ideal is grounded in a personal history that is informed by the visions and social actions of revered spokespersons of civil rights movements across time and around the world: Martin Luther King, Jr., Gandhi, and Jesus Christ. Richard "talks back" to the representations and reconciliations of difference in *Maniac Magee* by invoking the images and stories of those who led social movements. Although the leaders to whom he refers are individuals, like Maniac, they are not innocent or solitary heroes. The films Richard knows show people acting against racism in the midst of enormous social turmoil and at the risk of innumerable lives. With these references, Richard is able to more fully define the meaning of "being Black." He is clearly and positively aligned with an African American tradition of theology that strives for social justice and resists oppression. Together, Marisa and Richard rework the absence of context and history in *Maniac Magee* and construct a more viable setting for resistance to prejudices and racism.

TALKING BACK

Multicultural literature is often considered to be the primary symbolic material through which children might define and redefine meanings of difference. As we mediate this literature with children, it is critical that we recognize that they are not simply responding to these stories as if they are creations of a singular imagination. In the midst of discussions, children borrow and often "talk back" to constructions of difference found in literature, popular culture, and in the words of their classmates and teachers. In this chapter, I have examined the ways difference is constructed in one piece of children's literature and, in turn, the ways children spoke with and against the authority of those constructions.

When the literature itself is granted authority through its awards and position as the focus of discussion, it is often difficult for teachers and children to recognize and question the images and ideology inscribed within it. As a Newbery award–winner, *Maniac Magee* has considerable authority; it is among the elite few books for children that will remain in publication and in use in classrooms for years to come. Because it engages with racial differences and speaks from a child's perspective, it is akin to the much-loved (and critiqued) classic *Huckleberry Finn*. Yet, as in the case of *Huckleberry Finn*, as Morrison (1992) argues, it may be easy to overlook

> the implications of the Africanist presence at its center [because it] appears to assimilate the ideological assumptions of its society and culture; because it is narrated in the voice and controlled by the gaze of a child-without-status—someone outside, marginal, and already "othered" . . . and because the novel masks itself in the comic, parodic, and exaggerated tall-tale format. (pp. 54–55)

When I critique *Maniac Magee*, I "talk back" to a canon in order to awaken my own and others' awareness of the linguistic strategies that can bind and blind the complicated junctures of difference in our literature, in our lives, and in our classrooms. Furthermore, a critical awareness of an Africanist presence in literature enriches the literature and its infinite readings. As Morrison (1992) argues, "when one begins to look carefully, without a restraining, protective agenda beforehand . . . the nation's literature [is rendered] a much more complex and rewarding body of knowledge" (p. 53). Thus, it is not my intention to censor this or any literature for children, but rather to initiate a more complex dialogue about its representations of difference.

Popular cultural references were a significant medium through which children talked with and against the meanings of difference found in the story and among themselves. The reference points they used could be understood as cultural maps that allowed them to place the "new" story of Maniac Magee within an already familiar framework of relations and meanings of difference. For many of the European American children, cultural maps were based on popular images that treat whiteness as a norm. Through these maps children were able to both interpret the story and define differences within and among themselves. Richard and Marisa, on the other hand, referred to personal and historical cultural maps that allowed them to "talk back" to the ideal of a raceless society and thus create strong positions for themselves within a racialized society.

Children also transformed cultural products such as films and songs into cultural resources. As cultural resources, their citations were no longer benign interpretations of the story; they were powerful indicators of social alignments. In several respects, the children "talked back" to *Maniac Magee* when they used the story as a cultural resource to define themselves and others. The official world of our meetings was not, intentionally, about negotiating the meaning of racial differences. But that was, in fact, the subtext of the students' dialogue with one another, the author, and me.

What might be the teacher's and researcher's role amidst this matrix of ideologies, cultural references, and social positions? Some would argue that, regardless of a story's representations, it is always most important to develop enjoyment and appreciation of the literature so that children will continue to seek reading as an enriching activity. I have argued, however, that such enjoyment is made difficult when children are placed in positions that require them to align with problematic representations of themselves and others. Rather than mask these difficulties, we can begin to talk about the ways characters and characters' relationships are constructed. I believe such "talking back" to multicultural literature makes the literature more interesting and the possibilities and definitions of being a reader more empowering. Pleasure in a story can be related to both reading and talking back. It can be enjoyable and rewarding for children to recognize their own authority in relation to the significations and interpretations that accompany a story.

POSSIBILITIES AND IMPOSSIBILITIES FOR NEGOTIATING THE MEANING OF DIFFERENCE

If we hope children will tell their stories and "talk back" to literature, we have to learn what constrains and what opens possibilities for such performances. The construction of difference in a story raises two key questions for readers that might constrain or open the possibility of dialogue: Who is the audience for this book (Sims, 1982)? How does the portrayal of difference relate to a wider circle of sociohistorical attitudes and practices (Bourdieu, 1984; Morrison, 1992; Taxel, 1992)? In the case of *Maniac Magee,* readers might ask, "Is Maniac like me? Is Mars Bar like me? Is his story my story? Are his experiences ones I have had or would like to have?" These are questions implied by any reading, but they may be left unstated or unexplored. If we choose *not* to explore these questions with children, it seems to me that all of the negotiations of the meaning of difference will be left to those children whose cultural references and perspectives are most understood and valued within the classroom. Recent studies of process writing (Dyson, 1993b; Lensmire, 1994) suggest that this is, indeed, the case. Further research on children's response to literature could benefit from a similar analysis.

Part of classroom-based research would also examine the ways children and teachers use popular cultural and multicultural literature as resources to position one another and define differences. Because, in a sense, it is not what we think defines someone else that matters (because that is always shifting) but how we continually place ourselves and others in relation to those shifting definitions. Given this view, we may begin to study the ways children's ideas about differences within and among themselves are intentionally and unintentionally invoked by multicultural literature and how we can work together to call out the contradictory stories and relationships that lend more possibility to our places in the world.

NOTES

1. Multicultural literature is variously defined as that literature representative of the perspectives of people of color (Harris, 1992; Kruse & Horning, 1991; Bishop, 1994) and as literature that reflects the lifestyles and viewpoints of marginalized cultural or social groups that are traditionally underrepresented in publications, mass media, and school curricula (Banks, 1993). Scholars have also grouped the literature by genre and by its intention to represent primarily an insider's perspective, cross-cultural relationships, or root-culture stories and traditions (Cai & Bishop, 1994; Barrera, Liguori, & Salas, 1992).

2. It is curious to note that the key source for the character of Maniac Magee is actually a black child in Spinelli's childhood experience. It is not surprising that Spinelli would choose not to write from the black child's perspective given numerous and pressing questions about representation and authenticity of voice and experience (cf. Cai, Chapter 9, this volume). However, this reversal meant that Spinelli had to equate the white child's first encounters with racism with the black child's first encounters with racism. So then the question has to be answered: How does a black child's view of skin color equate with a white child's view? Are they comparable? Spinelli has created a character who refuses to see the differences as meaningful. He writes, however, that his friend Niki Hollie knew that skin color was meaningful: "There was a turnstile—only one child admitted at a time. When my friend's turn came, a brawny hand clamped the metal pipe and held it still. It would not move. And my friend, who until then had known merely that he was black, discovered now that it made a difference" (p. 430). The replacement of Niki Hollie's perspective with Maniac Magee's creates a significant shift in the story of racial segregation.

REFERENCES

Anderson, B. (1983). *Imagined communities: Reflections on the origin and spread of nationalism.* New York: Verso.

Banks, J. (1993). The canon debate, knowledge construction, and multicultural literature. *Educational researcher, 22*(5), 4–14.

Barrera, R., Liguori, O., & Salas, L. (1992). Ideas a literature can grow on: Key insights for enriching and expanding children's literature about the Mexican-American experience. In V. Harris (Ed.), *Teaching multicultural literature in grades K–8* (pp. 203–241). Norwood, MA: Christopher-Gordon.

Belsey, C. (1980). *Critical practice.* New York: Methuen.

Bishop, R. S. (Ed.). (1994). *Kaleidoscope: A multicultural booklist for grades K–8.* Urbana–Champaign, IL: National Council of Teachers of English.

Blume, J. (1970). *Iggie's House.* Englewood Cliffs, NJ: Bradbury.

Bourdieu, P. (1984). *Distinction: A social critique of the judgement of taste* (R. Nice, Trans.). Cambridge, MA: Harvard University Press.

Britzman, D., Santiago-Valles, K., Jiménez-Munoz, G. & Lamash, L. (1991). Dusting off the erasures: Race, gender and pedagogy. *Education and Society, 9*(2), 88–92.

Britzman, D., Santiago-Valles, K., Jiménez-Munoz, G. & Lamash, L. (1993). Slips that show and tell: Fashioning multiculture as a problem of representation. In C. McCarthy & W. Crichlow (Eds.), *Race identity and representation in education* (pp. 188–200). New York: Routledge.

Cai, M., & Bishop, R. S. (1994). Multicultural literature for children: Towards a clarification of the concept. In A. H. Dyson & C. Genishi (Eds.), *The need for story: Cultural diversity in classroom and community* (pp. 57–71). Urbana, IL: National Council of Teachers of English.

Dyson, A. H. (1993a). *Negotiating a permeable curriculum: On literacy, diversity, and the interplay of children's and teachers' worlds* (Concept Paper No. 9). Urbana–Champaign, IL: National Council of Teachers of English.

Dyson, A. H. (1993b). *Social worlds of children learning to write in an urban primary school.* New York: Teachers College Press.

Enciso, P. (1994). Cultural identity and response to literature: Running lessons from Maniac Magee. *Language Arts, 71,* 524–533.

Ferdman, B. (1990). Literacy and cultural identity. *Harvard Educational Review, 60*(2), 181–203.

Fiske, J. (1990). *Understanding popular culture.* New York: Routledge.

Hall, S., Critcher, C., Jefferson, T., Clarke, J., & Roberts, B. (1978). *Policing the crisis: Mugging, the state, and law and order.* New York: Holmes & Meier.

Harris, V. (Ed.). (1992). *Teaching multicultural literature in grades K–8.* Norwood, MA: Christopher-Gordon.

Kruse, G. M., & Horning, K. T. (1991). *Multicultural literature for children and young adults: A selected listing of books 1980–1990 by and about people of color* (3rd ed.). Madison, WI: Cooperative Children's Book Center.

Lensmire, T. J. (1994). *When children write: Critical re-visions of the writing workshop.* New York: Teachers College Press.

Morrison, T. (1992). *Playing in the dark: Whiteness and the literary imagination.* Cambridge, MA: Harvard University Press.

Narayan, K. (1993). How native is a "native" anthropologist? *American Anthropologist, 95,* 671–686.

Rosenthal, I. (1995). Educating through literature: Flying lessons from Maniac Magee. *Language Arts, 72,* 113–119.

Sims, R. (1982). *Shadow and substance: Afro-American experience in contemporary children's fiction.* Urbana–Champaign, IL: National Council of Teachers of English.

Spinelli, J. (1990). *Maniac Magee.* Boston: Little, Brown.

Spinelli, J. (1991, July/August). Newbery Medal acceptance. *The Horn Book Magazine,* pp. 426–432.

Stuckey, E. (1991). *The violence of literacy.* Portsmouth, NH: Heineman.

Taxel, J. (1992). The politics of children's literature: Reflections on multiculturalism, political correctness, and Christopher Columbus. In V. Harris (Ed.), *Teaching multicultural literature in grades K–8* (pp. 1–52). Norwood, MA: Christopher-Gordon.

CHAPTER 2

Re-Visioning Reading and Teaching Literature Through the Lens of Narrative Theory

WILLIAM McGINLEY, GEORGE KAMBERELIS, TIMOTHY MAHONEY, DANIEL MADIGAN, VICTORIA RYBICKI, AND JEFF OLIVER

AFTER READING *Song of the Trees* (M. Taylor, 1975), 10-year-old Joseph reconsidered the hardships associated with being separated from one's family and the experience of growing up apart from one's father or other family members. Specifically, in reading about the struggles that the characters Cassie, Stacey, Little Man, and Christopher-John experienced while their father was away from home searching for work, Joseph was reminded of the time when his own father left home. His comments further reveal the joy he shared with these children upon learning of their father's surprising return:

> These people, Casey, Stacey, Christopher-John, Little Man, momma, and pappa, their pappa has been away for many years. . . .'Cause he was looking to find a job and it took him that long. He had to work for some white men. . . . When I heard that, I wondered how could they miss their father that long. Christopher-John and the others didn't even know their father. . . . My first dad had been away, but see, he never came back. And I just liked it because it was about the whole family and the family meeting, like um, how the children met their father [in the end] and how the ma met, saw their father, saw their father again.

Similarly, after 8-year-old Jamar had finished reading *I Have a Dream: The Story of Martin* (Davidson, 1991) and *Encyclopedia Brown Gets His Man* (Sobol, 1982), he reflected on the meanings he associated with these books that allowed him to envision the possible selves and future responsibilities he might assume as a member of the African American community in which he lived:

> They [these books] make me think that I want to, that I could help the community or go up in space or be an actor or have all three. I have three choices to choose from [when I grow up], helping the community, going up in space, or being an actor. . . . See, if I think about my life, I only think about being an actor, but if I read Encyclopedia Brown or a book about Martin Luther King or Abraham Lincoln, it helps me to think about different things instead of being an actor.

When Joseph and Jamar read these and other stories, they were students participating in two different language arts classrooms in different regions of the country. As part of their participation in these unique programs, they were provided with opportunities to read, write, and talk about themselves, their family and peers, and their communities and cultures. Through a variety of instructional activities that encouraged them and other children to reflect on their own lives and experiences in response to their reading, they were introduced to the idea that stories can be a means of personal and social exploration and reflection—an imaginative vehicle for questioning, shaping, responding, and participating in the world. As Joseph, Jamar, and the many other children who were members of these two classrooms shared their thoughts and feelings about the stories they read, they brought to light a wealth of ways in which reading and responding to literature led not only to an understanding of the conceptual content of the stories but also to a process of reflection that helped them to understand themselves, others, and the world in which they lived.

Taken together, the written and spoken words of the children with whom we have worked over the past few years echo recent themes in the theoretical realms of narrative theory (e.g., Bruner, 1986) and transactional theory (e.g., Rosenblatt (1978, 1983). Collectively, these themes have spawned a renewed interest in the life-informing and life-transforming possibilities afforded by story reading that have only recently begun to be examined by researchers in literacy and literature.

In focusing on this dimension of children's reading, we draw upon data collected during several related ethnographic studies in the classrooms of Joseph and Jamar. Across these studies, we explored some of the ways that reading and writing functioned in children's lives as sources of personal, social, or political understanding and exploration. In addition, we sought to understand children's literacy as a function of the particular communities of practice in which they were socialized and enculturated to value reading and writing (McGinley & Kamberelis, 1992a; McGinley & Kamberelis, 1992b; McGinley & Kamberelis, 1996; McGinley, Mahoney, & Kamberelis, 1995). In this chapter, we draw upon this work in arguing that without a better understanding of the specific ways that stories may function as a means of organizing and interpreting experience, we stand to miss significant dimensions of students' development as readers, as well as an understanding of the possibilities that such reading might offer both children and adolescents who are also coming to know themselves, their family and peers, and the society in which they live. In addition, although conceiving of stories as a unique source of knowledge about self and world is certainly not a new proposition, a more complete understanding of the life-informing dimension of reading literature is essential if we are genuinely to evaluate, revitalize, and refine our understanding of the purpose for reading and teaching literature in school.

In the first part of the chapter, we review many of the constructs from the theoretical domains of narrative theory and transactional theory as they serve to outline the interdisciplinary framework and rationale with which we began our studies of the nature and meaning of children's story reading. Second, we present brief portraits of the classrooms of two teachers who sought to provide children with opportunities to reflect upon both literature and life. Third, we offer the written and spoken words of several children from these classrooms, communities, and cultures, as they provide insight into some of the ways that stories functioned as an imaginative resource for exploring, understanding, and re-creating themselves and their world. Finally, we conclude by discussing the implications of such findings for literacy pedagogy and for reconsidering the role and function of story reading in school and in students' lives.

PERSPECTIVES ON THE FUNCTIONS OF STORIES

The potential of narrative to function as a way of understanding one's own and others' experience has received renewed attention from scholars in both the humanities and the social sciences in recent years (e.g., Booth, 1988; Bruner, 1986, 1987; Carr, 1986; Martin, 1983; McAdams, 1993; Narayan, 1991; Ricoeur, 1984; Rosen, 1986; White, 1987; Witherell & Noddings,

1991). In general, these theorists have argued that because narratives are organized around the dimension of time in lived experience, they allow us to interpret our pasts, envision our futures, and understand the lives of others with whom we interact.

Participating in Storied Worlds

The importance of story or narrative in understanding both self and world has been given careful treatment by Bruner (1986, 1990). According to Bruner, the narrative models and procedures for interpreting and organizing experience are embodied in the written and told stories that a culture provides. Drawing on the work of Greimas and Courtes (1976), Bruner (1986) argues that the imaginative use of the narrative form in literature engages readers in the exploration of human possibilities by situating them simultaneously in a "dual landscape" of both action and consciousness. Stories, he explains, locate readers in a particular pattern or "grammar" of events, situations, and goals while also revealing the subjective worlds of characters who are involved in such events. In this way, stories provide "map[s] of possible roles and possible worlds in which action, thought, and self determination are permissible or desirable" (p. 66). In order to achieve such an effect, stories rely upon particular discourse properties that invite readers to enter into the fictional landscape and participate in the lives of protagonists. As Iser (1978) notes in *The Act of Reading,* the meanings of fictional texts are largely open-ended or "indeterminate." This "relative indeterminacy of text" provides readers with the incentive to develop or construct "a spectrum of actualizations" or formulations about themselves and the social world (p. 61). In sum, the discourse of a story invites a certain ambiguity of meaning and events that induces readers to participate in the production of meaning.

In building upon this idea of indeterminate meaning, Bruner (1986) emphasizes the notion of "subjunctivity" to explain the process through which readers enter a fictional landscape and experience or participate in the life and mind of story characters. Stories derive their power to render reality subjunctive or hypothetical through the depiction of the subjective consciousness of protagonists and the consequential alternativeness of the worlds they inhabit. Through the triggering of subjectification and the presentation of multiple perspectives, narrative discourse succeeds in "subjunctivizing reality" by "rendering the world of the story into the consciousness of its protagonists" (p. 28). As readers, we do not see the world through "an omniscient eye" but through "the filter of the consciousness of protagonists in the story" (p. 25) In this subjunctive state, we know only the realities and experiences of the story characters themselves and we are induced to identify with the plights in which they find themselves. Ultimately the "fictional landscape" achieves a reality of its own as readers construct and "act" in self-made story worlds. This power, Bruner (1986) insists, is at least partially dependent upon the subjunctive force or quality of a given narrative. The plights of characters must be rendered with "sufficient subjunctivity" so that their storied lives and experiences can be "rewritten" through the readers' own "play of imagination" (p. 35).

Moral and Ethical Functions of Stories

In relation to these points, several theorists have focused attention on life-informing and life-transforming possibilities that such a "play of imagination" might afford. For example, some scholars have foregrounded the ethical value of reading literature and the influence that stories may have on the development of an individuals' character or self. Coles (1989), for example, developed the idea that stories achieve their particular force through characters and events that engage readers in a psychological or moral journey. Such a journey or "personal expedition" allows readers to explore life's contingencies and dilemmas through the "moral imagination" of an author and, in so doing, enables them to "take matters of choice and commitment more seriously than they might otherwise have done" (p. 90).

According to Coles, the act of listening, reading, or responding to the stories of others can have important consequences for the ways in which we think about our own lives. The indirections and vicissitudes that inhabit a story and the lives of its characters become our own. A story's energy and emotion solicits our own involvement in the thoughts, feelings, desires, and fears of its characters. As Coles (1989) further explains:

> The whole point of stories is not "solutions" or "resolutions" but a broadening and even a heightening of our struggles—with new protagonists and antagonists introduced, with new sources of concern or apprehension, or hope, as one's mental life accommodates itself into a series of arrivals: guests who have a way of staying, but not necessarily staying put. (p. 129)

According to Booth (1988), the ethical and moral influence that stories exert on our lives and the development of our individual character is simply inescapable. In his exploration of the "efferent effect" or "carry-over" from our narrative reading to daily life and behavior, Booth explains that "anyone who conducts honest introspection knows that 'real life' is lived in images derived in part from stories" of themselves and others both real and fictional (p. 228). So spontaneous and unrehearsed is this narrative process that individuals often "cannot draw a clear line between what [they] *are*, in some conception of a 'natural,' unstoried self, and what [they] have become" as a result of the stories they have enjoyed, experienced, and appropriated over the course of their lives (p. 229).

Similar to Booth, other theorists have argued that individuals' understanding of both self and society is a function of the repertoire of stories that they have read, heard, and inherited throughout their lives (Bruner, 1990; MacIntyre, 1981; McAdams, 1993; Stone, 1988). As MacIntyre (1981) explains, these stories constitute the "dramatic resources" that individuals use in constructing their own moralities and evaluating the moral and ethical sensibilities of others in their world. Depriving children of stories of social traditions and moral life, he writes, "leave[s] them unscripted, anxious stutterers in their actions as in their words" (p. 201).

The personal, social, and moral functions of stories (or literature more broadly conceived) have also been a central focus among reader-response theorists (e.g., Beach, 1990; Hynds, 1990; Iser, 1978; Rosenblatt, 1978, 1983). According to these scholars, the literary experience can function both as a source of personal, social, and political exploration that provides readers with a means to interpret human experience and as a vehicle through which readers broaden their cultural understanding and sensibility. In her now classic work, *Literature as Exploration* (1983), Louise Rosenblatt argued that literature represents "an embodiment of human personalities, human situations, human conflicts and achievements" (p. vii). Through stories, Rosenblatt explains, we "do not so much acquire additional information as we acquire additional experience" (p. 38).

Similarly, Iser (1978) emphasized literature's power to reveal a "new reality" to readers—one that is different from the world they have come to know, such that the "deficiencies inherent in prevalent norms and in his own restricted behavior" are disclosed (p. xiii). More recently, Straw and Bogdan (1990) argued that the act of literary reading should be understood as "part of the lifelong experience of coming to know . . . part of a person's repertoire of experience to be remembered, reflected upon, and recomprehended" over the course of his or her life (p. 5).

In spite of these theoretical accounts of the processes through which narrative discourse succeeds in rendering reality subjunctive, as well as accounts of the moral, ethical, or political force that stories are believed to exert on our lives, several important questions remain concerning the kinds of insight into one's self and one's world that narrative experiences actually call forth. Though it may indeed seem from recent theoretical perspectives on narrative that children's story reading would be associated with particular life-informing possibilities, these theories are still largely without empirical foundation. In relation to this point, we might ask what the nature is of the understanding about themselves and the social world that young readers acquire as a result of their transactions with the stories they read and discuss in school. How do young readers emerge from the feelings and possibilities portrayed through the storied lives and experiences of the characters they encounter in books? In addition, according to a recent comprehensive study across a number of different schools (Applebee, 1993), knowledge of such theories is seldom reflected in current classroom approaches to the teaching and learning of literature. As a result, we know little about kinds of classroom practices and experiences that might engage students in reading both literature and life. These discontinuities among theory, research, and practice formed the basis for our initial interest and subsequent exploration into the nature and function of students' story-reading experiences in school.

STORIES OF READING IN TWO ELEMENTARY SCHOOL CLASSROOMS

Over the past several years, we have spent numerous hours on school playgrounds, on the floors of classrooms, in hallways, and in libraries, listening to children talk about a wide variety of books and stories. In sharing excerpts from students' written and spoken responses to literature, we hope to illustrate some of the ways in which stories provide them with a uniquely powerful means through which they might explore and reflect upon experience. In documenting the meaning that children in these classrooms evoked in relation to the literature they read, we relied upon our analyses of small- and whole-class literature discussions, children's literature journals and response notebooks, the in-depth interviews we conducted with children about their reading, and our field notes of classroom literature-related activities.

The Teachers and Their Classrooms

Vicki. Vicki was an experienced third- and fourth-grade teacher in a neighborhood elementary school in northwest Detroit. She had been living and teaching in the city for approximately 20 years. Throughout those years, she had devoted a considerable amount of her time and energy to trying to improve the community in which she and her students lived and attended school. In addition, she often provided children with rides to and from school; she took them to cultural and recreational events; she developed personal relationships with some of the children's parents; and she became involved with interest groups and activities in the local community. In the classroom, Vicki searched for ways to validate children's personal interests and experiences while also negotiating the numerous school district imperatives to improve children's standardized reading and writing scores. Although she made a special effort to prepare children for such tests, she also wanted students to view their own lives and experiences as important subjects about which they might read, write, and talk.

Motivated by her desire to provide her students with literate experiences that would involve reading and writing both text and life, Vicki searched for literacy activities that "would celebrate the children's voices"—voices that she believed teachers needed to listen to and encourage. Grounded in her "ethic of care" and based on her child- and community-centered educational philosophy, classroom activities were structured to provide children with reading and writing experiences that would be sensitive to their personal, emotional, and communal needs.

Three key events helped to initiate and anchor literacy instruction in Vicki's classroom. At the beginning of the year, Vicki arranged for the children to get to know one another by inviting each child to tell a story about him- or herself. In order to encourage the children and initiate the storytelling, she first asked them to think about what they do when they want to "become friends with someone." In response to this question, children offered a variety of ideas from "talking to them" to "sharing some things" to "asking their name." Vicki then suggested that we could also "tell a story about ourselves." The children then arranged their desks in a circle, and everyone shared some experience or details about themselves or their family.

Second, children were invited to plan and videotape a tour of the neighborhood where they lived and attended school. During the tour, children offered extensive commentary about a variety of local landmarks and related experiences that had particular meaning for them (e.g., churches, homes of relatives and friends, favorite restaurants, neighborhood stores, parks, abandoned homes, and local hangouts). This commentary included historical information about featured landmarks, as well as information about the personal, communal, and political significance of these sites.

Finally, Vicki involved the children in drawing and constructing a number of colorful signs or posters about the particular street where their own home was located. These signs were to be different from those commonly found in most neighborhoods. In constructing these "signs of community life," as she referred to them, children were encouraged to reflect upon and share those aspects of their community that they wished to celebrate, as well as those they wished to change. After sharing their ideas, the children were presented with the following question: "If we could place a sign in our neighborhood, what would it say?" Vicki then explained that the yellow-papered bulletin board in the back of the room would be like "house lights" illuminating their street signs and pictures. In a few days, these "signs of community life" were displayed across the bulletin board, revealing many of the children's hopes, interests, and concerns as they pertained to their lives and their community. The following examples were representative of the many messages and accompanying drawings that children constructed: "Please Don't Take Down The Basketball Rims," "Be Kind to One Another," "Stay in School," "Let's Clean Up Our Neighborhood," "Please Please Be Smart Don't Be a Drug Addict," "Don't Speed Down the Streets Watch For Children," "Keep Community Clean," and "Street of Peace."

Children in Vicki's classroom were also engaged in reading a variety of fictional and nonfictional texts.[1] In general, children's reading took three different forms: shared reading of stories from the classroom basal series, self-selected reading of school library books, and stories that Vicki elected to read aloud over the course of the year. In addition, as children's interest in reading developed, Vicki continued to supply them with books that represented the range of genres and topics in which they had expressed interest. On most days, children began by reading silently from a teacher-selected basal story or from self-selected books. In conjunction with this reading, they were encouraged to "reflect" or "write a sentence" in their reading-response journals about events or characters in the story that reminded them of experiences in their own lives. Each day after reading, several children were invited to share entries from their reading-response journals, and the other children in the class were invited to discuss these entries in small- and whole-group meetings. In both their written responses and in class discussions, Vicki encouraged children to reflect on and share their feelings in relation to particular texts by posing specific kinds of questions (e.g., "Reflect on what you read"; "How did the story make you feel?"; "What did the story make you think?"; "Did the story help you to imagine being a certain kind of person?"; "Did the story help you to imagine doing certain kinds of things?"). She also encouraged them to explore the reasons why an author might have written a particular piece (e.g., "Why do you think this author wrote this story?"; "What did the author want us to think, know, or do?"; "Is the author trying to change our minds about anything?").

Vicki's discussion of *To Hell With Dying* (Walker, 1988) was emblematic of many of the literature discussions in which the children took part. The story is about a loving relationship between a young child (Alice

Walker) and her aging friend (Mr. Sweet). Vicki began by asking the children to share their ideas about why the author might have written such a book. As the discussion developed, Vicki helped the children to identify the qualities and traits of the characters they admired and sought to emulate in this book as well as in other books. In this discussion, as in subsequent conversations about a variety of fictional and nonfictional texts, the children were frequently invited to "read" the experiences of such real and imaginary characters as Alice and Mr. Sweet, Rosa Parks, Harriet Tubman, Malcolm X, Sojourner Truth, Martin Luther King, Maniac Magee, Lulu and Sandy, Encyclopedia Brown, Romona Quimby, and Nate the Great as "dramatic resources" for reflecting upon important experiences and issues central to their own lives and the lives of their friends, families, and members of their immediate community.

Jeff. Jeff was a fourth- and fifth-grade teacher in Boulder who, like Vicki, was concerned with finding ways to help his students bring literature to life. We first met Jeff in 1992. He had been living and teaching elementary school in Colorado for approximately 20 years. In the classroom, Jeff devoted a considerable amount of time to fostering children's interest in reading by providing them with opportunities to understand and experience some of the ways that literature might function in their lives as a vehicle for examining and understanding experience. In particular, children in his classroom were often involved in wide-ranging, literacy-related activities designed to make literature and literacy a meaningful part of their lives both in and out of school. Among the many activities in which children participated, the following are examples of experiences that occurred regularly in Jeff's classroom: storybook read-aloud and personal story sharing in the group center, outdoor nature walks involving poetry reading and writing, storybook writing and reading projects with older adults in the community, student-organized story-reading clubs, student dramatizations of selected storybooks, composing original storybooks, in-class publication of student writing, independent reading, and visits from local writers, poets, musicians, and visual artists.

Although all children participated in these literacy activities over the course of the schoolyear, we became most interested in the story "read-aloud" time that took place in "the group center"—a small carpeted area separated from the rest of the room by a sofa, some chairs, and a bookshelf. On most mornings, children gathered on the floor of the group center to listen to Jeff read aloud from a children's storybook book or a young adult novel. These stories or novels were usually selected by Jeff and often related to particular themes or issues that he believed the children would enjoy discussing.[2] Once children were seated comfortably in a circle near their friends, story-reading time officially began with the ritual lighting of "the dreamer's candle" followed by the whole-class recitation of the poem "Invitation," by the well-known children's author Shel Silverstein (1974). The poem reads as follows:

> If you are a dreamer come in,
> If you are a dreamer, a wisher, a liar,
> If you're a hope-er, a pray-er, a magic bean buyer . . .
> If you're a pretender, come sit by my fire
> For we have some flax-golden tales to spin.
> Come in!
> Come in!

In conjunction with the stories he read and shared, Jeff often encouraged children to respond or react to such stories in particular ways. Similar to Vicki, Jeff's oral story-reading practices were frequently accompanied by invitations to the children to "read" or revisit their own lives and experiences through the lives and experiences of the characters they encountered in books. These invitations usually took the form of questions and often asked children to (1) tell a personal story related to particular story events, (2) share a related personal experience, (3) participate in the consciousness or subjective worlds of story characters, or (4) envision or celebrate a possible self or possible world in relation to a given story. Although Jeff frequently concluded each read-aloud session by asking children if they had "any comments, reactions, or responses," he often used these moments to model a way of reading and responding to literature that involved sharing a personal story or experience from one's own life. Consequently, after Jeff had narrated and shared an experience from his own life, children responded to his story by sharing a personal experience of their own or by responding to one of the specific questions that Jeff sometimes asked. Some of the most frequently asked questions included: "Does the story remind you of anything in your life?"; "Did anything like that ever happen to you?"; "Do you know anyone like that character?"; "What do you think that character is feeling or thinking about right now?"; "What would you do if you were in that character's situation?"; "What do you think the character will do next?"; "How is that character the same or different from you?"

Jeff's discussion of the novel *Everywhere* (Brooks, 1990) was emblematic of many of the literature discussions that took place in the group center each day. The story describes the experiences of a 10-year-old boy and his grandfather, who suffered a life-threatening heart attack. Together with his friend Dooley, the boy dreams of bringing his grandfather "back to life" by performing a "soul switch"—a magical process through which the soul of a dying person is exchanged with the soul of a particular animal with whom the person "got their soul mixed up . . . way back when the world was made" (p. 26). After sneaking a closer look at the grandfather's face, Dooley decides that a turtle would be the most appropriate animal for the switch. The first day's reading concluded with both boys searching for a suitable turtle at the foot of small creek in the woods filled with the wonderfully rich smells of "sap and waterlife" that often inhabit such places. As the grandson openly laments and regrets his decision never to have shown his grandfather this special place, Dooley turns to him and describes the way such places often get "captured" by those who visit them: "When a man gets to a certain spot and it strikes his fancy, he takes it on into his soul, see. It become his. And all the critters in that spot become his right along too" (p. 23).

Jeff initiated a discussion on this first day by asking a question ("Does that remind you of anything?") and then sharing the following memory or personal experience about the woods near his home in Virginia:

> I'll tell you what it reminded me of was, the place. The way he de-scribed the place reminded me of being in the woods in Virginia when I was probably about the age of the kids in the book. And seeing turtles and there was a little creek down there. But I liked the way he said, "you can take a place into your soul" because that's kind of how it feels to me even though, like now, when I go back, there are houses built on it, all in there and stuff. But I still feel like I carry around the place. I think that's what he meant by that. I don't know. Anyone else?

In response to Jeff's story and question, nearly every child shared a personal experience or told a story about a special place he or she had visited, often drawing connections to "that place" in the story. In addition, several of these children shared memories of their relationships with older adults (e.g., grandparents). In these accounts, they frequently reflected upon the importance of particular individuals in their lives, expressing personal regrets about missed opportunities for spending more time with older members of their family or immediate community. On this day, story reading was a imaginative vehicle through which students revealed themselves to one another as they shared and reconsidered the nature of their relationships with family members and friends.

On still another occasion, Jeff read *The Mountain That Loved a Bird* (McLerran, 1985), the story of a mountain made of "bare stone" that "stood alone in the middle of a desert plain." Each year a singing bird visits the mountain "carrying in her beak a small seed" that she tucks "into a crack in the hard stone." As years pass, plants begin to grow and eventually the mountain is no longer bare and alone. At the conclusion of the story, Jeff directed children's attention to the mountains they could see from the windows of their classroom. As the children looked out the window he asked, "What might the mountain be thinking?" At this point, children were invited to go outside to think and write in their "writer's notebooks." The invitation to write from the perspective of the mountain—to "experience" the "mountain's thoughts"—was just one of the more common approaches that Jeff used in helping children to understand the possibilities for re-creating and revisioning their world that were offered them by the stories.

Throughout the remainder of the school year, Jeff continued to question children and engage them in similar activities designed to help them draw upon the stories they read as a way to revisit and "experience" a number of important personal, social, and political issues. In reading the book *Teammates* (Golenbock, 1990), a story of the interracial friendship that developed between baseball players Jackie Robinson and Pee Wee Reese, students explored and discussed racism as it was "experienced" through the character of Jackie Robinson. In addition, they reflected on moments in their own lives during which they felt persecuted or oppressed.

The Children's Responses to Their Reading

The majority of students in Vicki's classroom were African American third- and fourth-grade children representing a wide range of academic abilities. The elementary school they attended drew its students from the surrounding neighborhood, a community largely comprised of African American families. The neighborhood in which the children lived and attended school was home to many of the social and economic problems that have become all too commonplace in large urban areas across the United States. Over the course of the year, the children in Vicki's class wrote and talked about many of these problems in response to the literature they read. Although such topics frequently captured students' attention and concern, story-related discussions also focused on the aspects of students' personal and community lives that they sought to remember, embrace, or affirm. Not surprisingly, conversations about family reunions and church gatherings, interesting or unique family members, African American leaders, vacations and family picnics, birthdays and holidays, personal goals and aspirations, and a variety of growing-up memories and experiences were equally popular topics of literature-related discussions.

The fourth- and fifth-grade students in Jeff's classroom were from predominately white, middle-class families. Similar to Vicki's classroom, these children represented a wide range of academic abilities and interests. The neighborhood in which the children attended school was adjacent to a major university campus. In general, although children in the surrounding community had little firsthand experience with many of the kinds of social and economic problems that children in Vicki's classroom experienced on a daily basis, many of their comments and reactions reflected a growing awareness of the problems and complexities associated with growing up in contemporary American society. More specifically, written responses and conversations throughout the year often touched on such problems and issues as poverty and homelessness, racial prejudice, ageism, environmental and conservation issues, health care, religious beliefs, and national and international conflicts as they were experienced at home, at school, in the immediate community, and on the pages of the local newspaper. In addition to these topics, story-related discussions in Jeff's classroom frequently focused on social relationships with family and friends, personal dreams and aspirations, favorite animals and pets, and a wide variety of memorable growing-up experiences associated with birthdays, vacations, holidays, and everyday events in children's lives.

Although the focus of children's writing and discussion about literature in both of these classrooms often differed in specific ways, our interactions and conversations with students over the course of the schoolyear provided insight into some of the humanizing and life-informing possibilities that children in each classroom had come to associate with the experience of reading and discussing stories. In presenting some of these possibilities, we draw upon children's written products, as well as the informal interviews we conducted with them. Our purpose here is not to provide an extensive account of the many ways that reading may function for children (for a more detailed discussion of this topic, see McGinley & Kamberelis, 1996). Rather, we intend to highlight some of the more salient ways that children in both classrooms seemed to use reading to explore and understand various aspects of their life and world.

In general, children's reading seemed to function in personal and social ways. Among the many personal meanings that story reading evoked in children, several emerged as the most salient. Specifically, children's reading often served as a means to envision and explore possible selves, roles, and responsibilities through the lives of story characters, both real and fictional; to describe or remember personal experiences or interests in their lives; and to objectify and reflect upon certain problematic emotions and circumstances as they related to important moral and ethical dilemmas in their lives. Reading also functioned in more social ways, providing children with a means to understand, affirm, or negotiate social relationships among peers, family members, and community members, as well as to raise and develop their awareness of significant social issues and social problems.

Exploring or Envisioning Possible Selves. Children's narrative reading provided them with opportunities to envision possible selves and celebrate particular role models—to adopt and imaginatively explore a variety of new roles, responsibilities, and identities derived from both real and fictional story characters. For example, after reading several books about well-known African American women, Mary wrote the following in her reading-response journal, indicating how the experiences of these women enabled her to reflect upon possible selves and possible roles for herself:

> Leontyne Price is a famous young lady. I read about her and sometimes I think I want to be like her. I read about lots of Black Americans like Duke Ellington, Barbara Jordon, and I forgot Phillis Wheatly. Some of these Blacks are dead already and I wish people would be alive. . . . Harriet Tubman Helped every one when it was slave wartime. I feel like I help people when I think about her.

Another classmate, Tanya, wrote about the biography of Diana Ross in her reading-response journal, emphasizing the qualities of independence and self-respect that she admired in the singer. She began her journal entry by copying a passage from the biography that described the family circumstances and living conditions of Diana Ross's childhood. Then she paraphrased another portion of the biography that juxtaposed Diana Ross's view of her home with that of the mainstream world. Finally, Tanya provided her own commentary on the singer's character:

> "After Diana [was born] came three boys and another girl. They all lived in a small apartment on the third floor of an old apartment house in the northern part of Detroit, Michigan. All the children slept together in one bedroom." I can see that being hard to sleep. The outsiders of Diana's neighborhood called it a ghetto, but Diana called it home. I really think Diana stood up for herself very well.

Remembering and Revisiting Personal Experiences. Children in both classrooms also used reading as a vehicle through which to remember, savor, and reflect upon personal experiences and interests or important people they had met or once known. For example, in an excerpt from her reading-response journal about *Bridge to Terabithia* (Paterson, 1977), Mari, a Japanese American student, wrote about the particular memories of friendship that the text brought to mind:

> When I was in 1st or 2nd grade I had a very close friend her name was Alice. I don't quite know what made he so speical, mabe it was because she was asian and I always felt a little more comfortable around asians. I might have liked asians because they seemed like part of my family.

Similarly, after reading *To Hell with Dying* (Walker, 1989), Gail revisited and reflected upon her relationship with her great-aunt Esther and her grandfather. In particular, she used the occasion to validate and reaffirm the importance of her past experiences with these elderly relatives. As she wrote in her response book:

> MR. Sweet reminds me of my great aunt ester, who dyed a cupple months ago. She was in the hospidle a few weekes and then she dyed and that reminded me of how MR. Sweet dyed. How he was sick and dockders [doctors] would see hem all the time and then he dyed. I thoat that the book was verry sad. and it also reminds me of how the girl would tickle MR. Sweet. I give my grandpa hi fives when ever we pass eachother and we started doing that at north carolina beech on vacation.

Reflecting upon Problematic Emotions. Children also found the experience of reading to be a useful way to objectify and reflect upon certain problematic emotions as they related to difficult or confusing circumstances in their lives. For example, Shanice described how reading *To Hell with Dying* (Walker, 1988) helped her to deal with the emotions she experienced in relation to the recent alcohol-related death of her uncle. In her reading-response journal, she drew a connection between her own experience and the experience of the author, Alice Walker:

> I like this book Because It tells you more what will happen to you if you do those kinds of things. When my uncle died from drinking. I was hurt. and I felt the same way as Alice Walker did. But when I went to the funeral I got Back home and I sat in my room and thought about it. then I learned how to deal with it.

Erika also wrestled with some important problematic emotions surrounding her relationship with her newly adopted infant brother in response to reading *The Cay* (T. Taylor, 1969). The story describes the developing friendship between a young boy named Phillip and his West Indian companion, Timothy. Shipwrecked and lost at sea, the two strangers endure a number of hardships that provide them with new understanding and insight into the differences that have characterized their separate lives. Specifically, the relationship of Phillip and Timothy served as an imaginative vehicle through which Erika revisioned and reconsidered the confusing and sometimes troubling behavior of her new brother.

> I cant sleep when my brother screems ispeshaley [especially] when we just got [adopted] him. he would screem and screem and I would just liy [lie] in my bed and wander what was rong and if I could help him because I felt bad that he had to go through so mach pan [pain] with being with 2 difrnt [different] people [families].

Participating in Imaginary Lives. Children frequently sought to share the exploits and experiences of the characters about whom they read. For example, while talking about the story *St. George and the Dragon* (Hodges, 1984), the story of a "brave and noble knight" who saves a kingdom of people from a "grim and terrible dragon" who was laying waste to their land, Jamar illustrated how the story functioned as a way for him to imaginatively participate in the lives and worlds of fictional characters quite different and removed from his own world:

> The story made me feel that I'd like to be both characters in the story. I would like to beat the dragon, and I would like to be the dragon. I'd like to know how it feels to be something, a giant animal, but then you're defeated by a little person. I'd like to know how it feels to be like, crush cities and stuff, but not hurt people.

Similarly, in response to a series of events in *The Cay* (T. Taylor, 1969), Christa imagined or re-created the "experience" of being lost at sea after Timothy and Phillip tried unsuccessfully to be noticed by a single rescue plane flying overhead. As she wrote in her reading-response journal:

> I would be feeling very sad that the plane had gone and I had been on the island for so long and I for some reason would be thinking

of Timmithy and the storm and the war, my mom and dad and just about my whole life.

Negotiating Social Relationships. Although our work in the classrooms of Vicki and Jeff revealed that children's reading was most often associated with these personal meanings, the children also invoked a number of social meanings that seemed particularly important to their development as readers and within various social groups. Among the most salient of these functions, reading presented children with a vehicle through which to understand, affirm, or negotiate social relationships among peers, family members, and community members.

Billy was one child who engaged in reading (and writing) in order to construct and affirm his relationship with members of his own family. Among the texts that Billy read, several included brief biographical accounts of the lives of famous African Americans such as Rosa Parks, Frederick Douglass, Harriet Tubman, Martin Luther King, Jr., and Malcolm X. When we asked him to reflect upon his reasons for both reading and writing about these texts, he often mentioned experiences and relationships that different members of his family had had with these individuals in the context of the civil rights movement. Thus, through his reading (and writing) he was able to celebrate, reflect upon, and deepen his affiliations with family members who valued and frequently discussed the lives and accomplishments of important African American leaders:

> [I like to read and write about black Americans] 'cause my mom met Rosa Parks and my grandfather he met Martin Luther King, and my dad tell me a story about Malcolm X. And then my dad, and my momma, and my grandfather met Martin Luther King. . . . And then after he was marching with Dr. Martin Luther King they wetted his shirt up. They wetted my grandaddy's shirt up when the firemen came. . . . And then, when my grandfather, he travels a lot, he went to Atlanta, Georgia, and then he put some sunflowers on his grave.

Children's reading also served as a means reflecting upon and rethinking the meaning and importance of friendships and relationships with peers. For example, *Lulu Goes to Witch School* (O'Connor, 1987) is the story of a young girl named Lulu and the difficulties she encountered with Sandy, another young girl who picks on Lulu during her first days at "witch school." In responding to the book, Tanya described how the storied experiences of Lulu and Sandy helped her to understand the difficulties she once encountered in school and the importance she assigned to her developing friendship with a classmate named Mary:

> It brought back memories, when I was little, not when I was little, back when people, when I was picking on people and people picked on me. . . . When I first read the first part of the book, it was talking about Lulu going to witch school and I predict, I said in my mind that this might be how my life was when I first came to school. . . . And as I read on, it kept talking about how I was when I first came to school.
> And then it came to the part where Mary [a new student that had just arrived in Tanya's class] came to school, and I started, started thinking on her [Mary]. And then it [the story] went on and on, and started, then we [Mary and I] started being friends.

In later conversations with Tanya, it became clear that reading about the friendship of Lulu and Sandy was a way for her to dramatically revisit the kind of friendship she had developed with Mary. In fact, we believe that in rethinking her relationship with Mary, she refashioned her ideas about the value and importance of friendship in general.

Understanding Social Problems and Social Issues. In addition to engaging in literate activity in order to explore and negotiate social relationships, reading was a means through which children could develop their political sensibilities, especially as it pertained to heightening their awareness of important social issues and social problems. For example, after reading *Farewell to Manzanar* (Houston & Houston, 1973), 9-year-old Mari talked about the experiences and struggles that other Japanese Americans were forced to endure as a result of their imprisonment in internment camps during World War II. In particular, she drew a connection between her own life and the experiences of a young girl named Jeane whose father was "sent away to an internment camp like my great grandfather." Mari used the story of hardship and separation that Jeane and her father experienced as a way of dramatizing and further understanding the difficulties that her own great-grandfather may have encountered in such camps. As she explained:

> The story *Farewell to Manzanar* starts out with an adult and she comes to Manzanar, when, after the war is all over and everything and then she remembers the whole story about when she was a little girl and that and how her father was sent away to an internment camp like my great grandfather was, and didn't come back

'till about five months after the war. . . . I was thinking that one of my great grandparents was this man [in the story] who was very proud, and it was very hard for him to be locked up in this place, so it made him kind of crazy. . . . [And there was a little girl in the story] and I thought that I might be very much like that if I was in the war, 'cause she didn't understand you know, what was happening and why her father was sent away, and what they were going to, like a camp, or something like that. . . . Even though it is something that happened a long time ago, it was a big thing, and it was hard, and I wanted to know just how they got through it.

As demonstrated in children's talk and text, the narrative reading in which they were engaged was associated with a number of life-informing functions and possibilities. As part of their participation in their respective classrooms, children were encouraged to practice and value a way of reading and discussing literature that involved reading both text and life. Over the course of the schoolyear, they used reading to explore new roles and social identities, to affirm their cultural identities, to understand and negotiate human experiences, and to wrestle with vexing social and political issues related to improving the quality of their life and world.

READING LITERATURE AND LIFE

In this chapter, we argued that a more complete understanding of the critical, humanizing, and life-informing dimensions of reading stories is integral to our efforts to further develop and extend our understanding of the meaning and importance of literature (or literacy) in students' lives. In addition, we argued that knowledge of this dimension of story reading is essential if we are to genuinely evaluate, revitalize, and refine our understanding of the role and function of reading and teaching literature in the school curriculum. Toward that end, we examined recent work in the area of narrative theory and reader-response theory as it serves to focus on the important role that stories play in helping us to organize and structure human experience. Although theories of narrative understanding and literary reading are indeed interesting, they have had little influence on the school literature curriculum and the specific manner in which stories are read and taught in classrooms. As Applebee (1993) found, literature instruction is still closely aligned with New Critical or more text-based approaches to literary reading. In the context of such approaches, students have little or no opportunity to experience or understand some of the possibilities for exploring self and world that both narrative theorists and reader-response theorists have come to associate with reading stories.

Unfortunately, recent research in the area of response to literature has done little to mitigate the apparent disjunction between narrative theory and the actual practice of teaching literature in school that Applebee describes. Although a fuller and more comprehensive awareness of the kinds of personal or social insight that literary reading might offer readers would certainly be useful in rethinking the role and importance of literature in the school curriculum, the majority of literature-related research has continued to focus on the *processes* that underlie students' literary transactions (e.g., Earthman, 1992; Garrison & Hynds, 1991; Hancock, 1994; Langer, 1990; Rogers, 1991). So, while some of literature's life-informing or life-transforming possibilities have been suggested by the data from previous studies of students' school-based story reading (e.g., Many, 1991; Many & Wiseman, 1992), few have been made explicit and many have remained largely unnoticed. For example, although many literature researchers have pointed out that children sometimes relate reading and personal experience, the functions of such relations have seldom been investigated.

In sharing a glimpse of the life and language that characterized the classrooms of Vicki and Jeff, we provided a unique look at some of the ways that children were encouraged to use and conceptualize story reading and story-related discussion as unique opportunities for interpreting, negotiating, and reconstructing experiences involving themselves, family members and peers, members of their immediate community, and the larger society. As we explored the talk and texts that emerged from children's reading of literature, we learned that such reading functioned primarily in personal ways. More specifically, children's reading was often related to exploring and envisioning possible selves and identifying with role models, objectifying and reconciling problematic emotions, and remembering and reconstructing important life episodes and events. In addition to these personal uses, children's reading functioned in more social ways, helping them to affirm or transform social relationships in their immediate worlds, to understand and consider possibilities for transforming social problems and injustices, and to fashion social and moral codes.

Through a variety of instructional activities that encouraged children to reflect upon their own lives and experiences in response to their reading, they were introduced to the idea that stories can be a means of personal and social exploration and reflection—an "imaginative vehicle," as Willinsky (1991) suggests, for questioning, shaping, responding, and participating in the world. As Joseph, Jamar, and the many other children who were members of these two classrooms shared their thoughts about reading, they brought to light a wealth of ways in which reading and responding to literature led not only to an understanding of the conceptual content of the stories they read but also to a process of reflection that helped them to understand themselves, others, and the world in which they lived. In sum, reading for these children involved not only constructing textual understanding of the literature they read but also constructing their identities, their moralities, and their visions for social and community life.

The written and spoken words of these children have a number of important implications for the reading and teaching of literature. In particular, children's experiences with stories in the classrooms of Vicki and Jeff suggest the need to reconsider once again the role and function of literature in the school curriculum—to rethink our current conceptions of what it means to read and study literature in classrooms. We believe that this reconsideration would involve shifting attention from comprehending, analyzing, or interpreting literature texts to reading life through texts and texts through life. Indeed, the children whose reading and responses we shared prefigured this shift in the ways in which they readily took up their teacher's invitation to read and talk about themselves, their friends, their families, their community, and their culture. In this regard, these children enacted what many narrative theorists and reader-response theorists have claimed to be one of the most fundamental dimensions of reading stories—their potential to engage readers in the exploration of possible selves and possible worlds through the depiction of the subjective worlds of protagonists. In relation to this point, it may be that literature instruction that focuses primarily on the analysis and interpretation of literary texts denies students access to significant personal, social, and political possibilities and consequences that might be afforded by adopting different and perhaps more life-informing perspectives concerning the functions of literature.

Surprisingly, although our understanding of this dimension of story reading remains only partially developed, assumptions about the life-informing and life-transforming function of literature continue to figure prominently in the conceptual frameworks of recent curricular reforms that fall under the rubric of multicultural education. Such reforms currently place considerable faith in the unique power and quality of literature to transform students' perceptions and understandings of individuals whose life histories, memories, and cultural backgrounds differ significantly from their own (see Desai, Chapter 7, this volume). Literature, from this perspective, is often linked to promoting cultural awareness among students as the basis for social change and the foundation for developing such democratic principles as social justice and equality for all citizens (e.g., Harris, 1993). These assumptions are clearly evident in a recent article by Yokota (1993) in which she revealed some of the more common transformative themes attributed to literature and story reading within recent multicultural pedagogies. As she explained:

> With the increasing cultural diversity of students in American schools, we as language arts educators face the need to provide literary experiences that reflect the multitude of backgrounds from which the children in our schools come. . . . For *all* students, multicultural literature provides vicarious experiences from cultures other than their own; and these experiences help them understand different backgrounds, thereby influencing their decisions about how they will live in this culturally plural world. (p. 156)

However, in a recent study Beach (1994; Chapter 3, this volume) found that mainstream students often develop "stances of resistance" to much of the multicultural literature they encounter in school. According to Beach, such findings raise important questions about the role of multicultural literature in combating racial stereotypes or prejudice. More specifically, several questions related to understanding the functions of stories suggest themselves: Can literary reading and study engender the kinds of transformative possibilities attributed to it by multicultural reformers? What are some of the meanings and functions that students actually evoke in relation to their reading of multicultural literature? In what ways does such reading inform students' lives, as well as their perceptions of others in their school and their world? What is the nature of the instructional context and practices in which students might experience and learn about this dimension of literature?

In light of these questions, possibilities, and consequences, we are led to underscore the importance of developing English or language arts programs that focus on the life-informing dimensions of literary reading and actively engage children in exploring some of the humanizing and transformative functions of stories or literature. The specifics of such programs and the kinds of understanding that literature makes possible are further discussed by Beach, Enciso, and Rogers (Chapters 3, 1, and 4, respectively, this volume). Indeed, we join these authors in suggesting that literature programs should be built upon an integration of the ideas and constructs embodied in the work of narrative theorists and reader-response theorists that we outlined in the beginning of this chapter.

Some of these ideas were embodied quite fully and explicitly in the classrooms of Vicki and Jeff. Others remained only emergent and partial. Yet by providing the children in these classrooms with personally and culturally relevant materials, occasions to read and talk about issues close to their own hearts and lives, we think that these teachers provided a catalyst for children's efforts to explore and understand some of the life-informing possibilities that might be associated with reading stories in school classrooms. As they became familiar with this aspect of reading stories, the children seemed to appreciate more fully the humanizing and transformative possibilities and consequences of such reading. The children's appreciation of these possibilities and consequences suggests the value of articulating, implementing, and studying the ways that stories may function in readers' lives. In addition, they suggest the need to better understand the kinds of pedagogical practices that make such possibilities a reality.

NOTES

The research on which this chapter is based was funded by the National Council of Teachers of English Research Foundation and the International Reading Association Elva Knight Research Award. Special thanks to Daniel Madigan for the intellectual energy he so willingly devoted to helping develop and implement the curriculum in Vicki's classroom. Also thanks to Lucia Kegan for her assistance in collecting and organizing data for much of this research.

1. Some of the more popular texts included *Here Comes the Strikeout* (Kessler, 1965), *Honey I Love and Other Love Poems* (Greenfield, 1978), *Harriet Tubman: The Road to Freedom* (Bains, 1982), *Encyclopedia Brown Gets His Man* (Sobol, 1982), *Diana Ross: Star Supreme* (Haskins, 1986), *To Hell with Dying* (Walker, 1988), *The Chalk Doll* (Pomerantz, 1989), *Ragtime Tumpie* (Schroeder, 1989), *I Have a Dream: The Story of Martin* (Davidson, 1991), and *Maniac Magee* (Spinelli, 1990).

2. Some of the texts that Jeff elected to read included *Bridge to Terabithia* (Paterson, 1977), *A Grain of Wheat: A Writer Begins* (Bulla, 1985), *The Mountain That Loved a Bird* (McLerran, 1985), *Heckedy Peg* (Wood, 1987), *My Name Is Not Angelica* (O'Dell, 1989), *To Hell with Dying* (Walker, 1988); *The Chalk Doll* (Pomerantz, 1989), *Ragtime Tumpie* (Schroeder, 1989), *Everywhere* (Brooks, 1990), *Teammates* (Golenbock, 1990), and *Uncle Jed's Barbershop* (Mitchell, 1993).

REFERENCES

Applebee, A. (1993). *Literature in the secondary school: Studies of curriculum and instruction in the United States.* Urbana, IL: National Council of Teachers of English.

Bains, R. (1982). *Harriet Tubman: The road to freedom.* New York: Troll.

Beach, R. (1990). The creative development of meaning: Using autobiographical experiences to interpret literature. In D. Bogdan & S. B. Straw (Eds.), *Beyond communication: Reading comprehension and criticism* (pp. 211–235). Portsmouth, NH: Boynton/Cook.

Beach, R. (1994, December). *Students' responses to multicultural literature*. Paper presented at the National Reading Conference, San Diego, CA.

Booth, W. C. (1988). *The company we keep: An ethics of fiction*. Los Angeles: University of California Press.

Brooks, B. (1990). *Everywhere*. New York: Scholastic.

Bruner, J. (1986). *Actual minds, possible worlds*. Cambridge, MA: Harvard University Press.

Bruner, J. (1987). Life as narrative. *Social Research, 54*(1), 11–32.

Bruner, J. (1990). *Acts of meaning*. Cambridge, MA: Harvard University Press.

Bulla, C. R. (1985). *A grain of wheat: A writer begins*. Boston, MA: Godine.

Carr, D. (1986). *Time, narrative, and history*. Bloomington: Indiana University Press.

Coles, R. (1989). *The call of stories: Teaching and the moral imagination*. Boston: Houghton Mifflin.

Davidson, M. (1991). *I have a dream: The story of Martin*. New York: Scholastic.

Earthman, E. A. (1992). Creating the virtual work: Readers' processes in understanding literary texts. *Research in the Teaching of English, 26*(4), 351–384.

Garrison, B., & Hynds, S. (1991). Evocation and reflection in the reading transaction: A comparison of proficient and less proficient readers. *Journal of Reading Behavior, 23*(3), 259–280.

Golenbock, P. (1990). *Teammates*. New York: Harcourt Brace Jovanovich.

Greenfield, E. (1978). *Honey I love and other tales*. New York: HarperCollins.

Greimas, A., & Courtes, J. (1976). The cognitive dimensions of narrative discourse. *New Literary History, 7*, 433–447.

Hancock, M. R. (1994). Exploring the meaning-making process through the content of literature response journals: A case study investigation. *Research in the Teaching of English, 27*(4), 335–368.

Harris, V. J. (1993). *Teaching multicultural literature in grades K–8*. Norwood, MA: Christopher-Gordon.

Haskins, J. (1986). *Diana Ross: Star supreme*. New York: Puffin.

Hodges, M. (1984). *St. George and the dragon*. Boston: Little, Brown.

Houston, J., & Houston, J. (1973). *Farewell to Manzanar*. New York: Bantam.

Hynds, S. (1990). Reading as a social event: Comprehension and response in the text, classroom, and world. In D. Bogdan & S. B. Straw (Eds.), *Beyond communication: Reading comprehension and criticism* (pp. 237–256). Portsmouth, NH: Boynton/Cook.

Iser, W. (1978). *The act of reading: A theory of aesthetic response*. Baltimore: Johns Hopkins University Press.

Kessler, L. (1965). *Here comes the strikeout*. New York: HarperTrophy.

Langer, J. A. (1990). The process of understanding: Reading for literary and informative purposes. *Research in the Teaching of English, 24*(3), 229–257.

MacIntyre, A. (1981). *After virtue*. Notre Dame, IN: University of Notre Dame Press.

Many, J. E. (1991). The effects of stance and age level on children's literary responses. *Journal of Reading Behavior, 23*(1), 61–85.

Many, J. E., & Wiseman, D. L. (1992). The effect of teaching approach on third-grade students' response to literature. *Journal of Reading Behavior, 24*(3), 265–287.

Martin, N. (1983). *Mostly about writing*. Montclair, NJ: Boynton/Cook.

McAdams, D. (1993). *Stories we live by: Personal myth in the making of the self*. New York: Morrow.

McGinley, W., & Kamberelis, G. (1992a). Personal, social, and political functions of reading and writing. In C. Kinzer & D. J. Leu (Eds.), *Yearbook of the National Reading Conference: Vol. 44. Literacy research, theory, and practice: Views from many perspectives* (pp. 403–413). Chicago: National Reading Conference.

McGinley, W., & Kamberelis, G. (1992b). Transformative functions of children's writing. *Language Arts, 69*, 330–338.

McGinley, W., & Kamberelis, G. (1996). Maniac Magee and Ragtime Tumpie: Children negotiating self and world through reading and writing. *Research in the Teaching of English, 30*, 75–113.

McGinley, W., Mahoney, T., & Kamberelis, G. (1995). Reconsidering stories. *Statement: Journal of the Colorado Language Arts Society, 31*, 9–16.

McLerran, A. (1985). *The mountain that loved a bird*. New York: Scholastic.

Mitchell, D. (1993). *Uncle Jed's barbershop*. New York: Scholastic.

Narayan, K. (1991). "According to their feelings": Teaching and healing with stories. In C. Witherell & N. Noddings (Eds.), *Stories lives tell: Narrative and dialogue in education* (pp. 113–135). New York: Teachers College Press.

O'Connor, J. (1987). *Lulu goes to witch school*. New York: HarperCollins.

O'Dell, S. (1989). *My name is not Angelica*. New York: Dell Yearling.

Paterson, K. (1977). *Bridge to Terabithia*. New York: HarperTrophy.

Pomerantz, C. (1989). *The chalk doll*. New York: HarperCollins.

Ricoeur, P. (1984). *Time and narrative* (Vol. 1) (K. McLaughlin & D. Pellauer, Trans.). Chicago: University of Chicago Press.

Rogers, T. (1991). Students as literary critics: The interpretive experiences, beliefs, and processes of ninth-grade students. *Journal of Reading Behavior, 23*(4), 391–423.

Rosen, H. (1986). The importance of story. *Language Arts, 63*(3), 226–237.

Rosenblatt, L. M. (1978). *The reader, the text, the poem*. Carbondale: Southern Illinois University Press.

Rosenblatt, L. M. (1983). *Literature as exploration* (4th ed.). New York: Modern Language Association.

Schroeder, A. (1989). *Ragtime Tumpie*. Boston: Little, Brown.

Silverstein, S. (1974). *Where the sidewalk ends*. New York: HarperCollins.

Sobol, D. (1982). *Encyclopedia Brown gets his man*. New York: Bantam.

Spinelli, J. (1990). *Maniac Magee*. New York: HarperCollins.

Stone, E. (1988). *Black sheep and kissing cousins: How our family stories shape us*. NY: Penguin.

Straw, S. B., & Bogdan, D. (Eds.). (1990). *Beyond communication: Reading comprehension and criticism*. Portsmouth, NH: Boynton/Cook.

Taylor, M. (1975). *Song of the trees*. New York: Bantam.

Taylor, T. (1969). *The Cay*. New York: Avon.

Walker, A. (1988). *To hell with dying*. San Diego: Harcourt Brace Jovanovich.

White, H. V. (1987). *The content of the form: Narrative discourse and historical representation*. Baltimore: Johns Hopkins University Press.

Willinsky, J. (1991). *The triumph of literature and the fate of literacy: English in the secondary school curriculum.* New York: Teachers College Press.

Witherell, C., & Noddings, N. (1991). *Stories lives tell: Narrative and dialogue in education.* New York: Teachers College Press.

Wood, A. (1987). *Heckedy Peg.* New York: Scholastic.

Yokota, J. (1993). Issues in selecting multicultural children's literature. *Language Arts, 70,* 156–167.

CHAPTER 3

Students' Resistance to Engagement with Multicultural Literature

RICHARD BEACH

As LITERATURE TEACHERS begin to incorporate more multicultural literature into the curriculum, they are encountering increasing resistance from
students (Jordan & Purves, 1993; V. Lee, 1986; Sharpe, Mascia-Lees, &
Cohen, 1990). When asked to give reasons for their resistance, students
cite their difficulty understanding the linguistic and cultural practices
portrayed in the texts (Jordan & Purves, 1993). They are also uneasy with
discussing issues of racism, particularly when these discussions challenge
middle-class students' privileged perspectives on the world. These students may also respond negatively to literary texts perceived as challenges to their privileged stance, apply negative stereotypes to portrayals
of cultural differences, and avoid thoughtful discussion of issues of race
and class.

Why this resistance? In this chapter, I discuss some of reasons why
students adopt what I am defining as stances of resistance to multicultural literature. I then suggest ways to help students move beyond resistance to develop a more positive engagement with multicultural literature.

STANCE AS IDEOLOGICAL ORIENTATION

For the purpose of this chapter, I am defining stance to mean the ideological orientations or "subject positions" students bring to their response to
literature (Beach, 1993; Bennett & Woollacott, 1987). These stances reflect
the beliefs and attitudes students apply to texts. Students judge characters' actions and infer thematic meanings according to their beliefs and

attitudes. For example, in responding to more "traditional" romance novels, students who bring feminist attitudes to these texts may be critical of the heroine's adherence to patriarchal values.

Students are socialized or positioned to adopt stances associated with their memberships or status in certain communities. These communities subscribe to certain cultural maps (Enciso, Chapter 1, this volume) or discourses constituting ways of knowing or organizing the world (Gee, 1990; Lemke, 1995). By responding in ways consistent with the values of a community, readers demonstrate their allegiance to a community's values. For example, members of fundamentalist religious groups may be socialized to read the Bible as "God's truth." They then affirm their group allegiance by sharing their literal interpretations of the Bible with these groups.

Stances as Constituted by Discourses of Gender, Racial, and Class Differences

Students' stances are constituted by ideological discourses of gender, class, and racial differences. Take, for example, a group of adolescent males watching and responding to a television program. In sharing their responses, these males are primarily concerned with maintaining their own masculine image (Buckingham, 1993). They are reluctant to express their emotional reactions to characters, particularly female characters, for fear of being perceived by their peers as unmasculine. To avoid risking their masculinity, they opt to play it safe by ridiculing or vilifying characters as "stupid" or "ugly." Similarly, female adolescents adopt a gendered discourse based on either/or oppositions between what is considered to be "female"—being outgoing and relating to others—and being "male"—managing events (Cherland, 1994). They also respond to characters in terms of oppositions between "good-girl" or "saintly" behaviors and "bad-girl" or "sinful" behaviors. These male and female adolescent groups are both adopting a stance reflecting a discourse of gender difference that privileges a male perspective (McIntosh, 1989).

As part of acquiring a sense of male privilege, males learn to adopt a "male gaze" stance associated with the masculine practices of assertiveness, physical prowess, and emotional detachment (Bennett & Woollacott, 1987). In a study of adolescents' responses to stereotypical portrayals of females in teenage magazine ads (Beach & Freedman, 1992), secondary school male students frequently described their responses in terms of metaphors of domination and male privilege. Few if any students in the study—male or female—were critical of the gender stereotyping in the

ads. Further, some males expressed their resistance to what they characterized as "feminist" perspectives on these gender portrayals.

Readers' stances are also shaped by discourses of class difference.
Readers applying middle-class values may object to portrayals that resist
these values. In a study of editors' decisions about the selection of books
for Book-of-the-Month Club members, Janice Radway (1988) found that
the editors preferred those books that did not offend or challenge what
they perceived to be their members' middle-class sensibilities. These editors were therefore reluctant to select novels that were experimental or
that portrayed topics deviating from middle-class values, anticipating potential resistance from club members to material that challenged the privileged middle-class worldview.

In secondary school settings, students' stances are shaped by a system of ability grouping or tracking that privileges some students over
others. It is often the case that students from middle-class backgrounds
are placed in "honors" or "advanced" ability groups and students from
working-class backgrounds, in "regular" or "vocational" ability groups
(Eckert, 1989; Oakes, 1985). From their experiences in these ability
groups, students acquire different attitudes toward their own status or
privilege in the school. These differences are evident in a study I conducted on students' responses to Richard Peck's (1989) short story "I Go
Along" (Beach, 1995). This story contrasts two different groups of high
school students: advanced and regular students. I asked students in advanced and regular tenth- and eleventh-grade classes to respond to this
story. In the story, Gene, a member of a regular English section, decides
to accompany the advanced students on a field trip to a poetry reading
at a neighboring college. Gene ends up being the only student from the
regular class who goes on the trip. While he is befriended by one of the
most popular girls in the school, Sharon, and he enjoys the poetry reading, he recognizes the fact that he lacks the social status associated with
being a member of the advanced class.

The regular and advanced students differed in their responses to the
story, differences that reflect their stance of privilege. The regular students noted: "I'm glad they have high-potential classes because I
wouldn't want to drag anyone back because of my rate of learning." "I
used to be in honors classes and then when I switched to regular classes,
my teacher was not as nice and treated me and others like us as stupid
and as failures." They also perceived the advanced students as being
more popular in the school than the regular students. One regular student
noted, "Most of the popular kids would not want to sit by a person who
is not popular; Gene was amazed that Sharon would sit by him." Another
regular student noted that "people who are 'above everybody' usually

don't talk to people like Gene." Advanced students attributed Gene's status as a regular student to his lack of motivation; for instance, one said, "I have run across many Genes in my 10 years of schooling and none of them are in advanced classes even though they should be. The average Gene dresses sloppily and doesn't act like they have a care in the world."

These students' responses reflect their beliefs and attitudes regarding power and privilege. Most of the students in the study also conceived of the characters as motivated primarily by their own individual attitudes, as opposed to institutional forces. Few of the students focused on the institutional system of ability grouping or tracking that shaped the characters' actions. Similarly, in responding to multicultural literature portraying racial conflict, students may conceive of racial conflict and prejudice primarily in terms of differences in feelings or opinions as opposed to institutional forces. They may explain instances of racial discrimination as a matter of individual prejudice deriving from a failure to recognize that "we are all humans." Their responses reflect the perspective that Henry Giroux (1983) describes as "private authority"—that subjective responses are constructed primarily by individuals as opposed to institutional or ideological forces. For Giroux, this perspective serves to "suppress questions of power, knowledge, and ideology" (p. 3).

This "individual prejudice" stance is prevalent in mass media analyses of the issue of racism. For example, a "Racism in 1992" series on "The Oprah Winfrey Show" treated the issue of racism as a reflection of individual opinions, rights, and experiences (Peck, 1994). This individualistic perspective reflects a therapeutic model of racism. In that model, racism is defined as an "illness" cured through confessions, release of anger, empathetic understanding of others, and forgiveness. By conceiving of racism as a matter of individual prejudice, whites avoid equating racism with themselves. This allows whites to "assume that every group is racist and to avoid acknowledging the power differential between whites and groups of color" (Sleeter, 1993, p. 14).

For John Fiske (1993), this attitude represents a "new racism" that goes beyond notions of racial superiority. This "new racism" has to do with "the struggle over the power to promote social interests that are always racial but never purely so and that function by putting racial difference into practice" (p. 252). Fiske argues that, rather than a matter of acts of individual discrimination, racism is an institutional phenomenon that privileges those in power, that is, whites. This power has to do with how

> certain social formations, defined primarily by class, race, gender and ethnicity, have privileged access . . . which they can readily turn to their own

economic and political interests. [It is] a systematic set of operations upon people which works to ensure the maintenance of the social order (in our case of late capitalism) and ensure its smooth running. It is therefore in the interests of those who benefit most from this social order to co-operate with this power system and to lubricate its mechanisms. (pp. 10–11)

Fiske cites the example of the initial Rodney King trial that led to the acquittal of the police officers who beat King. The trial was moved to a suburban site in which jury members would be more likely to side with the police officers, a reflection of the power associated with the Los Angeles Police Department relative to the power of a black man.

Beverly Tatum (1992) distinguishes between white racism as an institutional force that operates to benefit whites as a group and prejudices, defined as misconceptions or preconceived opinions that all groups may hold. She argues that the prejudices espoused by whites, given their social power in the system, are more likely to be taken seriously than prejudices espoused by other groups. However, whites are often not aware of the power of their prejudices. She also finds that as soon as her white college students begin to sense that they are part of this system of advantage, they deny any personal connection to racism as a system that serves to perpetuate their own economic privilege. While some of her students may perceive the influence of racism on others, particularly people of color, they do not necessarily examine its influence on their own attitudes and behavior. Tatum (1992) notes that students explain their interest in enrolling in her course on racism "with such declaimers as, 'I'm not a racist myself, but I know people who are, and I want to understand them better'" (p. 8). However, their understanding is based on a belief in a just meritocracy in which individual achievement is rewarded, and they are uncomfortable with the idea that society unjustly rewards those who are in power.

One reason for the prevalence of this "individual prejudice" stance is that those students who benefit from institutional power are rarely aware of the advantages of privilege. White students often take for granted their own white privilege because, in their largely homogeneous suburban communities, they are socialized to assume that white privilege is the norm (Scheurich, 1993). In their experience with the mass media, with films such as *Dances with Wolves,* the dominant system of representation positions people of color relative to a white perspective that is presented as the norm (McCarthy, 1993).

These mass media representations are based on essentialist, fixed categories regarding race. As Ann Louise Keating (1995) argues, "despite the many historic and contemporary changes in racial categories, people generally treat 'race' as an unchanging biological fact. Often, they make simplistic judgments and gross overgeneralizations based primarily on outer appearances" (p. 914). Such stereotypical thinking reduces exploration of issues to a sharing of master stereotypes such as "welfare recipient" or polarizing issues such as "affirmative action" (Goebel, 1995). Students may also be reluctant to challenge simplistic equations between academic achievement and race. In a critique of Ogbu and Fordham's notion of the "burden of acting white" hypothesis, Joyce King (1995) argues that this hypothesis assumes that in order to do well in school, students have to "act white." This further assumes the converse: that "acting black" represents a resistance to the school culture and is associated with low academic achievement. However, as King argues, such resistance often stems from students' attempts to protect themselves from exclusionary schooling practices that devalue African American cultural perspectives. Further, the notion of the "burden of acting white" may also include whites who may "experience being and acting white as a 'burden,' particularly in situations where they may begin to feel guilty when learning about 'white privilege,' or having to develop and/or resist 'racial awareness'" (King, 1995, p. 161).

These attitudes were reflected in an unscientific "write-in" survey of 248,000 secondary students conducted in 1995 ("Teens and Race," 1995). About half of the students experienced racial discrimination; 80% of students believe that their peers harbor some form of racial prejudice; 64% hang out with peers of their own race; 47% feel more comfortable with these peers than with peers of another race. These attitudes reflect adults' racial attitudes—64% of students shared their parents' attitudes. The increasing racial polarization in America is evident in changing attitudes toward affirmative action programs. A poll conducted by the Times Mirror Center for the People & the Press (1994) indicates that 51% of whites surveyed agree that equal rights have been pushed too far in this country. This result of 51% contrasts with 42% in 1992 and 16% in 1987, indicating a decline in whites' positive attitudes toward affirmative action programs.

A STUDY OF STUDENTS' RESPONSES TO MULTICULTURAL LITERATURE

All of this raises the question of how these stances of resistance shape students' reactions to portrayals of racial conflict in multicultural literature. In a study of students' responses to multicultural literature (Beach, 1994), I asked eleventh- and twelfth-grade students in three different high schools and in a university course to respond in writing to a range of different multicultural texts. These students also responded to two short stories by African American writers about African American adolescent males. One story, "Judgment" (Thompson, 1990), portrays tensions associated with an interracial relationship between a black male and a white female on a small college campus in the 1980s. (Current attitudes toward interracial dating reflect generational differences; the "Teens and Race" (1995) poll indicated that while 70% of students would date someone of a different race, 51% of their parents would either oppose or disapprove of their doing so.) The other story, "The Kind of Light That Shines on Texas" (McKnight, 1992), is set in a junior high school in the 1960s. It depicts a conflict between a black student and a bigoted white student who bullies the black student. Selected students also participated in taped small-group discussions and were interviewed about their responses to these texts.

It is important to note that the three high schools varied considerably in terms of their racial diversity. Two of the high schools were located in largely white suburban communities and had few students of color. In contrast, the third high school, given its location in an urban area, had a relatively high percentage of students of color. Content analyses of the students' responses indicated that while students in the urban high school were more likely to adopt an "institutional racism" perspective (Beach, 1994), students in the suburban schools were more likely to adopt one of the following "individual prejudice" stances associated with resistance to multicultural literature.

Backlash to Challenges to White Privilege

A number of students were openly resentful of implied challenges to their sense of white privilege. For example, one student, Andy, notes that he is "proud to be white and I'm not going to say oh I want to be something else." Given this stance, he reacts negatively to implied accusations regarding racist or sexist behavior, noting that "when I get accused of something I don't do, I don't like that and I get really violent."

He also defines the relationships between characters in highly competitive, individualistic terms. In responding to the white bully, Oakley, who harasses the black student, Clinton, in "The Kind of Light That Shines on Texas," he notes:

> I have no time for people like that, none at all. I was picked on when I was a kid all of the time just because I was different. There is a time when I wanted to be cool and change, like Clinton expressed that he wanted to be white, even though now I am glad

that I didn't change, because I am now proud to be an individual, not a number in a large group. I can do what I want, by myself. I don't rely on others for decisions.

Andy's backlash is also evident in a small-group discussion about "The Kind of Light That Shines on Texas" with three other students, Jody, Lori, and Jason. In this discussion, Jody argues that "females are minorities in that they are treated the same ways as blacks were treated back then."

> LORI: This is like a big picture of everybody who has been discriminated against in their lives.
> ANDY: Yeah, but it's not just women. Everybody is discriminated against.
> LORI: Women are discriminated against more than a white male.
> ANDY: By some people.
> LORI: By most people. Women still make less than males do.
> ANDY: I've seen some females get jobs on the basis that they are females.
> LORI: That's good. It's about time women rise to power.

Andy's reaction to Lori reflects his defensiveness regarding his own white male status. Later in the discussion, the group discusses Jason's claim that males prefer science:

> JASON: Like you can take science and you can find out how you can make your car faster or how you can hit somebody harder but . . .
> LORI: Because guys aren't sensitive at this age. All they have in their heads is girls and football.
> ANDY: That's prejudice right there.
> JASON: That's a stereotype right there.
> LORI: I don't think it is, though; it's true.
> ANDY: You think it's true about every single male in the school?
> LORI: Not every single male but most of them. Don't tell me that you guys don't think about sports and cars and girls more than your school work.

Running through all of Andy's comments is a resentment toward implied generalizations about groups, particularly white males. Thus, in responding to literature, Andy resents implied generalizations from white characters' behavior to the larger white population: "I hate reading stories that tell me that the whole race is to blame; I treat each individual as a person. . . . This story isn't saying that every white person is this way, it is the teacher and Oakley and a couple of other people."

In contrast, Matt, a college student, is more open to discussing issues of racism than is Andy. He recognizes his own sense of privilege: "I'm actually rather lucky and privileged. It stands better generally to be white because we don't have as high of a mortality rate. And we don't have institutional racism against us as much, so I feel very lucky." At the same time, his sense of white privilege leads him to object to having to read texts in which authors portray their victimization according to their race. In responding to Native American poet Diane Glancy, Matt notes:

> I am sick of victimization writers. It seems we moved from centering on the individual to centering on the group, and now we focus on the victim in the arts and Diane Glancy is just another of the various tag-alongs. And where does she get off being this Champion of the Native American plight when only one of her many grandparents was a Native American, Cherokee? Because of this she writes that she has always felt this presence inside of her. Give me a break. One of my grandparents was one-hundred percent German, yet I have never once felt any hatred toward the Jewish. What I mean is this, often when someone is so wrapped up in something they are unable to see very clearly. They can only look for the inside out and not vice versa. . . . She is too close to her subject.

Matt is irritated with Glancy's portrayal of herself as "victim." He seems uneasy with her openness in discussing her "presence inside of her"—her feelings about her victimization. He also resents having to read the Japanese American writer David Mura, "because it makes me feel as though no matter how hard I try I will always be racist, my society will always be unfair. I get apathetic and start seeing all the instances of domination throughout history." While Matt identifies instances of racism, he is reluctant to empathize with others' experience of racism, empathy that might lead to an analysis of institutional causes of racism.

Denial of Racial Difference

Another stance of resistance reflects students' denial of racial difference. In adopting this stance, students minimize the role of race, assuming that racial differences can be bridged simply by changing how people perceive or feel about each other. In response to the story about interracial dating, Kari notes that: "I think that if two people love each other, it shouldn't matter what color they are. To me, love doesn't see color. It just sees what's inside . . . for the most part we're all the same." Similarly, Amy posits that "People are people, why should it matter . . . maybe someday, we will also grow to a point where everyone believes in equality." And Nicole argues that "in the book that we're reading now, you don't see black and white; it's like it can be anybody. You can get into their role . . . I don't see any racial differences so I get into it. Like in *Sula*, I didn't feel like she is a black character. I felt like she could be anybody, Indian, white." She interprets a scene in "The Kind of Light That Shines on Texas" in which Clinton is "looking out the window and seeing prisms of all different colors" as representing the need for people not to "see because of somebody's color of skin that they are different. Everybody would be the same; he wanted everyone to be the same."

Denial of racial difference reflects a moral relativism—the assumption that everyone has the right to espouse their own feelings about race as individual opinions even if these opinions reflect a racist perspective. For example, because Mike assumes that individuals have a right to their own opinions, expressions of prejudice do not disturb him. As he notes:

> I don't care too much about what people say. I'll laugh or I don't really take it offensively. A lot of jokes don't really bother me because I don't really act stupid. My dad's a successful businessman and Polish. I think it's all in people's head what they think and it's their problem. I mean I don't get into people's problems; people believe what they want to believe.

Assuming that everyone is entitled to their own opinions serves to circumvent consideration of ideological issues associated with racism.

The extent to which students deny or accept racial differences is related to the degree to which they define their own identity in ethnic or racial terms (Helms, 1990; Phinney, 1992; Tatum, 1992). As they develop a sense of their racial or ethnic identity, they become increasingly aware of how their ethnic orientation shapes their responses and perceptions. These developmental phases have been explicated by Janet Helms (1990) in her model of white racial identity development. In the initial "contact" phase of Helms's model, white students lack awareness of or deny their own privileged status and often perceive people of color in stereotyped ways. They are also less likely than students of color to perceive themselves as part of a racial group, acknowledging their own racial attitudes only when challenged by alternative perspectives (Ferdman, 1990). At the subsequent stage, "disintegration," white students experience a sense of guilt or shame related to their own advantages as whites, but they still deny their own privileged stance. At the "reintegration" stage, students blame people of color for their discomfort and anxiety. At later stages, white students abandon their sense of white superiority, seeking out information about racism and openly confronting racism in their daily life. In a related study, 65% of first-year college students' thinking about racism was characterized as that of an "individual prejudice" perspective (Bidwell, Bouchie, McIntyre, Ward, & Lee, 1994). This suggests that many secondary and even college students conceive of racism in terms of dualist categories of victim/victimizer having to do with an individual's bias or discrimination. As they then acquire more information about racism through their own experience or in reading literature portraying racist actions, they begin to conceive of racism as a more complex phenomenon involving a range of factors within a larger social context.

Voyeuristic Reaction to False Portrayal of "the Other"

Students may also respond to portrayals of racial difference with a voyeuristic fascination, particularly in responding to texts such as gangsta rap music that seemingly portray a cultural world different from their own middle-class, suburban worlds. However, simply being fascinated by a sense of difference or "the other" does not necessarily lead to an examination of the issues of racism. It may even serve as a false substitute for grappling with authentic portrayals of racial difference.

The popularized versions of gangsta rap music that appeal to these students differ considerably from music geared to a black audience that directly confronts issues of institutional racism. This popularized version is marketed primarily to appeal to suburban students' adolescent fascination with images of deviant macho gangsters. Ewan Allison (1994) describes this appeal as based on

> a long-established romanticization of the Black urban male as a temple of authentic cool, at home with risk, with sex, with struggle. Mimicry is rife: baseball caps turned backwards; street mannerisms learnt from watching Yo MTV raps!: "wack", "dope", "chil", "yo", uttered with blackward prowess. These safe voyeurisms of rap allow whites a flirtation with the coolness of ghetto composure, the hipness of an oppositional underclass, without having to deal with the actual ghetto. (p. 445)

This romanticized portrayal of racism provides middle-class adolescents with a stereotyped conception of blacks in urban settings as "the other" without having to examine the underlying economic and political causes for the decline in urban life. As David Samuels (1991) argues,

[T]he more rappers are packaged as violent black criminals, the bigger their white audience became . . . rap's appeal to whites rested in its evocation of an age old image of blackness: a foreign sexually charged and criminal underworld against which the norms of white society are defined, and by extension, through which they may be defined (p. 25).

The emotional appeal of this gangsta rap not only serves to perpetuate stereotypes of black males as being predominantly criminals; more importantly, it diverts attention away from the institutional critiques found in other rap music. Further, students may pretend to "understand" racial issues simply because they listen to rap, without any reflection on their own privileged middle-class status. They may also avoid music that deals explicitly with racism, particularly when they sense that this music is not rhetorically geared to a middle-class audience. As Allison (1994) notes, "[T]he muteness of so much in hip-hop to white ears comes down in part to the ghetto's economic, political, and geographic and even legal dislocation from the rest of America" (p. 453). Middle-class adolescents' alienation from this more authentic form of rap music reflects their resistance to all forms of multicultural texts.

Reluctance to Adopt Alternative Cultural Perspectives

In responding to literature, students enter into a different cultural world, requiring them to suspend their disbelief and accept alternative cultural perspectives. For example, in responding to "The Kind of Light That Shines on Texas," set in the 1960s, students needed to adopt the perspective of a different historical era, one in which racial discrimination was blatantly and openly expressed. However, many students in the study had difficulty entering into what was an alternative fictional world of the past. In explaining this difficulty, they cite their lack of background knowledge of cultural differences given the lack of attention to diversity in their school curriculums. When, for example, a speaker at one of the suburban high schools analyzed Christopher Columbus from a more imperialist perspective, the students in the audience were astounded by the fact that in all of their history courses, they had never been exposed to such an interpretation. To their credit, these students were beginning to sense the need to broaden their perspectives, recognizing that they need to begin somewhere in their understanding of diversity.

Other students refer to their lack of direct experience with diversity. For example, Melissa notes, "I don't think I have a deep knowledge of any other culture or experience feeling of being in the minority; it is hard for me to relate to multicultural literature without very much background information." However, her conception of what constitutes cultural difference reflects a parochial conception of diversity. She describes herself as

> mostly Swedish and Polish and I don't feel like it has a big effect on me, but I think it's because I'm in the majority. There is one time that I had an allergic reaction—my lip swelled up and it is so different for me to feel like people are staring at me and like there is something wrong with me. That's one of the few experiences that I've has where I felt not mainstream.

Her conception of diversity is limited to observing surface behaviors. This was evident in her comment that "I went on a field trip to [the urban school in this study] the other day to see the different cultures and the ethnic diversity." Given her somewhat superficial conception of diversity, she may have difficulty adopting an alternative cultural perspective. Adopting an alternative perspective requires momentarily assuming a cultural worldview based on differences in beliefs and attitudes, as opposed to phenomena such as observed physical appearance.

Reluctance to Challenge the Status Quo

Another stance of resistance is related to a sense of paralysis that stems from students' sense of guilt or shame about their newfound sense of racism. Students certainly recognize instances of racism in their schools. As Matt notes:

> One thing that's gotten into is the idea of white bashing because our class is almost entirely white persons. A lot of people get really defensive when we see people depicting white people in a derogatory way. I'll admit to it and agree that's not very good, but even as white people we have to admit that our culture has done a lot of really negative things in the past and they have oppressed a lot of cultures . . . it hits us right at home.

However, students then have difficulty knowing how to act on or channel their guilt or shame in responding to racial conflict. In some cases, they espouse simplistic solutions to racial conflict, such as the use of physical violence. In responding to Mrs. Wickham, the teacher in "The Kind of Light That Shines on Texas," who tells racist jokes at the expense of the three black students, David comments that "I felt like if I was one of the black students I would have knocked Mrs. Wickham out. I couldn't believe that the teacher is this mean and racist." Other students were more perplexed about their own feelings. Roman (1993) argues that white students need to focus on their own sense of shame, analyzing reasons for their shame in terms of a social structure that privileges them:

> If white students and educators are to become empowered critical analysts of their/our own claims to know the privileged world in which their racial interests function, then such privileges and the injustices they reap for others would necessarily become the *objects* of analyses of structural racism. This allows white students and educators, for example, to move from *white defensiveness* and *appropriate speech* to stances in which we/they take effective responsibility and action for "disinvesting" in white privilege. (p. 84)

Students in the study explain their reluctance to act openly on their beliefs as based on fear of social repercussions. In response to the story about interracial dating, Heather notes:

> I look at black students or people of different color and wish to date one of them, but know deep in my heart that if I did my parents would scream at me, my friends would look at me funny, and people would stare, even though I think it might be fine to date a person of another color.

Similarly, Dan observes that "I don't worry about racism because you can't really do anything by worrying about it. . . . I just go with the flow because I just don't like a lot of controversy." In response to the portrayal of interracial dating in "Judgment," he recalls his own experience of social embarrassment:

> A girlfriend dumped me to go with a black male, for which I took some harassment at school. We broke up and two weeks later I met her at a summer baseball game or something. She has a black boyfriend and she introduced me and he seemed like a nice guy; I really never got to know him that well. But you say to yourself all those things under your breath and you kind of walk away. It's just that your own people stared at him, and you're just, like, "Well that's the way the ball bounces."

His reference to his peers as "your own people" reflects his concern with his own status with his white peers. The fact that Heather and Dan are reluctant to openly challenge their peers' racist views reflects their social concern with their peers' perceptions.

These, then, are some of the stances of resistance students adopt in responding to multicultural literature, stances that serve as barriers to exploring cultural perspectives that transcend an "individual prejudice" perspective. These stances of resistance mirror the larger society's reluctance to critically examine those institutional forces that serve to perpetuate racism in American society.

MOVING BEYOND RESISTANCE: EXPLORING ALTERNATIVE STANCES

In Chapter 2 of this volume, McGinley and colleagues argue that responding to literature entails more than simply reacting to a text. Responding also entails a range of life-transforming functions by which students construct alternative versions of reality and self. Central to this transformation is an awareness of how one's own ideological stance shapes the meaning of one's experience with literature.

Some students in the study moved beyond stances of resistance to assume a more transformational perspective. By openly exploring their beliefs and attitudes regarding racism as an institutional phenomenon, they reflect on the implications of portrayals of racism for changing their own attitudes and behaviors.

Empathizing with Experiences of Discrimination

In order for students to break down resistance to engagement with multicultural literature, they need to empathize with characters grappling with racism and then connect that experience to their own real-world perceptions. These vicarious experiences are certainly no substitute for the actual experience of discrimination. For example, a suburban student, Josh, describes his experience with working with low-income people: "I worked with the elderly, battered women and children, lower-income housing kids, and the Native Americans who go to Red Cloud School; and then I've worked in a reservation in South Dakota." He then connects his experience working on the reservation with his responses to characters who suffer from similar racial and economic discrimination. He also reflects on the limitation of his own perspective. As he notes, "I'm advantaged given my background . . . while I have a house, car, and shoes, and breakfast every morning, we had to give these kids in the housing projects their breakfast." Josh recognizes his own stance as that of an "advantaged" student. Similarly, by comparing her experiences in a private and a public school, Elizabeth perceives the relationship between institutional attitudes and racism: "In private school, they are racist and a little bit cocky . . . it opened up my eyes because I have always been around diversity. It is just interesting to see how the other half of the world lives . . . it just didn't feel like the school knew anything about the real world." Jason, an African American student, contrasts his experience of living in the city and the suburb: "I really learned what a stereotyped black is when I moved into the city. Because there you've got the gang bangers and all of that in the neighborhood and that's why my mom pulled me out of the neighborhood, because I started to turn into one." He notes that in the suburb he was "trying to play the 'Tom' role, something I remember doing when I was young. I didn't really know that is what I was doing until I moved into the city and started to learn different ways of acting other than what my parents are teaching me." Jim, an "American-Mexican" who was born in Mexico and lived his first five years in Mexico City—which he visits every summer—notes that his experiences in Mexico shaped his perceptions of racial and social discrimination: "You realize that a lot of these countries need a lot of help in order to make themselves better." He attributes his attitudes to experiences such as hearing jokes about Mexicans: "People remember that I come from Mexico and look at me and say, 'no offense intended,' or 'not of course you.' But I know that if I wasn't in the room they wouldn't say we mean this about all Mexicans except for Jim over there." Given these experiences, he is aware of how racism is shaped by institutional forces. In reacting to the portrayal of the teacher's discrimination against black students in "The Kind of Light That Shines on Texas," he notes that "the teacher seemed to care more about the twenty-seven white students than the three black students. And the rest of the community or society just seemed to let this happen."

Some of the female students in the study link their experience with gender discrimination to racial discrimination, seeing both as being shaped by institutional forces. For example, Lori notes:

> It's bad enough to be a white woman in the work force but to be a black woman in the work force is even worse. Race and gender kind of mix in together because both minorities and females feel the same kind of racial and sexist tension in the work place or in school, sports especially.

While the two forms of discrimination certainly differ in many ways, by linking the two, these students begin to define larger institutional forces shaping both gender and racial discrimination. As Pam notes,

> Thirty years since the beginning of the civil rights movement, women still don't have equal right to men. Even white women who are part of the majority race aren't treated equally. I couldn't imag-

ine being a minority race and being a woman. As a young female, I see that I'll have many odds stacked against me.

These students are not reluctant to challenge the status quo, even though they are discouraged from doing so. For example, Lori recalls her experience with confirmation class:

> I'm Catholic and I'm very pro-choice on abortion. Last year I went through a confirmation class and the issue for one night was abortion. I did voice my opinion but I was shunned because right away I'm perceived to believe in killing and all of this so I could not voice what I wanted to say because it was against my religion. So you have to keep your mouth shut.

In describing these experiences, students begin to recognize that discrimination derives from dominant institutional forces, whether they be racial, patriarchal, or religious.

Recognizing the Limitations of One's Cultural Stance

In addition to connecting one's experiences to portrayals of racism, some students are able to stand back and reflect on the limitations of their own stance as cultural outsiders. As Jamie notes in reading *Sula*, "it might be hard to read from a nonwhite point of view. None of us know what it feels like to be black. We just assume that they think and feel the same things that we feel. Maybe they do, maybe they don't." In describing her response to *The Joys of Motherhood* (Emechete, 1979), a novel about Nigeria, Elizabeth perceives herself as "an intruder: I'm trying to learn about Nigeria and it just doesn't seem right sometimes. I feel bad because we make so many assumptions about blacks like in *The Joys of Motherhood* what it is they are feeling." In defining her role as an "intruder," she notes that she is adopting "an objective, sterile, controlled viewpoint of a white middle-class female." She perceives herself as "a scientist, observing, picking apart, and categorizing multicultural literature as if I'm not a part of it, only looking down and observing and only being objective." She therefore realizes that understanding a different cultural perspective requires some understanding of how those norms shape people's lives.

Students also recognize their ambiguous attitudes toward experiences with racism. For example, regarding her upbringing in a small North Dakota town that was "generally pretty racist," Andrea, a college student, believes that "because of my socialization I make a conscious effort to not make assumptions about other people." When asked in an

interview to recount an incident in which she had difficulty openly challenging racist actions, she recounted her experience of going to a nightclub with a Philippine male. While at the nightclub, she noticed that another male with the same appearance as her partner was harassing some
females. She was approached by a female employee of the nightclub, who
asked her if her partner was bothering her and, if so, whether she wanted
him removed from the premises. She then realized that the woman had
confused her date with the other male in the nightclub primarily because
he was also a Philippine male. She then reflects on whether she should
have confronted the woman who had falsely accused her partner because
of his race:

> I thought if she wants to think that he's like this and I'm a certain
> way for being with him, then that's her problem. I just didn't want
> to deal with it. And I just told her fine, don't worry about it, I'll
> keep an eye on him. She left and I felt really bad afterwards be-
> cause I really wished I would have said something because it
> would have been one more person on his side. . . . It really annoyed
> me but what was I really going to do about it? In a way I really
> didn't feel like I had a right to say anything because as a woman I
> was glad she was there. If I was having problems with somebody,
> she would get rid of them. So it took me a minute to think now
> wait a minute, where did that come from. So who was I to stick my
> face in there and say anything?

Andrea is reflecting on her own shame in not confronting the woman
about her racist assumptions. She is conflicted about the differences between her own sense of being insulted by the woman and her need for
protection. She is also aware of her concern with potential social embarrassment from openly challenging the woman's implicit racism. Examining these tensions leads her to reflect critically on her own stance.

Reflecting on One's Stance as a Privileged White

In responding to portrayals of white privilege in texts such as Conrad's
Heart of Darkness (Conrad 1902/1990), students begin to reflect on their
own stance of white privilege. In her response to that novel, Elizabeth
examines the nature of a white European colonialist perspective:

> *Heart of Darkness* can be seen as making a very strong case against
> colonialism, not only through the symbolism of Kurtz/Europe in a
> savage land, but also through the constant images of waste and

death. The black African's victimization is obvious; the picture that sticks with Marlow is that of the pristine accountant who writes numbers all day long while outside there are moaning, dying people. . . . When Europeans go to places where their own society is unknown, they lose themselves.

Elizabeth then considers whether Conrad himself is racist, but has difficulty coming up with a definitive answer. She notes:

There are two basic elements of prejudice: ignorance and fear. We might call Conrad ignorant or Eurocentric, but he and his hero Marlow do not hate or fear the Africans; indeed, they admire their strength and grace. I suppose that it's as racist to stereotype positively as it is to stereotype negatively. So is Marlow/Conrad racist? Not hatefully so. Almost forgivably so. But, yes.

By analyzing Conrad's racism, Elizabeth is defining a historical perspective that helps her perceive racism as constituted by institutional forces.

Other students examine the ways in which school-endowed privileges represent a form of institutional racism. In describing the racial diversity in the urban high school, Alison also notes that the ability-grouping system in the school creates classes that are not racially balanced, something that bothers her:

I really think that part of your education is not the classes you take but that you're learning to deal with all kinds of different people. The classes here are not racially diverse at all and I'm not sure why. I think that maybe we don't like to talk about class in our society, but most of the kids in this class are probably from upper-middle-class backgrounds . . . maybe we aren't as multicultural as we could be here.

From her analysis of institutional structures such as the ability-grouping or tracking system, Alison perceives how race and class intersect in the school to create structures that privilege certain groups.

Students are also aware of how punitive administrative policy can create conflict between racial groups in schools. As Jim notes:

We get privileges taken away, and sometimes people base that on a group or something. They say "Oh, well, it was these people," and then everybody turns you against them. I think that's kind of a pass-

word that this group did this and this group did that and then it
starts to become discrimination.

Jim is recognizing that discrimination stems from "competition among
and inequality across groups . . . that results from group conflict much
more than natural endowment or individualistic factors" (Sleeter, 1993,
p. 14).

Thus some students are able to move beyond stances of resistance to
explore how experiences in their own lives, and with texts, are shaped
by ideological forces. These students then examine how their own behaviors as well as those of characters are shaped by institutional racism.

HELPING STUDENTS MOVE BEYOND RESISTANCE TO ENGAGEMENT

The students in this study who resist engagement with multicultural literature either see little reason for caring about the plight of characters or
react defensively to challenges to their own sense of white privilege. As
a result, they rarely grapple with issues of institutional racism. In contrast, those students who are engaged with multicultural literature are
more likely to reflect on their own perspective as privileged whites. By
empathizing with characters who are victims of discrimination, they begin to vicariously experience the impact of institutional racism. This may
then lead to some self-reflection on their own perspective of white privilege.

These findings suggest the need to help students empathize with
characters' perceptions and analyze how those perceptions are shaped by
institutional forces. For example, students could read August Wilson's
play *Fences* (Wilson, 1986), about an African American working-class family living in Pittsburgh in the 1950s. The play revolves around conflicts
between a domineering father and a rebellious son who returns home
after serving in the military. Both the father and the son are angry about
their treatment in a racist society. As in all of Wilson's plays, characters
frustrated with their inability to vent their anger on the outside society
turn this anger inward in self-destructive ways.

In responding to the play, students could write a narrative from the
perspective of the son who is returning home from the military and confronting his father. For example, a student could depict the son's anger
with his controlling father as well as his father's reluctance to attack racism. Students could then write a narrative about their own autobiographical experience evoked by their description of a character's experience.

Students could also engage in role-play activities in which they adopt a character's role. For example, students could assume roles in which they confront one of their own parents regarding that parent's racist statements. At the completion of the role-play, students could stand back and reflect on the positions they assumed in the role-play and discuss how those positions are linked to allegiances to certain social groups. For example, a student could adopt the role of a parent who seeks to prevent low-income housing from being built in a suburban community because of the need to limit potential crime. That student could link such a stance to racist assumptions equating low-income people and crime. By reflecting on these links, students could begin to examine how their own perceptions are related to institutional perspectives.

Students could then reflect on their narratives or role-play in terms of the competing voices or ideological stances adopted in their narrative. In doing so, they could consider the following questions:

Who is speaking and in what voices?
What attitudes and beliefs are being espoused?
What are the motives for assuming a certain voice?
How do these voices reflect attitudes toward gender, class, or race?
How are these voices constituted by discourses of religion, the law, education, management, merchandising, and so forth? (Gee, 1990; Lemke, 1995)

By reflecting on these voices and the implied attitudes, they may begin to recognize ways in which their voices represent certain institutional forces or allegiances. Or, as did Andrea, they may recognize ways in which they are silenced by a concern with offending or criticizing certain institutional forces.

Discussing Issues of Race

While many students in my study are often reluctant to openly share their opinions about race with others, they do perceive a need to discuss an issue that shapes their everyday lives. Given this need, students, teachers, or administrators may want to create a forum in a school that serves to promote such discussions. When, for example, the students in the urban high school in my study experienced an incident involving written racial slurs in the lavatories, they organized a series of forums to discuss ways of combating such incidents (Tevlin, 1994). At the university level, Joe, a college student, in commenting about his willingness to openly discuss issues of racism, recalled his participation as an intern in a Diversity Institute in his university. In the Institute, they "discussed issues and listened to speakers who would tell you about racism being institutional and that you can't be racist unless you have the power to affect other people."

These forums can also provide ways to help students discuss strategies for actively coping with racism. For a number of students in my study, their sense of guilt simply immobilizes them from taking action to cope with their concerns. This suggests the need for what Beverly Tatum (1994) describes as "white allies" who would provide the necessary support for sharing concerns about racism. These allies consist of role models in biographies or autobiographies or in real-world contexts who reflect white practices that are nonoppressive. For example, Tatum asked a antiracist political activist to speak to her class at Mt. Holyoke College about her own awareness of racism and coping with the social repercussions of taking antiracist stands. One of her students commented that this person's presentation highlighted the need for a

> support group/system; people to remind me of what I have done, why I should keep going, of why I'm making a difference, why I shouldn't feel helpless. I think our class started to help me with those issues, as soon as I started to let it, and now I've found similar support in friends and family. They're out there, it's just finding and establishing them—it really is a necessity. Without support, it would be too easy to give up, burn-out, become helpless again . . . when the forces against you are so prevalent and deep-rooted as racism is in this society (Tatum, 1994, p. 23).

These "white ally" role models provide students with what, for Tatum, is a sense of hope for combating racism.

Students can also examine portrayals of discrimination in literature not simply as expressions of individual prejudice, but as manifestations of institutional power. Fiske (1993) defines these top-down expressions of institutional power as "imperializing ways of knowing [that] tend to produce cultures of representation, ones that reproduce both a sense of the world and the power to control that world" (p. 15). These "imperializing ways of knowing" are often insensitive to "localizing ways of knowing" that are based on the particulars of unique cultural and economic circumstances. For example, in discussing issues of welfare, conservative politicians represent single mothers in a manner that fails to appreciate the particular circumstances of these women's lives as part of their daily need for survival.

One aspect of representation has to do with the selection of multicultural literature in the literature curriculum. A number of the students in the study, particularly middle-class African American students, noted that most of the characters they were reading about were victims of oppression. The very selection of these texts may itself reflect a process of representing racial groups in a manner that serves those in positions of power. For example, African American characters in literature antholog-ies or frequently used novels in secondary and college literature classes are typically shown as poor and/or working-class. Also, background in-formation about authors of color often tends to emphasize their own struggles with poverty. Having documented the existence of numerous African American middle-class writers who are usually not taught in schools, McHenry and Heath (1994) argue that multicultural literature is often represented for students as written by writers who are not middle-class and who lack "the same degree of variation in class, region, and ideology as other writers" (p. 437). They note that the choices of multicul-tural texts in the literature curriculum reflect a much narrower socioeco-nomic range, such that middle-class African American writers are ig-nored:

> The major choices as exemplars of African American literature tend to depict characters whose impoverishment and exploitation challenge them to survive as individuals that rise out of and above the circumstances of other victims of discrimination. The writings of Harriet Jacobs as an ex-slave are far more often read and referred to than those of Ida B. Wells as newspaper publisher and lecturer. Stories of Zora Neale Hurston's background in poor rural areas of north Florida receive much more attention than accounts of the elite back-grounds of her Harlem Renaissance contemporaries, such as Dorothy West or Jessie Fauset. (p. 437)

In examining this exclusion of middle-class African American writers as an issue of representation, students might question whether these cur-riculum decisions are themselves a reflection of institutional racism. The exclusion of these writers itself serves the larger goals of perpetuating the value of white, middle-class attitudes as the norm. Students might also reflect on how their attitudes toward class differences shape their responses to multicultural literature.

By participating in activities such as these, students may learn to be engaged with multicultural literature in ways that lead them to decons-truct their own white perspective of privilege that underlies much of their resistance to reading multicultural literature.

REFERENCES

Allison, E. (1994). It's a black thing: Hearing how whites can't. *Cultural Studies, 8*, 438–456.

Beach, R. (1993). *A teacher's introduction to reader response theories.* Urbana, IL: National Council of Teachers of English.

Beach, R. (1994). *Students' responses to multicultural literature.* Paper presented at the National Reading Conference, San Diego.

Beach, R. (1995, December). Applying cultural models in responding to literature. *English Journal, 84,* 87–94.

Beach, R., & Freedman, K. (1992). Responding as a cultural act: Adolescents' responses to magazine ads and short stories. In J. Many & C. Cox (Eds.), *Reader stance and literary understanding* (pp. 162–190). Norwood, NJ: Ablex.

Bennett, T., & Woollacott, J. (1987). *Bond and beyond: The political career of a popular hero.* New York: Methuen.

Bidwell, T., Bouchie, N., McIntyre, L., Ward, L., & Lee, E. (1994, April). The development of white college students' conceptualization of racism within the context of cultural diversity coursework. Paper presented at the annual meeting of the American Educational Research Association, New Orleans.

Buckingham, D. (1993). Boys' talk: Television and the policing of masculinity. In D. Buckingham (Ed.), *Reading audiences: Young people and the media* (pp. 89–115). New York: Manchester University Press.

Cherland, M. (1994). *Private practices: Girls reading fiction and constructing identity.* London: Taylor & Francis.

Conrad, J. (1990). *Heart of darkness.* In C. Watts (Ed.), *Heart of darkness and other tales.* Oxford, England: Oxford University Press. (Original work published 1902)

Eckert, P. (1989). *Jocks and burnouts.* New York: Teachers College Press.

Emechete, B. (1979). *The joys of motherhood.* New York: Braziller.

Ferdman, B. (1990). Literacy and cultural identity. *Harvard Educational Review, 60,* 181–194.

Fiske, J. (1993). *Power plays, power works.* London: Verso.

Gee, J. P. (1990). *Social linguistics and literacies: Ideology in discourses.* New York: Falmer.

Giroux, H. (1983). *Theory and resistance in education: A pedagogy for the opposition.* South Hadley, MA: Bergin & Garvey.

Goebel, B. (1995). "Who are all these people?": Some pedagogical implications of diversity in the multicultural classroom. In B. Goebel & J. Hall (Eds.), *Teaching a "new canon"?* (pp. 22–31). Urbana, IL: National Council of Teachers of English.

Helms, J. (1990). Toward a model of white racial identity development. In J. Helms (Ed.), *Black and white racial identity* (pp. 78–94). New York: Greenwood.

Jordan, S., & Purves, A. (1993). *Issues in the responses of students to culturally diverse texts: A preliminary study.* Albany, NY: National Research Center on Literature Teaching and Learning.

Keating, A. (1995). Interrogating "whiteness," (de)constructing "race." *College English, 57,* 901–918.

King, J. (1995). Race and education: In what ways does race affect the educational process? In J. Kincheloe & S. Steinberg (Eds.), *Thirteen questions: Reframing education's conversations* (pp. 159–180). New York: Peter Lang.

Lee, V. (1986). Responses of white students to ethnic literature. *Reader, 15,* 24–33.

Lemke, J. (1995). *Textual politics: Discourse and social dynamics.* Bristol, PA: Taylor & Francis.

Many, J., & Cox, C. (Eds.). (1992). *Reader stance and literary understanding.* Norwood, NJ: Ablex.

McCarthy, C. (1993). After the canon: Knowledge and ideological representation in the multicultural discourse on curriculum reform. In C. McCarthy & W. Crichlow (Eds.), *Race, identity, and representation* (pp. 289–305). New York: Routledge.

McHenry, E., & Heath, S. B. (1994). The literate and the literacy: African-Americans as writers and readers—1830–1940. *Written Communication, 11,* 419–444.

McIntosh, P. (1989). *White privilege: Unpacking the invisible knapsack.* Philadelphia: Women's International League for Peace and Freedom.

McKnight, R. (1992). The kind of light that shines on Texas. In R. McKnight, *The kind of light that shines on Texas: Stories* (pp. 59–64). Boston: Little, Brown.

Morrison, T. (1974). *Sula.* New York: Knopf.

Oakes, J. (1985). *Keeping track: How schools structure inequality.* New Haven, CT: Yale University Press.

Peck, J. (1994). Talk about racism: Framing a popular discourse of race on Oprah Winfrey. *Cultural Critique, 27,* 89–126.

Peck, R. (1989). I go along. In D. Gallo (Ed.), *Connections: Short stories by outstanding writers for young adults* (pp. 184–191). New York: Dell.

Phinney, J. (1992). The Multigroup Ethnic Identity Measure: A new scale for use with diverse groups. *Journal of Adolescent Research, 7,* 156–176.

Radway, J. (1988). The Book-of-the-Month Club and the general reader: On the uses of "serious" fiction. *Critical Inquiry, 14,* 516–538.

Roman, L. (1993). White is a color! White defensiveness, postmodernism, and anti-racist pedagogy. In C. McCarthy & W. Crichlow (Eds.), *Race, identity, and representation* (pp. 71–88). New York: Routledge.

Samuels, D. (1991). The real face of rap. *The New Republic, 34,* 21–26.

Scheurich, J. (1993). Toward a white discourse on white racism. *Educational Researcher, 22,* 5–10.

Sharpe, R., Mascia-Lees, F., & Cohen, C. (1990). White women and black men: Differential responses to reading black women's texts. *College English, 52,* 142–158.

Sleeter, C. (1993). Advancing a white discourse: A response to Scheurich. *Educational Researcher, 22,* 13–15.

Tatum, B. (1992). Talking about race: Learning about racism: The application of racial identity developmental theory in the classroom. *Harvard Educational Review, 62,* 1–24.

Tatum, B. (1994, April). *Teaching white students about racism: The search for white allies and the restoration of hope.* Paper presented at the annual meeting of the American Educational Research Association, New Orleans.

Teens and race. (1995, August 18–20). *USA Weekend,* pp. 5–10.

Tevlin, J. (1994). Fast times, good times at Henry High. *Minnesota Monthly, 28,* 80–85, 149–150.

Thompson, C. (1990). Judgment. In T. McMillan (Ed.), *Breaking ice* (pp. 615–629). New York: Penguin.

Times Mirror Center for the People & the Press. (1994). *Americans' political attitudes regarding current issues.* Washington, D.C.: Author.

Wilson, A. (1986). *Fences: A play.* New York: New American Library.

CHAPTER 4

No Imagined Peaceful Place

A Story of Community, Texts, and Cultural Conversations in One Urban High School English Classroom

THERESA ROGERS

THIS CHAPTER TELLS a story (not *the* story) of a teacher and her eleventh-grade English class in a midwestern urban high school. The teacher, Chris, developed her practices not out of any theoretical epiphany as a result of university courses, but out of a shared need among her students and herself to reform the kind of reading and writing instruction that typically takes place in classrooms such as hers.

It is important to set this story in the context of the 1990s debates, or, as they have been labeled, "culture wars," surrounding the teaching of English at all levels. While these debates have varied manifestations when it comes to policy, there is basically an argument on one side for the canon, basic instruction, and the pursuit of truth through literature. On the other side is a plea for the recognition of cultural difference, the awareness of subjectivity in relation to truth, and an expanded canon. As Peter King (1993) argues in the introduction to a book on critical teaching in England, teachers may be forgiven for becoming cynical about both extremes, but "nevertheless they must be urged not to . . . turn away to seek some imagined peaceful place of straightforward teaching" (p. xiii).

It is unlikely that teachers such as Chris would or could turn away. They are there in the classroom looking out at the faces of young adults who demand something different. They will ultimately have much more influence on these students and, as a result, on the larger society, than those of us in academia. Many of Chris's students had what would be

their last school literature lesson in her classroom, since there is a high
dropout rate: Many don't even reach eleventh-grade English. Some came
to class only occasionally and then not at all. So what does it mean to be
an urban English teacher at the end of the twentieth century in the United
States, standing in front of students whose mere presence demands something different?

THE TELLING OF THE STORY

This is primarily my story, since I am telling it, but it is integrated with
Chris's story and the students' stories by the intermingling of their voices.
A colleague and I visited Chris's classroom regularly over the course of
a year and documented what we saw, heard, and felt in journals, transcripts, videotapes, and field notes. Chris also kept a journal and occasionally provided time for us to interview her on audiotape. Some students were also interviewed. This chapter explores the nature of the
literacy or interpretive community that was built during the year we visited, with a particular focus on *what, how,* and by *whom* texts were read,
written, shared, and critiqued.

The class consisted of 34 students of "average" ability at the beginning of the year, about equally divided between white and African American, with one Asian student. About half of the students were girls. The
majority of African American students were bused in from an inner-city
housing project. The white students generally came from the neighborhood—so students came from a mix of poor, lower-middle-class, and
middle-class families. Chris is a white teacher who, although now firmly
a middle-class professional, grew up quite poor in the south side of the
city. She has often been recognized by colleagues as a particularly dedicated and compassionate teacher. In fact, in her journal and interviews,
she often spoke of teaching as a spiritual calling (cf. McLean, 1991). In
every other way, this classroom was a fairly typical urban English
classroom.

The story begins with a discussion of the notion of an interpretive
community as it is proposed by reader-response critics—the usefulness
of the concept in general as well as the ways in which it falls short of
actually shedding light on what it means to be part of a contemporary
urban high school English classroom.

REAL CLASSROOMS AND THE IDEA OF AN INTERPRETIVE COMMUNITY

At the center of reader-response theory is the notion that it is the reader who creates literary meaning (e.g., Bleich, 1987; Fish, 1980), given that literary texts themselves are indeterminate (Iser, 1978). However, in recent critiques of reader-response criticism as it is manifested in classrooms, a focus on personal responses as the basis for community responses is seen as somewhat limited. For example, Willinsky (1991) eloquently argues that students and teachers "should look up from their private and shared responses, to study how a poem is part of a larger literate enterprise . . . to trace texts out into the world" (p. 190). He also argues that works of literature should no longer be seen apart from other kinds of texts as though they are written or read in a social or cultural vacuum, as we sometimes pretend to be the case in English classrooms. In such classrooms, there is a focus on authoritative interpretations rather than on inquiry into texts as personal, social, and cultural constructions.

Students learn ways of reading from the particular contexts of the classroom communities in which they reside (e.g., Rogers, 1991); however, they also draw on previously learned conventions of reading and writing as well as on cultural situatedness, such as race, class, and gender (cf. Rabinowitz, 1987). Classrooms may include students and teachers who take on various identity or subject positions in relation to a particular literary work, and these positions may complement or even contradict one another (cf. Beach, Chapter 3; Enciso, Chapter 1; Hines, Chapter 5; all in this volume). Reader-response critics fail to acknowledge this "struggle of interpretations" of texts within communities or institutions that may result when "certain meanings are elevated by social ideologies to a privileged position" (Eagleton, 1983, p. 132).

In fact, literature study is increasingly viewed as the study of culture (cf. Smithson, 1994; Trimmer & Warnock, 1992), because literary texts are, in fact, cultural texts and because readers read from various cultural positions. Therefore literary works and readings can be seen as symbolic constructions of particular cultural meanings (cf. Campbell, 1994). In the communities constructed in English classrooms, students and teachers are necessarily negotiating social and cultural meanings and discourses as they engage in literary study.

What kinds of interpretive communities, then, are urban high school classrooms? How are they socially constructed? What are the boundaries? Are these communities sites of consensus or sites of struggle? How does the teacher affect this community and how do the students? What counts as text? What role do the texts of students play in these communities?

How are texts talked about, and how do they get "traced out into the world"? In what configuration do issues of culture or of race, class, and gender enter into the conversations? We felt that many of these questions could best be explored in the specific, or the case—that is, the particular instantiation of one classroom in one year. As Brodkey (1994) has argued we have too long reified theory while separating it from, and devaluing, local acts and local practice.

This chapter explores these questions through three lenses: through the study of the kind of literacy or interpretive community that was built among the teacher and students in this classroom from a sociolinguistic perspective; through a close look at the relationship of texts, or intertextuality, in the classroom; and through an examination of the cultural content of classroom discussions. The chapter is structured such that these issues are described as they unfolded across the academic year.

One Classroom, One Interpretive Community: Beginning Steps

We spent time in Chris's classroom in order to see how she and the students constructed a literacy community through their spoken interactions. Drawing on a sociolinguistic perspective (e.g., Bloome & Green, 1984; Saville-Troike, 1982; Weade & Green, 1989), we analyzed how classroom norms were created through these interactions across the year. This perspective illustrates how the rules for interacting in classrooms (such as who can talk to whom, about what, when, and for what purposes) are socially constructed through talk. "From this perspective, members of a classroom form a social group in which a common culture is constructed" (Green & Meyer, 1991, p. 141). In earlier analyses, I have illustrated how norms of literary interpretation are typically constructed in English classrooms through social interactions such as questioning cycles (Rogers, 1991; Rogers, Green, & Nussbaum, 1990).

To begin to understand this classroom culture, we recorded everything that was said during the first few weeks and systematically recorded for the rest of the academic year. We listened in particular to what Chris said about how classroom life would be managed, and *what, how, and by whom* texts would be composed, shared, and critiqued (Rogers & McLean, 1993). That is, we were interested not only in the building of literary interpretations but also in the interrogation of the ways of reading and interpreting in a particular community (Rabinowitz, 1987).

One of the first things we noticed in Chris's classroom was her constant and consistent attempts to build a particular kind of classroom literacy community. This was explicitly articulated through many specific comments on what kind of classroom she was hoping to create in general and what kinds of literacy events she was attempting to bring to life. Her comments signaled to the students that she hoped to construct a community in which members listened to each other and honored what they heard. In literacy events, she signaled a true personal interest in what the students had to say as well as a concern that they become skilled readers and writers with "voice" as well as mastery of conventions. For instance, an example of how literary texts were to be read in this community is illustrated in an early example across two days in September in which she models for them her way of reading a poem:

> When I read anything I try not to think too much about it when I read it for the first time . . . so take a couple of minutes to look over—begin first with the title. I think titles particularly have a lot to say . . . If you could read the poem once silently through . . . Is there anyone in here who would feel like they would need to read this a second time to get a better understanding or do you all feel like when you read a poem that immediately the meaning comes to you? Can I just get your initial reaction?. . . . Anything else . . . any other sort of feeling about this?

Here Chris seems to be both directing their attention to specific aspects of the text (thus to particular meanings) *and* encouraging immediate personal responses. She goes on to say:

> Now I always hated teachers when I was in school that used to rip poetry apart and then it was like you talked about it so much you never wanted to read another poem in your life. I really believe that poetry like other literature speaks to you as an individual. That your interpretation might be a little different from my own, but I don't think mine is necessarily better than yours. There are specific things that I should be able to ask you and you should be able to get from this and . . . there are some terms . . .

Again, Chris is displaying to the students the seemingly conflicting aspects of a literature curriculum in which students are encouraged to give individual, subjective responses but must also display knowledge of literary conventions and the ability to extract "an interpretation." Yet her overriding concern is that students be given a chance to construct their own meanings while moving herself away from the role of the interpreter, and so she provides them with models or ways of reading that would facilitate that process.

Let me say I don't have the right answer and that this group may
have a different view from that group, but I think that is sort of interesting. . . . See, the value of talking with other people is that ideas
come out that you may never have thought of . . . and I really want
you to know that you far surpassed my reading of it.

In her journal from that time, Chris expresses her concern about the
silence of some students even in the face of her continual prodding: "I
am concerned that a few students respond and *many* are silent" (journal,
9/6). And still a few weeks later, the concern appears in her journal that
the students are still looking toward her as the interpretive authority: "I
realize that if I speak, the group takes on my views and abandons their
own" (journal, 9/18).

By November, however, students who are interviewed recognize
Chris's efforts to build a particular kind of community. Jimmy (from the
inner city and the first male in his family who didn't drop out and who
had hopes of going to college—in part, so that he could set an example
for his younger cousins) comments:

Well, OK, she'll have like a class discussion and like she wants to
learn from what you say and we learn from each other. And she's always asking questions. Makes you want to listen. Wants to add little comments and then we learn off each other. I like that.

Even so, it is not until later in the year that she begins to hear the
kinds of responses or "voices" that she hopes to hear. This usually happens in the context of discussions in which students reveal their personal
responses, freely relate their own texts and other kinds of cultural texts
to literary texts, and respond in ways that reflect their social and cultural
stances in the world. In other words, it is not until the texts of the classroom "were traced out into the world" that Chris feels she is hearing
what the students have to say.

Texts and Intertextuality in One Classroom Community

The texts in Chris's classroom include a traditional American literature
anthology, student writings, a multicultural reading list, and movies,
magazines, and other noncanonical bits of literacy that serve the purpose
of creating responses and dialogue among students. The first thing Chris
notices about the new anthology is who is represented and who is not:

I think what's interesting is when I go through the textbook it started out with the pilgrims and haven't we left someone out? The American Indians. Are there American Indians here? (class, 9/5)

In her journal (9/4) she writes:

The materials [in the anthology] are in chronological order, but the text has omitted Native American Literature. . . . I want them to be able to compare the Puritans' view of America and the Indians', versus the Indians' values and beliefs. I want the students to compare these to their own values.

Simple decisions and recognitions such as this in a classroom become political acts for teachers such as Chris. Indeed, as bell hooks (1994) has argued, no education is politically neutral. Chris's notion of what counts as texts worthy of sharing and interpreting, both within and beyond the canon, is also open and fluid. Student texts, in particular, are seen as the stuff of the curriculum, and much time is spent carefully modeling ways in which students can respond to each other's work. In one example, which we call "Larry's story," a student's story is held up for sharing and critique in a writing lesson, and then it is briefly reintroduced in the context of a discussion of a canonical poem.

Larry's Story. The following excerpt, from one of Chris's early transcripts, is part of a lesson in which she asks student volunteers to share their written "memory pieces." She gives the autobiographical assignment to get "some insight into who they are and what they think/feel" (journal, 9/3). This is the first piece of writing to be included in their portfolios, and it is also a way for Chris to come to know the students and for the students to come to know each other. The students share stories about a range of experiences, including being seriously injured in a sports-related accident, giving birth, and, in Larry's case, being shot.

CHRIS: I'm real anxious to hear some of your memories. Larry, you decided to go first. All right.
LARRY: I did mine on the worst memory I ever had. It was May 4th, 199—. I got shot three times. . . . It was my oldest brother's birthday that day. I stayed home most of the day waiting for a phone call. . . . Around 10:30 I left and went over (inaudible) and she was already drinking some beer and I had some and I drove home. . . . Deana and I got punked up a little bit. I got real high. I thought I was bad and my little brother came over and we was all sitting

down talking and he pulled out a gun from nowhere and I was like I don't believe it was real so I asked to see it and it was real and it had six bullets in it. From there he asked me if I wanted to go to a party and so I went to a party again. After I left the party I went to another party and then I saw a guy that spit on me and I was going to beat his—you know so when I seen him you know that's what I did. I kicked him bad. Then he was holding on to me for some reason and then the next thing I know he just pulled out a gun and shot me in my arm and my chest. The next thing my little brother heard the gunshot. He turned around and pulled his gun and shot me in my leg while shooting the other guy. Then from there—I've got more but that's all I wrote because I didn't have enough time to write the rest.

CHRIS: So Larry, how did you feel? This is terrible to have to ask one of my students this, but how does it feel to have a bullet in you?

LARRY: Still in. They took one of them. I got shot in my arm right here and then they had to cut me open because of the bullet. He shot me with a hollow-tip bullet and the first one is inside my stomach. He cut me from here (*gestures*) all the way down. My little brother shot me with a .38 in my leg and the gun that he shot me with was a .22. I got shot three times. It was a mistake but if he wasn't there I would probably be dead.

During his sharing of his story, there are signs that in this early draft Larry is already creating a text that has a personally transforming function (McGinley & Kamberelis, 1992; McGinley et al., Chapter 2, this volume) for him. That is, the classroom dialogue helps him to reflect on the incident, on the irony of thinking his brother was killing him but was actually perhaps saving his life. He brought up the incident again in his interview and reflected on how the incident made him realize he wanted to do something with his life—"I don't want to be a bum. I don't want to live off other people." He also talked about how it changed his attitude toward conflict: "Now I don't care if somebody spit on me. They can spit on me. I just wipe it off and keep going. Not important to me anymore. Not if my life is involved."

CHRIS: Larry, I'm curious. This is such a terrible thing. I mean I'm glad you survived that and it would make a great story if you ever decided to write a short story. I think this would be a great story where you actually could tell what people said and what happened and carry that thought over. . . . Thanks for being willing to share that with everybody. That's a scary thing. . . . Probably a lot of you have personal experiences. . . . Are there any questions you thought to ask Larry when he was reading his story?

STUDENT: Did it hurt?

LARRY: I thought my little brother was trying to kill me and the other guy tried to kill me but when the doctor put the tubes in my body that was the worst part of all.

CHRIS: What was the worst part?

STUDENT: Just the IVs hurt?

LARRY: The whole thing. (*Many people talking.*)

CHRIS: I can visualize that, can't you? I want to thank those people who volunteered to read. I know that it is not always easy to do in front of your peers . . . but sometimes it's easier to take criticism from your peers than from a teacher. The one thing I try to point out by asking you if there were any questions that you had as you were listening is that, like in any good story, a good teller never leaves out the details. And they were obviously important enough for people to ask. . . . Larry, what you were feeling physically was something that I wanted to know and maybe that was something you would include in your story, but like any writer you always have the option to accept someone's advice or to disregard it. . . . We are going to be doing a lot of writing. We are going to be doing a lot of sharing of our writing with other students and you have to learn that criticism isn't something to hurt you. Hopefully, it will be used to improve your writing. We'll be talking more about that later.

Chris displays her many reasons for sharing and critiquing student texts: to build community, to make them feel like writers, to help them with the skills of writing, and to connect their lives to the more traditional curriculum. Aware of the need to make these connections between what the students experience and what they read, Chris provides opportunities to make these links explicit. In the following discussion, which took place almost three months later, Chris asks the students to write a journal entry on their thoughts about or experiences with death prior to reading "Thanatopsis" by William Cullen Bryant. During their sharing of journal entries in November, a student spontaneously reintroduces Larry's story into the discussion.

STUDENT 1: I'm not scared of [death]. I don't want to die right now but I'm not going to be scared when it comes.

STUDENT 2: You can't be scared of something that has to happen to you at a certain time in your life.

STUDENT 3: Until you've got children or a whole family. . . . Somebody comes to you and says . . .

STUDENT 1: I know what you're saying.

STUDENT 3: . . . if you don't give me your money then I'll shoot you, you ain't going to be ready to leave.

STUDENT 2: I just don't see why I would be—I'm not scared. I don't see why people would be scared of something that has to happen.

STUDENT 4: (inaudible) in a painful way. It's not that they're scared of dying. It's just dying in a painful way.

CHRIS: Well, see, you know what my fear is? It's like Joe says—you die and we really don't know what happens because no one has really come back to tell us so I think for myself—I can only speak for myself—the fear is not knowing.

STUDENT 4: That's normal.

CHRIS: That's what you're scared of?

STUDENT 1: But I go on faith because I don't know the specifics but I know there is a better place and I have faith in at least that. Whether it's going to be some cloudy place where I float around with planes . . .

CHRIS: Uh huh (*Laughs.*)

STUDENT 1: . . . or just living out the fantasies of my life or whatever. Maybe as a spirit living it out the way I want to live . . .

STUDENT 5: I have a question for Larry. When you were shot did they put you under anesthesia in the hospital?

LARRY: Yeah.

STUDENT 5: You could have died. . . . So when you were put asleep did you have a feeling like you would come back?

LARRY: I was praying. I was afraid I wouldn't come back.

CHRIS: You know what's interesting is when I talk with young people, in my mind I still think that you haven't had a lot of experiences with death and after talking with young people that's so untrue. Because many of you have had such close experiences with death. Some of you have had surgery. Some of you have had near-death experiences with being shot or in auto accidents. Some of us have had a lot of experience. . . . Well, I really want to read these [journal entries] and if you want to finish that thought or idea and then turn them in tomorrow to me that's fine. If you're finished if you wouldn't mind I would like to see them. Um, the poem we are going to read today—it's really interesting and the reason I like it is because supposedly the author was about your age . . . and he was contemplating this very thing. He was contemplating death and he was thinking, gosh, I wonder what is going to happen ... and he was considered a deist and I'm not expecting you to call that up in your memory but what do you surmise he might think about death based on that. Just knowing he is a deist?

STUDENT 6: That once he's dead, it's over with ... (inaudible). Is that a deist?

CHRIS: Uh ... that God sort of created things and then he let them follow their natural order and what is that—natural order?

STUDENT 6: That's what I just said.

CHRIS: Right. You said it. There is a belief in God but not in predestination. Just sort of a cycle. The natural cycle of things (*compares to cycle of seasons*). If our author sort of believes in the natural cycle of things—if he believes this then we're going to guess now what is his perception of death, or how does he view death. Can we—can we speculate? Your speculation is as good as anyone else's. Someone said when you're dead, you're dead. Someone else said reincarnation and there might be some others. Actually, what he does is he goes out and he is sort of wandering and he starts looking at these things in nature and evidently he wrote this poem after that experience and in this poem nature speaks. Could we have a nature speaker?

After reading and discussing the poem, including the author's view of death, Chris says:

> Someone said to me yesterday, "Miss Gibson, are we going to read poetry and enjoy it or are we going to rip it apart?" I don't want to rip it apart. I just wanted to show you that this man at 16, 17 was having some thoughts about death and this was his belief or explanation. This is how he dealt with it and I'd like to talk, after I have a chance to look at your responses, about how this compares to your view.

In these excerpts Chris again signals the worth of the students' own responses, which are "as good as anyone else's" and indicates that part of the process of reading in this classroom is to set their own beliefs against those articulated in texts. In this way she keeps an unswerving and sympathetic eye on what the students are expressing personally about themselves and their lives and their beliefs, while at the same time she is able to see these expressions as texts worthy of analysis, comparison, and critique. In this classroom, then, we begin to see an intermingling of texts: of students' written and spoken texts, canonical texts, and the texts surrounding those primary texts, so that authors and readers become members of the same community (Rabinowitz, 1987). In their interviews many students feel that Chris is mixing up history with English in her attention to authors' social and cultural backgrounds, and at the same time they feel, as one student said, "she is more of a real person interested in us." What Chris is beginning to accomplish is to create a community in which authors are readers, readers are authors, and both readers and authors are seen as situated in particular social and cultural places from which they can construct particular meanings about their lives and the lives of others.

Social and Cultural Conversations in One Community

In February, Chris reads student responses to F. Scott Fitzgerald's *The Great Gatsby* and feels once again that there is a lack of "voice" in their writing and that they miss the race and class implications in the novel. So on the advice of a friend she shows them a documentary film called *The War Between the Classes* and then distributes a survey to get their responses. When there still isn't much discussion, Chris thinks, "Now I know they have had similar experiences but maybe I'm treading too close . . . I know they want to say something but they are hesitant."

Eventually, as Chris encourages them to share their survey responses, the discussion becomes a lively debate. At one point, a student says he agrees with the student in the film who says people don't want to be responsible for historical racism and prejudice. Chris responds by acknowledging his comment and bringing up a comment by another student in the film who had talked about the subtleties of contemporary racism.

> CHRIS: You know, I think there's a point here. We're saying OK, we're not putting Asians in camps anymore, enslaving blacks and we're not. . . . I hear there clearly is a difference but I think the subtleties that Ann is talking about, unless you walk in someone's shoes it can be a little difficult to understand and I think that's why the teacher [in the film] went to the extreme he did to make the point about what it is like to be a victim of racism.
>
> SUSAN: It's like they're trying to say they're not enslaving people, putting them in a place and saying you do this, but they give them these jobs and it's hard for them because like they put them in poor conditions. Like Jesse's mom [in the film] wasn't a slave but she got paid minimum wage and they wanted her to do extra

work and she had to do it or lose her job. That's enslaving her right there.

SAM: I don't think you should live that way. I don't think you should worry about what happened 20 or 30 years ago. Worry about what will happen now and how you're going to change that.

CHRIS: And Adam [in the film] says that. He says I don't know why you're bringing up all this old stuff, all these old feelings. Bob, you made a comment to that point.

BOB: I don't think you should forget it either. The human race isn't perfect and I believe that if you forget about something you will probably fall back into that pattern again. You have to rehash the mistakes of the past.

After a brief discussion on the acting in the film, another student, Susan, suddenly shifts the topic to a current concern of the students: a new proficiency test that would be tied to high school diplomas throughout the state.

SUSAN: What I gotta say is not pertaining to this movie, right? They say racism and prejudice is not going on. But this proficiency test ... in a couple of years from now, people that live in the lower class, they gotta go out and make money you know, but if they can't pass that test that's keepin' them down in the lower class ...

CHRIS: Right, you see, my purpose in showing you this film was not to talk about the film, per se, but to get you to think and write about your own experience and Susan, I'll tell ya, that's my fear as an educator, and there are a lot of educators out there expressing the same fear of this proficiency test and what it does to keep people where they are and keep people under control. . . . Is this test designed to keep you at a certain level? That's something that affects you people directly, and Susan, you may want to write about that.

BOB: And they published those scores and like ———— [a suburb] had like 99% and in city schools, there's like 16% that passed and it went down from the ones that had money to the ones that had nothing. The ones that have money have the grades and the ones that have nothing have nothing.

CHRIS: And do you think the people in ———— are more intelligent than you?

STUDENTS: No.

CHRIS: Then why do they do better on the test?

JAY: They have the support they need.

Joe: I think the parents push them more. There's more influence to do well.

Ann: I used to go to school there and it was, like, what are you going to do tonight and they would say, "I'm gonna do my homework" and it's like they know their parents got to where they are and they want to get there, too.

Chris: It's that self-fulfilling prophecy. It's understood you will do well. It has a lot to do with environment.

Joe: Yeah, like my mom has to work and she doesn't have time to help me. I'm not putting her down or anything, but she can't help me and stuff. So like in ———, they've got all the money and maybe those parents have time to sit down with them and show them how to do it. My parents, they don't have enough time. Not that they don't care or don't want to but they're tired when they come home.

Carl: I'll go with Joe. People in ———, I mean everyone is success-ful around there and they've got good school buildings, every-thing. But if they had to live in my neighborhood and see what I see every day they would probably lock themselves in their house and cry. There wouldn't be anything to do because they couldn't deal with it.

Chris: I don't know—if some of the things that some of you live with I don't know if I could get up in the morning. I've even said that out loud to people. Sometimes when I think about your experi-ences I try to put myself in that experience and I say, "Could I get up in the morning and go on?" I'm not sure. I'm not so sure about that.

At this point the discussion turns to opportunities for work and college, focusing on the relative difficulties of blacks and whites to "make it," with various personal anecdotes to illustrate points made. One anecdote from the film centers on a humorous story that also contains a racist inci-dent, to which Chris responded:

Chris: We laugh about that but if you remember what Amy said in the film, she said I smiled but I cried inside. . . . I wanted to give you a thought before the bell rings. Really, truly, my purpose in the film was to give you some things to think about. . . . And if you would talk or write about an experience that you have had or that someone you know had I would like you to begin drafting and I would like you to bring that draft tomorrow. I think when you open your feelings . . . you took a lot of risks here today and

I'm asking you to risk something in writing. I don't think these are issues to be resolved easily and I think the teacher in the film was saying this is only a beginning. I think what we have done here in a small way is to make people aware, maybe a little more sensitive. There are going to be people in this room that will just walk away. I would like you to draft something. If you have had any experience that you would like to talk about and maybe it's dialogue you want to write or maybe a conversation. Maybe something that happened at work or in your neighborhood. Would you bring that back tomorrow?

Afterward, in an interview, Chris says, "I was excited about their understanding of social issues and what these mean in their own lives." Initially, the students, for whatever reason, make no connection between race and class issues in the novel and similar issues in their own lives. What Chris is able to do is to find another kind of cultural text (the film) that would stimulate these connections, which spontaneously extends the inquiry into the ways in which social issues are related to literacy practices—that is, the assessment of literacy by the state actually serves to reinforce both inequities due to race and class (Rogers & McLean, 1991) and, for some children, the related discontinuities between home and school (Heath, 1983). In supporting this kind of discussion, Chris gives the students an opportunity to critique texts and discourses, such as the "violent" (Stuckey, 1991) discourses of assessment, as well as to respond to them, making literacy "discourses themselves the object of study" (Luke & Baker, 1991).

The intertextual nature of the discourse in this classroom provides a place where the students can begin to see the relationships between the texts of their own lives and the lives of others who are like them as well as different from them—which eventually enables them to connect to texts across historical, cultural, and social borders:

> When we isolate literature from the world, allowing only for a brief background of the author and the times to introduce the work, students have little chance of understanding how books work and how readers make something of real importance out of them. . . . What is public, historical, and cultural about [the literary transaction] is most often left unspoken, although these are arguably aspects of literary accomplishment. (Willinsky, 1991, p. 195)

The writings the students bring in the next day range from brief historical analyses of racism related to the present, to personal experiences with racism or prejudice, to inequities between working men and women.

Chris feels that their writings reveal understandings that they gained from the discussion that followed the film, and she encourages the students to revise and include them in their writing portfolios (Gibson, 1991).

By the end of the year, students are able to share the personal, social, and cultural nature of their responses or their identity positions openly, but not without some struggle of interpretation. During a sharing of poetry projects in May, for instance, an African American girl presents her research on Countee Cullin to the class. She reads two poems, "Tableau"—about the response to a white boy and a black boy walking arm in arm—and "The Incident."

> DAWN: I'm not a reader of poetry but this really involves—he writes about something that had to do with like blacks and whites. It really makes the poem interesting. The first poem is "Tableau." As I read it, think about it. I'm serious, really do think about it (*She then reads the poem.*) Do y'all have thoughts about this? You have to think about what it means. . . . What I got out of it was there was a black boy and a white boy . . .
>
> STUDENT: Were they holding hands or something . . .
>
> DAWN: Just walking along like past houses or villages or something and that people out of their houses were looking out of their blinds not understanding why a black and a white was walking with each other. I'm serious. I'm serious. It's more common maybe if a white and a white walk together or a black and a black but they couldn't see—they just couldn't understand. Okay, the next one is called "The Incident." I really liked this one.
>
> "The Incident"
>
> Once, riding in old Baltimore,
>   Heart-filled, head-filled with glee,
> I saw a Baltimorean
>   Keep looking straight at me.
>
> Now I was eight and very small,
>   and he was no whit bigger,
> And so I smiled, but he poked out
>   His tongue, and called me "Nigger."
>
> I saw the whole of Baltimore
>   From May until December;
> Of all the things that happened there
>   That's all that I remember.

What do you all think about that one? Now that was deep. I'm serious. It is deep.

AIMEE [another African American girl]: Everybody's had an experience like that. If you ever went somewhere, you know, you just happen to be there and somebody—they ain't going to stick their tongue out and call you nigger. They're just like (*turns her head and stares*) "what're you doing here?"

DAWN: There are just certain things, like places you'll go when you're younger you remember every detail. Like if you go somewhere fascinating, a lot of fascinating . . .

SARAH [a white girl]: I was going to say if you go someplace—well, he's so excited to see this place and it's new and everything, but out of his time there's this one thing that brought him down and it ruined his whole time down there.

DAWN: Well, sort of. See, everyone has their own opinion about stuff but what I was saying is like when you're young you block out stuff. There is just a certain thing in your life you'll always remember. You know she'll always remember this guy calling her a nigger. Out of all the things that happened in her life, she'll never forget someone calling her a nigger.

TIM [a white boy]: Isn't she just asking why? Wondering why this happened?

DAWN: I know a lot of y'all have been places but it's just one thing, one instance that may have happened that you'll always remember. I liked both these poems because it had to do with blacks and whites. Not because they were short but they were interesting. The last poem really gets to you. You've got to take time out to read them.

This exchange is particularly interesting because of the kind of struggle for meaning it represents. Dawn is trying to situate the poem in the context of the profound effects racism can have on a child; and, in fact, in the middle of her speech she begins to reference the speaker of the poem as "she." In this way it becomes her own experience, "populating it with [her] own intention" so that the poem "lies on the borderline" between herself and the narrator (Bakhtin, 1981). Aimee attempts to expand the conversation by suggesting that racism is still a common experience even if it may take more subtle forms; yet the white students seem to want to understand the poem in a more restricted context. They want to understand the incident as isolated and as affecting the narrator's experience in a more circumscribed way—that it ruined his or her trip, or that it was somehow momentarily puzzling. While Dawn attempts to share her understanding of the poem again, from her identity position, as a powerful statement on the personal effects of racism, the issue is essentially left unresolved apart from a plea for them to read it (again). This plea echoes Chris's earlier comment that some will just walk away from this kind of conversation but that she hopes they will be more aware.

This discussion illustrates a kind of resistance by some students to hearing or understanding Dawn's response to the poem. Resistance to certain understandings takes many forms and can be understood only by examining the context of classrooms in which it is manifested. In her work in another high school classroom, Fairbanks (1995) describes what she calls the "relational waters of culture, context, and gender" that shape classroom interpretations of literary works (p. 50). By studying one African American girl's response to *The Bluest Eye* by Toni Morrison, Fairbanks takes a closer look at these relational waters in order to understand the girl's uncharacteristically resistant stance to the story as a situated act. As she argues, students need curricular spaces in which they can explore complex and conflicting images in their social and cultural worlds, and in which they can communicate with others about matters that concern them.

RE-PLACING TEXTS

Across the year in Chris's classroom curricular spaces were gradually opened up so that literature became a subject of critical and social as well as literary inquiry, rather than an exercise in close reading of texts that remain irrelevant to students' experiences—an exercise that directs attention to "words on the page rather than to the contexts which produced and surround them" (Eagleton, 1983, p. 44). As Poovey (1992) points out, when culture is put at the center of classroom inquiry, we can begin to understand historical transformations and the place of texts considered to be "the best that has been thought or said" (p. 5). When the traditional canon is decentered, a focus on student voices is a natural consequence. Indeed, embracing multiculturalism compels educators to ask who speaks, who listens, and why (hooks, 1994).

Over time, Chris carefully crafted a community in which responses that reflected some risk-taking on the part of the students could be voiced and were encouraged to be voiced. She did this by gradually shifting textual interpretive authority away from herself and back to the community, and by gently encouraging the most personal responses so they could be understood in the larger social and cultural realm. At the same time, the literary canon was shifted away from center in favor of an intermingling of texts and voices both within and beyond the classroom and discourses of critique and resistance as well as consensus. Without developing this kind of community with an emphasis on intertextual readings, it is unlikely that expanded cultural conversations such as these could take place (Greene, 1994).

This kind of teaching is not sanctioned by the larger culture of high schools and by the norms for teaching reading or English in the United States. Many high school English teachers still view their job as one of transmitting culture rather than critiquing or transforming it and of teaching the skills of reading and writing as though they were not themselves cultural artifacts—products of particular ways of doing literacy in schools. That is, few teachers see issues of culture (e.g., race, class, and gender) or literacy practices themselves as open to critical inquiry in the classroom (cf. Bigler & Collins, 1995; Fine, 1987).

Teachers like Chris are not starry-eyed about what the task in front of them consists of. As Chris (Gibson, 1991) wrote of the students,

> They are there in school, for whatever reason: for the free lunch, for the heat, for the escape from responsibility, for the attention. . . . While they are in my class they are going to learn. I can't control their environment, take them home with me, give them money, but I can try to teach them to read and write. (p. 4)

Nor do teachers like Chris turn away from cultural difference, from the role of power and ideology in social institutions and interactions, or from the facts of racism, violence, poverty, and discrimination in hopes of finding some timeless truth in texts and some imagined peaceful place of straightforward teaching.

NOTES

A very special thank you to Chris Gibson for allowing us to spend time in her classroom and for responding to an earlier draft of this chapter.

Chris's real name has been used in this and in other reports with her permission. The names of the students have been changed to protect their anonymity.

Other reports from this project have provided a glimpse into the teaching characteristics of Chris and her colleagues (Rogers & McLean, 1994), the ways in which they themselves are at risk for dropping out of the system (McLean, 1991), a more complete analysis of the classroom transcripts (Rogers & McLean, 1993), and the teachers' own descriptions of their practice in an edited journal (Rogers & McLean, 1991).

REFERENCES

Bakhtin, M. M. (1981). Discourse in the novel. In M. Holquist (Ed.), *The dialogic imagination: Four essays by M. M. Bakhtin* (pp. 259–422). Austin: University of Texas Press.

Bigler, E., & Collins, J. (1995). Dangerous discourses: The politics of multicultural literature in community and classroom. Report series 7.4, National Research Center on Literature Teaching and Learning, State University of New York at Albany.

Bleich, D. (1987). *Subjective criticism.* Baltimore: Johns Hopkins University Press.

Bloome, D., & Green, J. (1984). Directions in the sociolinguistic study of reading. In P. D. Pearson, R. Barr, M. Kamil, & P. Mosenthal, (Eds.), *The handbook of reading research* (pp. 395–422). New York: Longman.

Brodkey, L. (1994). Lecture at Ohio State University.

Campbell, R. (1994). Cultural studies. In *The encyclopedia of English studies and language arts.* New York: Scholastic.

Eagleton, T. (1983). *Literary theory: An introduction.* Minneapolis: University of Minnesota Press.

Fairbanks, C. M. (1995). Reading students: Texts in context. *English Education, 27* (1), 40–52.

Fine, M. (1987). Silencing in public schools. *Language Arts, 64* (2), 157–174.

Fish, S. (1980). *Is there a text in this class: The authority of interpretive communities.* Cambridge, MA: Harvard University Press.

Gibson, C. (1991). Listening to what they say: Using portfolio evaluation with "at-risk" high school students. *Literacy Matters, 3*(2), 4–8.

Green, J. L., & Meyer, L. A. (1991). The embeddedness of reading in classroom life: Reading as a situated process. In C. Baker & A. Luke (Eds.), *Towards a critical sociology of reading pedagogy* (pp. 141–160). Philadelphia: John Benjamin.

Greene, M. (1994). Multiculturalism, community and the arts. In A. Dyson & C. Genishi (Eds.), *The need for story: Cultural diversity in classroom and community* (pp. 11–27). Urbana, IL: National Council of Teachers of English.

Heath, S. B. (1983). *Ways with words: Language, life and work in communities and class-rooms.* Cambridge, England: Cambridge University Press.

hooks, b. (1994). *Teaching to transgress: Education as the practice of freedom.* New York: Routledge.

Iser, W. (1978). *The act of reading: A theory of aesthetic response.* Baltimore: Johns Hopkins University Press.

King, P. (1993). Introduction to N. Peim, *Critical theory and the English teacher: Transforming the subject* (pp. xiii–xvi). New York: Routledge.

Luke, A., & Baker, C. (1991). Toward a critical sociology of reading pedagogy: An introduction. In C. Baker & A. Luke (Eds.), *Towards a critical sociology of reading pedagogy* (pp. xi–xxi). Philadelphia: Johns Benjamin.

McGinley, W., & Kamberelis, G. (1992). Personal, social, and political functions of reading and writing. In C. Kinzer & D. J. Leu (Eds.), *Literacy research, theory, and practice: Views from many perspectives* (Forty-first yearbook of the National

Reading Conference) (pp. 403–413). Chicago, IL: National Reading Conference.

McLean, M. M. (1991) *The plight of the at-risk teacher.* Unpublished doctoral dissertation, Ohio State University, Columbus.

Poovey, M. (1992). Cultural criticism: Past and present. In J. Trimmer & T. Warnock (Eds.), *Understanding others: Cultural and cross-cultural studies and the teaching of literature* (pp. 3–15). Urbana, IL: National Council of Teachers of English.

Rabinowitz, P. (1987). *Before reading: Narrative conventions and the politics of interpretation.* Ithaca, NY: Cornell University Press.

Rogers, T. (1991). Students as literary critics: A case study of the interpretive experiences, beliefs and processes of ninth grade students. *Journal of Reading Behavior, 23,* 391–423.

Rogers, T., Green, J. L., & Nussbaum, N. (1990). Asking questions about questions. In S. Hynds and D. Rubin (Eds.), *Perspectives on talk and learning* (pp. 73–90). Urbana, IL: National Council of Teachers of English.

Rogers, T., & McLean, M. (Eds.) (1991). Theirs are voices we need to hear: Teaching literacy in urban high schools [Special issue]. *Literacy Matters, 3*(2).

Rogers, T., & McLean, M. (1993, December). *Reading, writing and talking our way in: The social construction of literacy communities in three urban classrooms.* Paper presented at the annual meeting of the National Reading Conference, Charleston, SC.

Rogers, T., & McLean, M. (1994). Critical literacy/Urban literacy: A case study of three urban high school English teachers. *Urban Review, 26*(3), 173–185.

Saville-Troike, M. (1982). *The ethnography of communication: An introduction.* Oxford: Blackwell.

Smithson, I. (1994). Introduction: Institutionalizing culture studies. In I. Smithson & M. Ruff (Eds.), *English studies/ Culture studies: Institutionalizing Dissent* (pp. 1–22). Urbana: University of Illinois Press.

Stuckey, J. E. (1991). *The violence of literacy.* Portsmouth, NH: Heinemann.

Trimmer, J., & Warnock, T. (1992). *Understanding others: Cultural and cross-cultural studies and the teaching of literature.* Urbana, IL: National Council of Teachers of English.

Weade, R., & Green, J. L. (1989). Reading in the instructional context: An interactional/sociolinguistic perspective. In C. Emihovich (Ed.), *Locating learning across ethnographic perspectives on classroom research* (pp. 17–56). Norwood, NJ: Ablex.

Willinsky, J. (1991). *The triumph of literature/ The fate of literacy: English in the secondary school curriculum.* New York: Teachers College Press.

CHAPTER 5

Multiplicity and Difference in Literary Inquiry

Toward a Conceptual Framework for Reader-Centered Cultural Criticism

MARY BETH HINES

I think they don't want me to make it. I mean they just want me to stay low. . . . They all have me down. They all . . . think I'm gonna be a junkie or something. I just think what I can. If I keep on keeping on, I can leave. . . . School's for stupid people.
—Kevin, a 14-year-old African American student

They don't be treating us right in schools and stuff. They say the only way a black person can be real good or make the grades is like they gotta act white or something. All the black people who got good grades, they ain't been suspended, they ain't been in trouble, and they don't act like their self. They try to fake it and be somebody else. . . . I know they do it to get along; I see it every day. . . . They gotta suck up, and I mean they act like other white students and stuff; they act like the teachers and stuff. Well, they gotta suck up to the teachers, and they don't be their self—they act all stupid.
—David, a 15-year-old African American student

FOR DAVID AND KEVIN, middle school students living in a housing project nestled against a row of brick colonial homes with manicured lawns, "school's for stupid people." Consequently, they choose the margins and refuse to "act like other white students . . . and teachers" because such behaviors seem antithetical to the social and cultural traditions they value, those that texture their daily experiences and provide a grid of intelligibility for their lives as African American adolescent males living in a housing project. To "fake it," by being successful in school, as David explains, is to not "be their self."

Given these views, it should not surprise us that, although bright, both boys have failed a series of classes, garnered a string of truancies, and tendered a number of disciplinary infractions—all before the eighth grade. School is a "battle ground," as Kevin says, where race, class, gender, authority, and ideological issues intersect, circulate, and escalate in school halls and classrooms. The boys, in turn, respond with a variety of forms of resistance to those who want them to "stay low." Although the boys seem headed for failure, they are fighting furiously to stay in school, determined to graduate from middle school and eventually attend a post-secondary institution. During that schooling process, however, they have no intention of surrendering their racialized identities, and they speak disparagingly of teachers and students who thwart their efforts to learn about African American culture.

But if David and Kevin's efforts to retain, rather than to obscure, their identities remind us of the value of community and the importance of selfhood to adolescents, they also remind us that we have failed in some ways to make schools in general, and English classrooms in particular, spaces of community for nonmainstream and oppositional students. As is obvious, David and Kevin's alienation will constitute the "prior knowledge and experience" that they bring to their respective English classes. As a result, their behaviors, attitudes, and practices may complicate or deflect efforts by the district's English teachers to "build community," "foster success," and "honor differences," as our slogans go, even when their English teachers stand firmly committed to multicultural education.

As David's and Kevin's teachers move beyond the narrow confines of the canon, they might also enrich inquiry by cultivating new understandings of what it means to know texts, selves, and culture. In this chapter, I draw from case studies of four literature classrooms to illuminate the principles of a reader-centered cultural criticism, informed by recent work in literary and cultural studies and focused on the concepts of multiplicity and difference. In conceptualizing interpretive communities that foster appreciation for multiplicity as they sensitize students to diversity, teachers can make spaces for David and Kevin in the name of effective literary inquiry.

EXPLORING TEXTUAL AND ACTUAL WORLDS

Because our ways of reading are always inherently linked to our ways of seeing society, current approaches to texts can be examined for the ways in which they explicitly and/or tacitly promote particular conceptions of the world. Belsey (1980) explains:

> No theoretical position can exist in isolation: any conceptual framework for literary criticism has implications which stretch beyond criticism itself to ideology and the place of ideology in the social formation as a whole. Assumptions about literature involve assumptions about language and about meaning, and these in turn involve assumptions about human society. (p. 29)

This chapter uncovers the "assumptions about human society," as Belsey says, that are tacitly and explicitly promoted in literature discussions, shaped by the teacher's understanding of multiplicity and diversity. I trace the conceptions of multiplicity and diversity issuing from literature classrooms taught by Barb, a middle school teacher; Paul, a high school teacher; and Richard and Michael, college instructors. Despite variations in their approaches, all take the view that knowledge, language, and truth are socially constructed; thus students can assert, contest, and complicate truth claims in the classroom. All believe that effective literary inquiry invites discussion of personal, social, cultural, and textual matters in communities where the teacher makes interpretive priorities and practices explicit through his or her discourse. In naming the salient principles of a reader-centered cultural criticism, I hope that we can begin to imagine new possibilities and responsibilities for English/language arts classrooms, just as we can begin to create homespaces in English classrooms for David, Kevin, and their friends in the housing project. In the next sections I turn to the four classrooms to consider the "assumptions about human society" at play in those particular interpretive communities.

A NEW CRITICAL PERSPECTIVE

Paul, an Anglo teacher of an American literature class for high school juniors in a predominantly Anglo, middle-class suburban district, advocates the text-centered practices of New Criticism as a way of knowing literature. Thus he engages in practices that reflect and constitute the current-traditional text-centered and teacher-led orientations to literature instruction that prevail in the research on literature classrooms (Applebee, 1993; Marshall, Smagorinsky, & Smith, 1995). From Paul's perspective, a multiplicity of responses can be generated by students who use social, economic, and historical knowledge to better comprehend the text. He explains:

> I know that with *The Great Gatsby* I'm trying to decide how much I teach from the book, what—do I point out every little detail—and you know, I feel compelled to do so. You know, there's a great little line here, and a great one there; Fitzgerald writes these magnificent little lines. . . . What I want to do is to ask a question that forces students to look at the novel as a whole piece of work rather than asking yes-or-no questions. . . . I wonder if it's a bias on my own part. I'm very much interested in the techniques that an author uses in a novel, and particularly Fitzgerald with his use of symbolism and characterization and all that. How else can you discuss it without looking directly at it?

For Paul, the formal properties of a text provide entrance into the social and culture worlds created by an author. "Knowing" in this case focuses on "symbolism and characterization" issues that, in turn, prod students into looking at the "techniques that an author uses" or "the novel as a whole." We can see the logic of this approach in the following excerpt, where Paul and his students explore *The Great Gatsby* (Fitzgerald, 1925/ 1953) and learn about its sociohistorical context:

> PAUL: Let's finish up on our characterization of Tom. . . . What's the one word you'd use to characterize Tom after he talks about this book [Goddard's *Rise of the Colored Empires*]?
>
> MEGAN: He's a bigot.
>
> BILL: He's racist.
>
> PAUL: (*Sarcastically.*) Yeah, you know, blacks are going to take over. We gotta watch out. It's in the book; it's scientific. I've read it. Whatever is in the book must be right. OK, now you have to wonder how he could get an attitude like that. He's a relatively educated man. I mean, he graduated from Yale, and it helps to know a little bit about the 1920s, the attitudes about the times. To help me with that will be Bob and Carrie, who have done some research about the KKK and racism in the 1920s. Go ahead and tell us what you know.
>
> CARRIE AND BOB READING ALTERNATE SECTIONS: The KKK was the Ku Klux Klan in the 1920s. The reason of this was that people were worried that the United States was going to this industrial business and what not, and there was more immigration coming in

with the blacks of South Africa and what not, and they were worried about the takeover of the blacks, so they formed the KKK and in a way to make them [blacks] feel uncomfortable and not to try going out and taking over the United States. The KKK was basically a group of prejudiced white people, and they'd start with their children basically. Even the older people from the KKK would bring their children to the meetings and burn crosses, carry torches. They'd go around sometimes and torch 'em, sometimes with a Negro on them. They'd drag them behind cars and do all sorts of bad things basically to try to drive them from the community.

PAUL: Did you see that movie on cable the other night, *Mississippi Burning?* . . . That, of course, took place in the 1960s; it wasn't that long ago. . . . The KKK is still prevalent today; the numbers are greater, I think, than they ever were. You'd think what happened 70 years ago we could forget about; it still continues. The KKK was prejudiced not only against blacks but against who else, Mike?

MIKE: Minority groups.

PAUL: Yeah, OK, anyone who wasn't . . .

MIKE: Anglo-Saxon.

PAUL: Yeah, have you heard this term before, WASP? W–A–S–P. Do you know what that stands for? What's the term for that acronym?

SUE: White, Anglo-Saxon.

TERRY: Protestant.

PAUL: Protestant, right. So not only that any immigrant came in, but anyone who is Catholic, Jewish, black. Minorities could take over the country, all right, so we gotta watch out. It's been proved in this book by Goddard. I don't know who he is, but it's proof. All right, Tom literally, physically pushes people around. Mentally, he is not very open-minded; he is unwilling to accept other people that are different from him, and that's shown in his belief in this book, *Rise of the Colored Empires.* Thank you for that presentation, very well done. OK, that's all for Tom, so let's move on to Jordan.

This excerpt suggests several of Paul's priorities. First of all, he encourages multiplicity by providing an array of inroads into the nature of Tom's character. He invites connection to the quality of "bigot" by evoking a movie, by appealing to the antiracist sentiments of students, by noting the prevalence of racism in contemporary culture, and by asking for clarification of terms.

In this section Paul also tacitly and explicitly conveys his attitudes about diversity. He playfully picks up on the racism suggested by the texts and times evoked in *The Great Gatsby* ("Minorities could take over the country, all right, so we gotta watch out."). Implicit in his ironic tone is an antiracist sentiment that becomes manifest in his follow-up questions about the KKK's targets. His mention of the popular movie *Mississippi Burning* suggests not only the resurgence of KKK affiliations but also his antiracist convictions ("You'd think what happened 70 years ago we could forget about; it still continues.").

In this exchange Paul and his students also dramatize Belsey's (1980) claim that a specific way of reading a text also promotes a particular way of seeing the world. For instance, students are invited to contribute to the discussion of racism, but they simply recall and recite facts and definitions, that is, "w–a–s–p," missing opportunities to hypothesize and problematize social, historical, and cultural forces in their own worlds as well as that of *Gatsby*. Paul's first and last turns in this episode suggest that the knowledge generated in relation to racism is rendered to understand Tom. That is, Paul does acknowledge racism, but he and his students construct it as a character trait, an attribute of Tom's persona. Hence inquiry about racism folds into a lesson on characterization.

As this exchange illustrates, inequities are elicited and acknowledged, but they are glossed over, appropriated as cues to analyzing the textual world, its characters, and events. If Paul's students explore social and historical issues, they do so within the context of learning about a textual universe, given the framework that guides and shapes Paul's understanding of literary inquiry. In light of the limits of teacher-led, text-centered approaches, many experts now turn to reader-response theories because they promote multiplicity and figure readers into "the meaning" of texts, as the next section illustrates.

A READER-RESPONSE ORIENTATION

As Paul invites his secondary students into a community where textual knowledge is privileged, Michael encourages his college literature students to join a classroom community where reader knowledge and experience are valued dimensions of the reading experience. Michael, an exemplary, award-winning teacher, attempts to enact lively discussions by invoking Rosenblatt (1938, 1978) in a transactional version of reader response. Michael encourages students to bring their prior knowledge and experience to bear on the text, recognizing "both the openness of the text, on the one hand, and on the other, its constraining function as a guide or check" (Rosenblatt, 1978, p. 88).

However, Michael is not only interested in promoting multiplicity in response to texts; he is also particularly aware of diversity issues. An Anglo male who recently married a woman of a different race and culture, he is working in both personal and professional ways on multiculturalism. In Michael's view there is a direct connection between promoting multiplicity and encouraging sensitivity to linguistic and cultural diversity. As students generate multiple ways of seeing society, texts, and citizens, they gain a greater understanding of diverse selves, societies, and texts, thereby gaining a greater understanding of difference.

In spite of his personal and professional priorities, Michael nonetheless objects to those who would measure a teacher's commitment to multiculturalism by the number of noncanonical texts students read in a course. He argues that classroom social dynamics, rather than the array of texts used in a curriculum, offer a more accurate index to an instructor's commitments to social justice:

> Just because he's teaching *Sula* and I'm not doesn't mean I'm less politically conscious. Does that make his class more politically correct? Somehow there's a slippage of logic, but that's what goes on. . . . You bring your questions, your interests, and we'll see what we'll do with them. If somebody says gender issues are important here, it's theirs; and then I can say, "What can we do with it?" . . . It's more important for me to echo what other people say about a text or about an idea. So I'm not saying, "I'm a feminist; therefore, I'm interested in issues of gender." I'm saying, "We're going to read closely. We're going to learn to read, and we're going to talk about the things you're interested in [with] this text."

His taking the role of facilitator allows students to bring various perspectives to the class, just as it enables Michael to enact his commitments to democracy—intent as he is on returning power and authority to students by vesting in them responsibility for discussion. Consequently, issues of social justice enter the classroom as students, not the teacher, raise and discuss them. "If you try to look at the story through somebody else's eyes, you will see some other picture," he explains. That new image, he believes, will lead to greater understanding of social, cultural, and individual differences.

Michael believes that patterns of language and patterns of society are necessarily linked. Consequently, as he says, when students "look closely at language," they can "question the construction of ideas, the ways we inherit certain ways of seeing things." If students do this, then it might be through the promotion of multiple perspectives that students can come to understand other ways of seeing things. However, Michael wants students to freely choose "without thinking about the political implications" of a differential system of values or knowledges because, as he explains, he isn't after "disruption and destabilization."

We can see the effects of his priorities in this excerpt from a discussion of Ellison's "Battle Royal" (1947/1990) with his predominately Anglo, middle-class students:

LINDA: What does he mean by "keep this nigger boy running"?

JASON: I kind of thought it was motivation. It was kind of like the message said it will always be like that. It was a general thing to say keep running. If you persist, you'll make it through. If you don't make huge strides, if you at least persist, then you've won.

MICHAEL: Sort of like the war is never over.

JASON: The war is never over. If you give up, you've lost; but if you don't give up, that's good.

MICHAEL: Add on to that?

JAY: You see "keep the nigger boys running." You see that in society anywhere throughout the history of the blacks. You fight it through your meekness. If you fight it through your meekness, you'll never get anything accomplished. So that's where he has to contemplate being meek or actually doing anything about it. It's a struggle.

MICHAEL: It is. Lee is still struggling with it, right? How many of you have seen *Do the Right Thing?* Martin Luther King and Malcolm X both on one wall of a building. The one preaching passive resistance and the other preaching take arms. Is there a point at which passive resistance no longer works? That seems to be what you're getting at. You're wondering if in here somewhere the story isn't suggesting "be hoping up to a point and when you're ready, take arms." I'm not sure if that's there or not. It's tricky.

JAY: I was just going to say that black people have, like you said, two selves, their outer self and their inner self. I think that represents white people, too. They try to be nice to black people on the outside, but behind closed doors they say the opposite. Sort of the same way on both sides.

This dialogue illustrates the ways in which students understand multiplicity. As Linda initiates the exchange with the question that sparks a discussion of racism, Jason elaborates by focusing on the theme of persistence as a key to overcoming oppression. Michael then "reads back" Jason's comment, prompting Jay to analyze the value of another trait, meekness, in relation to black history. Students explore racial difference by tracing it through what they know and believe about history, media, and psychology, generating similes and expressing their prior experiences and understandings. Meekness, persistence, history, and culture are all glossed, thereby evoking multiplicity in the spirit of Rosenblatt.

But if we also use this excerpt to understand how racial difference is constructed in this discussion, then we see both the power of reader response and its limits. For instance, when Jay and Jason speak, they conceive of racial difference in terms of individual personality character-istics—meekness, passivity, resistance, honesty. In articulating a liberal-humanist view—that individuals are "free" to lift themselves up by their bootstraps—students miss opportunities to explore the complex ways in which social, historical, ideological, economic, institutional, and material forces affect and constitute the self and society (cf. Beach, Chapter 3, this volume). The view that life is "sort of the same on both sides," issuing from students, actually fails to take difference into account because it obscures and appropriates the specific struggles and experiences that mark the lives of persons of color. Racial difference is repressed as human sameness is promoted; oppression is named but not analyzed.

In celebrating multiplicity with Rosenblatt—or any of the first gener-ation of reader-response theorists (Tompkins, 1980)—we need to consider that there are no theoretical linkages that systematically move from *ac-knowledgment* to *analysis* of social justice issues. That is, reader theories do not take up the political dimensions of reading texts, selves, and worlds; they do not explore how access to opportunity is structured dif-ferently for those who are not male, not Anglo, and not middle-class het-erosexuals (Mailloux, 1990; Pratt, 1982; Tompkins, 1980). Therefore such issues are, at best, glossed by politically oriented students or, at worst, occluded from view.

Given changing demographics and the importance of multicultural education, we need to create reader-centered approaches with conceptual frameworks for "reading" the histories, lives, and literacies of linguisti-cally and culturally diverse students, characters, and citizens. By explor-ing the interplay of complex and contradictory forces in various arenas—ideological, material, social, historical, and institutional—students can not only learn to respond to textual worlds; they can also be challenged to assume responsibility for their world.

From this perspective, reader response might best be viewed as a necessary but not sufficient set of principles to explore social justice is-sues; however, multiplicity can be recuperated by articulating it with a theory of difference, as it is elaborated by materialist-feminists and others in cultural studies (e.g., Barrett, 1988; Brodkey, 1989; Newton & Rosenfelt,

1985). Teachers can undertake analyses of the social, historical, material, and discursive forces at play as certain individuals and groups gain power and privilege at the expense of others, typically those who are not of the dominant race, class, and gender. While "liberal" versions of multicultural education encourage students to "see and even honor cultural differences," they do not require them to "examine, change, or be responsible to the economic and political power structures difference [that] is entangled within" (Hennessy, 1993, p. 11). However, to understand difference is to invite students not only to acknowledge diversity but also to trace the effects and sources of difference through cultural, economic, and political spheres. From this vantage point, the focus is on "acquiring the critical frameworks to understand how and why social differences are reproduced" (Hennessy, 1993, p. 11) in order to challenge instances in which diversity equals inequity. In the next section, we turn to teachers who dramatize forms of reader-centered cultural criticism capable of acknowledging, honoring, and interrogating difference.

A SOCIAL JUSTICE FRAMEWORK

Barb is an eighth-grade teacher in David's and Kevin's school. Committed to social justice, she spends summers developing curricula on thematic units related to diversity issues. For instance, her students recently completed a unit on gay and lesbian issues, and they have read texts about apartheid in Africa and Bosnia. She has taught units on the physically and mentally challenged as well. Like Michael, she values multiplicity in classroom discussion, and she believes that the experience of reading literature can be transformative because it offers possibilities for students to imagine lives and experiences that may be unlike their own:

> When you read, when you're exposed to literature, you can be anything and anywhere. You can have any experience in the world. And you take on points of view that you normally don't, because when you read a book, in effect, you become the character for a little bit of time. . . . For example, in *Monsoon* when you experience what the young girl does when she goes to India—the rampant hunger—it makes a stronger impression on you than seeing coverage in the news or reading it in a newspaper because it's *you* who becomes affected.

For Barb, a literary text provides a personalized transaction not simply with a text, but with a world, a personalized cultural odyssey. Therefore, in her view, literary inquiry can foster respect for and understanding of those marked as "other," those different from the culturally diverse urban students she teaches:

> What kinds of citizens will they become? How will they react to social issues? I totally believe in putting your money where your mouth is. I see certain problems with my world, and I want to help fix them. Teaching English is the best way I know how to do that. . . . Our world is about choices. But too many people don't have choices.

Consistent with her commitments to social justice, her students discuss the differences in experiences between male and female Delaware and Navajo Indians in relation to *Sing Down the Moon* (O'Dell, 1970) and *A Light in the Forest* (Richter, 1953). After small-group discussions, students present their opinions to the class and then attempt to defend their stances on how gender roles in the two tribes resulted in gendered divisions of labor. Barb then shifts the focus from textual to social issues, inviting students to make personal connections with the text by turning to an exploration of contemporary gender roles:

> BARB: Do you think they covered everything? Do you believe everything that James just said? What do we have to add from the book? Do you think that men and women today are completely equal?
>
> STUDENTS: (*Multiple students shouting indignantly.*) No! No way! No!
>
> BARB: Young women in the class, do you think that you are completely equal to the young men?
>
> STUDENTS: (*Multiple students.*) No! No! No!
>
> MARK: I was going to say like with football and basketball games on TV, there's no way that women can join these teams!
>
> SUE: We can't play!
>
> JOHN: Y'all can play!!
>
> BARB: Please be quiet, everyone, and let Glenda speak.
>
> GLENDA: My dad told me that they tried to let women in the NBA, only they didn't have enough money or spectators as the men's stuff.
>
> BARB: Why do you think that is?
>
> GLENDA: Because I mean—not me—but not a lot of people think this way, but some do: Some of it has to do with that they don't, they think we are as good as men and that the men are *more interesting* to watch.

JOSH: I just think that girls can play any sport, like girls playing hockey— a girl plays hockey, and we don't think it's nothing.

MAX: I think . . . now that women are equal and have every right to be equal and everything, they are like—grrrrr!—now WE'RE better than you! . . .

RONA: It's not that, "Oh yeah, we are better than you or anything," but it's just that we are sick of people—guys—saying that we are afraid that we are going to break a nail or something. (*Students clap enthusiastically.*)

JOSH: (*Standing, gesturing to gain the floor.*) That's a ster–e–o–type!!!!

BARB: Great, you are referring to a lesson we had before. Explain how.

JOSH: You are saying "guys." Like every male, all guys—

TRAVIS: Just like saying *all* of us are brutal!

This episode of discussion occurs between episodes in which students closely analyze the details of the two texts to illustrate social and cultural traditions in the tribes. Barb's initial question sparks a heated discussion in which speakers contribute with enthusiasm. Like Michael's discussion, this one, too, places an emphasis on multiplicity. Students not only volley back and forth with "yes" and "no," but they supplement those opinions with knowledge of sports, with knowledge of how "ster–e–o–types" circulate through popular culture as "one man" becomes "all men" in gross overgeneralizations. While in prior and subsequent episodes students focus closely on the text, in this exchange they consider social and cultural patterns.

Barb's turns in this episode suggest that she ostensibly works as a facilitator in many of the ways that Michael does, nudging students to elaborate and defend positions. But like Paul and unlike Michael, it is she who introduces the topics, that is, gender roles in the American Indian tribes and U.S. culture. While she promotes multiplicity, she also intervenes in discussions of diversity by raising social justice issues and by providing classroom time for students to "read" culture. Like Paul and Michael, Barb sees herself as a facilitator; but unlike them, she does not see herself as value-free. As a teacher who values and respects others enough to insist that her students do likewise, she consciously formulates questions that provide opportunities for students to crystallize their views on social justice issues. Obviously, the momentum of the episode suggests that students were excited and engaged, practicing "uptake" by elaborating on one another's comments and filling in words before speakers on the floor would ever have the chance (Nystrand & Gamoran, 1991).

The excerpt also suggests how students conceptualize and construct difference. Students highlight the variable and differential access to sports available to men and women in our society, and they suggest a variety of reasons for such inequities—revenues from media coverage, attitudes about women's abilities, and competing conceptions of women in the larger society. Glenda holds the view that "not a lot of people think this way, but some do," while Rona, Josh, and Travis collaboratively construct and explain the notion of stereotypes in relation to gender issues. Although these culturally diverse students do not complicate their analyses with overlays of class, race, ethnicity, and so forth in this instance, they explore competing ideologies and argue that gender differences result in and reinforce variable access to opportunity. In short, difference is not only acknowledged, it is also analyzed. In the next section, I turn to a classroom in which discussions of difference are mediated by a teacher who is able to advance a more sophisticated version of cultural critique because he teaches college students.

CULTURAL CRITICISM

Richard, a literature teacher who, like Barb, is committed to social justice, explains his priorities in an interview:

> If you go into your classroom and say that we're going to talk about how this piece of literature enriches us all as human beings, how it teaches us all as human beings to respond in the same way to love or to death—big universals—then that is very biased because it allows the political status quo in society—which exploits women, which exploits through the class system—to continue. It doesn't engage with them at all, and it doesn't even try. It says we're all the same, which of course we're not—you're a different class, a different color, and I would say, then, that your relationship to love and death is different.

While Paul wonders if his approach to literature is biased because it focuses on textual details, Richard suggests that approaches rooted in liberal-humanist tendencies—"We're all the same"—obscure diversity issues by refusing to take into account the ways in which individual, social, and cultural differences complicate and shape one's perceptions of "love and death," for instance. For Richard, challenging and critiquing received "ways of seeing" is at the heart of the literary enterprise. As he explains in an interview:

Teachers have been taught to believe that in literature classrooms we don't bring in too much of the outside world because that is not something that you teach. We're supposed to be teaching what's in the novel, the play, or the poem ... digging out. ... What I explain is that we're not interested in formal ways of writing, how great a text is put together, or anything like that. We're interested in the message that's being sold to us. ... What I'm really doing is not teaching text, but context, so I'm decentering the text. I'm saying that it is a catalyst. ... I want to stress that the text is a social construction, and if it's a social construction, then who constructed it, what's it doing, and what are the mechanisms that are at work here?

Richard's orientation to reading texts and worlds stands in almost direct opposition to Paul's. If Paul emphasizes the world in order to illuminate the text, then Richard uses the text to focus on the world, "the mechanisms that are at work." Like Barb, he is passionately committed to social justice, seeking to make visible the marginalized and obscured, infusing discussions with popular culture, media, social issues, and history.

In fact, his students learn to generate multiple responses to texts as they explore issues of difference. A good example of this process is the way they responded to the following passage from *Out of Focus* (Davies, Dickey, & Stratford, 1987), discussing the *Oxford English Dictionary* (*OED*):

> Its definition of the verb "to beat" is truly unbelievable (or is it) in these supposedly enlightened days: "to beat—to strike repeatedly, as in to beat one's wife." Not only does this show the presumed sex of the reader (at least one-half of the population does not have a wife), but it also clearly demonstrates that beating "one's" woman is an acceptable way for men to behave. Would it not otherwise have been struck from the "thinking man's bible"? (p. 98)

The discussion that ensued opened up the perspective:

> GREG: On page 98 talking about wife beating, "not only does this show the presumed sex of the reader ... but it also clearly demonstrates that beating 'one's' woman is an acceptable way for men to behave." I can't draw that conclusion from what's found in the dictionary.
>
> RICHARD: Why would they put that in the dictionary? It makes it very commonplace. As in beating one's wife. Like it happens all the time, right? And the dictionary is supposed to be the definitive meaning of the word.

JAN: The author sends subtle unconscious messages which shape our attitudes.

GREG: But a dictionary isn't the place where you make comments.

STAN: When you're little you don't hear them say to a little girl, "You're not supposed to hit little boys." But it comes to that; little boys aren't supposed to hit girls, but they play with GI Joes and stuff. So the whole thing is that they get those messages when they're little, from basketball players or cartoon characters, who are mostly male. A kid is too little to say, "Yeah, but that's not the way real life is." That's the point of the cartoon character. It is directed toward little kids, and that's the way life goes on.

JAN: When we look in the dictionary, what you see is what you believe. That's what you're taught. I think that what they're trying to say in this one quote is that something like that in there almost condones it. Like it's OK. Like a message if you're male it's something that is done or is OK to be done. It's tied in with a definition. It's just a message. But it's there. . . .

LINDA: By being in the dictionary it's something that people look at every day; they are stating that it's commonplace. You open a dictionary every day. If you read "beating one's wife," it may seem that that's what happens. . . .

TODD: It's kind of, I guess to add on to this, I was looking in my friend's room the other day and on his bulletin board, Charles Barkley, the NBA basketball player—I guess he was losing a game and was talking to a reporter and said, "Yeah, this is the kind of game that after you're done with it you go home and beat your wife." . . . The newspaper person was like, do you want me to just quote you on that or do you want it off the record. He said, no just quote me on that. That's kind of glamorizing. That it's OK. Some little boy might think, Charles Barkley is my hero, my idol, after a game you just go beat your wife. This kid will grow up and think that's OK. . . .

GREG: I sort of find it degrading to women, but some people do beat their wives, and it does explain the word *beat*. Striking repeatedly. But as I see it, they're putting the word *beat* in a certain context, and I don't think they should have used it. But at the same time I don't necessarily think it is a statement that it's OK to beat your wife.

JAMES: I think they have a valid point; I can see the point. But my question is, how are we supposed to respond to the knowledge that we have? How are we supposed to change ourselves and our attitudes? How do we go about doing that?

RICHARD: ... I don't think there are any ready-made solutions. But I think the biggest step is to be aware of this stuff.... The next step is to tend to your own ways of seeing and to tell other people to change their ways of seeing.

Salient here are distinguishing features of a reader-centered approach that fosters cultural critique (see also Rogers, Chapter 4, this volume). First of all, the discussion explores a multiplicity of meanings and purposes for the use of "wife-beating" as part of an OED definition. Students in this class understand that texts—and dictionaries—not only carry meanings, but also serve ideological functions in the larger society. That is, as cultural artifacts, they do cultural work by promoting, in subtle ways, a set of values. As Richard says in his interviews, he wants students to understand texts as social constructions so that they can question those values. In this exchange, personal experience, opinion, and popular culture infuse the "knowing" of texts, thereby complicating and enriching the discussion of the representation of women in various texts. Gender issues then become a point of analysis, resulting in cultural criticism and the interrogation of misogynistic forces that circulate in texts, media, toys, families, and history. As a result, gender is "read" as a set of complex, frequently conflicting set of material and ideological forces, visible in institutions, sports, and families as well as in dictionaries.

READER-CENTERED CULTURAL CRITICISM AND SOCIAL JUSTICE INQUIRY

We can, with Paul, Barb, Michael, and Richard, construct approaches that not only acknowledge and honor diversity but also interrogate its effects on selves, worlds, and texts. If David and Kevin remind us of what's missing from our current conceptions of the English classroom, then Paul, Michael, Barb, and Richard invite us to consider how we might reenvision instruction to make it relevant, engaging, and productive for these students. David and Kevin signal how important it is for English/language arts teachers to "honor students in all their pluralities" (Greene, 1993), just as the four case study teachers remind us to value texts in all their multiplicities. In so doing, Kevin and David can, as Kevin says, "keep on keeping on," cultivating new possibilities as they explore texts and worlds in their English classrooms.

REFERENCES

Applebee, A. (1993). *Literature in the secondary school: Studies of curriculum and instruction in the United States*. Urbana, IL: National Council of Teachers of English.

Barrett, M. (1988). *Women's oppression today* (2nd ed.). London: Verso.

Belsey, C. (1980). *Critical practice*. London: Methuen.

Brodkey, L. (1989). Opinion: Transvaluing difference. *College English, 51*, 597–601.

Davies, K., Dickey, J., & Stratford, T. (Eds.). (1987). *Out of focus: Writings on women and the media*. London: Women's Press.

Ellison, R. (1990). Battle royal. In P. J. Annas & R. C. Rosen (Eds.), *Literature and society: An introduction to fiction, poetry, drama, nonfiction* (pp. 62–75). Englewood Cliffs, NJ: Prentice-Hall. (Original work published 1947)

Fitzgerald, F. S. (1953). *The great Gatsby*. New York: Scribners. (Original work published 1925)

Greene, M. (1993, April). *Reciprocity, an ethic of care and social justice*. Fourth Annual Joshua Weinstein Memorial Lecture, presented at the University of Houston.

Hennessy, R. (1993). *Materialist feminism and the politics of discourse*. New York: Routledge.

Mailloux, S. (1990). The turns of reader-response criticism. In C. Moran & E. Penfield (Eds.), *Conversations: Contemporary critical theory and the teaching of literature* (pp. 38–54). Urbana, IL: National Council of Teachers of English.

Marshall, J., Smagorinsky, P., & Smith, M. (in collaboration with Dale, H., Fehlman, R., Fly, P., Frawley, R., Gitomer, S., Hines, M. B., & Wilson, D.). (1995). *The language of interpretation: Patterns of discourse in discussions of literature*. Urbana, IL: National Council of Teachers of English.

Newton, J., & Rosenfelt, D. (Eds.). (1985). *Feminist criticism and social change: Sex, class and race in literature and culture*. New York: Methuen.

Nystrand, M., & Gamoran, A. (1991). Student engagement: When recitation becomes conversation. In H. Waxman & H. Walberg (Eds.), *Contemporary research on teaching* (pp. 257–276). Berkeley: McCutchan.

O'Dell, S. (1970). *Sing down the moon*. Boston: Houghton Mifflin.

Pratt, M. (1982). Interpretive strategies/strategic interpretations: On Anglo-American reader response criticism. *Boundary 2, 11* (1–2), 201–231.

Richter, C. (1953). *A light in the forest*. New York: Knopf.

Rosenblatt, L. M. (1938). *Literature as exploration* (4th ed.). New York: Modern Language Association.

Rosenblatt, L. M. (1978). *The reader, the text, the poem: The transactional theory of the literary work*. Carbondale: Southern Illinois University Press.

Rosenblatt, L. (1985). Viewpoints: Transaction versus interaction—A terminological rescue operation. *Research in the Teaching of English, 19*, 96–107.

Tompkins, J. (1980). *Reader response criticism: From formalism to poststructuralism*. Baltimore: Johns Hopkins University Press.

PART II

Authors, Teachers, and Texts

CHAPTER 6

Exploring Multicultural Literature as Cultural Production

ARLETTE INGRAM WILLIS

THOSE OF US IN teacher education are preparing a predominantly white teaching force of preservice educators to teach an increasingly culturally and linguistically diverse student body. My crusade for improving the current generic approaches to literacy training of preservice teachers is both professional and personal. Professionally, I believe as teachers in institutions of higher learning we should equip our "charges" to meet the challenges of tomorrow—the challenges of cultural and linguistically diverse students—armed with theories and practical experiences that are inclusive. Personally, I want the future teachers of my own children to understand that children bring with them rich and culturally mediated language, experience, and knowledge to the classroom. Furthermore, I want these future teachers to understand that language and culture are inseparable. That is, the manner in which culturally and linguistically diverse students give meaning to the world is culturally understood and may differ from a mainstream perception. In addition, I want my preservice teachers to respect, value, and affirm the culturally mediated knowledge that my children (and others like them) bring to the classroom and to know how to build upon that knowledge for literacy development.

I use multicultural literature as an avenue to traverse the chasm between formal definitions of literacy and school realities of literacy (Willis, 1995). Moreover, in the undergraduate preservice classes I teach, I use multicultural literature to open discussions of history, knowledge, power, culture, language, class, race, and gender.

One of my goals is to sharpen the ability of my students to think critically about the choices they make when teaching literacy. Giroux (1987b) puts it this way: "The task . . . is to broaden our conception of

how teachers actively produce, sustain, and legitimate meaning and experience in classrooms" (p. 14). The task, I believe, can be performed with
the sagacious use of multicultural literature. I encourage and challenge
my students to become informed decision makers about the instruction
and use of multicultural literature for positive social change.

A CRITICAL PEDAGOGY

In addition to Freire, I ground my work in the thinking of the critical
pedagogues Macedo, Giroux, Shor, and McLaren, among others. My interpretation of Freirean theory, as applied to the instruction and use of
multicultural literature, begins with the adoption of the definition of literacy offered by Freire and Macedo (1987). They write of literacy as "a set
of practices that function either to empower or disempower people. In
the larger sense literacy is analyzed according to whether it serves a set
of cultural practices that promotes democratic and emancipatory change"
(p. 14). Further, they clarify their position on literacy by noting that "for
the notion of literacy to become meaningful it has to be situated within
a theory of cultural production and viewed as an integral part of the way
in which people produce, transform, and reproduce meaning" (p. 142). I
see multicultural literature as an artifact of cultural production. As such,
multicultural literature is an expression of how groups outside of the
dominant culture view themselves and their life experiences, of how they
read the world. All multicultural literature, in my opinion, must be evalu-
ated in light of what Freire (1994) calls the "complex set of circumstances"
(p. xi) that gave rise to it. In my courses the importance of attending to
the relationships among ideology, history, power, and knowledge in the
reading of multicultural writings is emphasized. I believe that it is important for students to be knowledgeable of the historical significance of
how those holding certain ideologies and positions of power have determined who can be literate, what is important to learn in literacy, how
literacy is to be learned, and when one is said to have become literate.
Exclusive use of Western Eurocentric ideology, situated in a celebratory
description of its historical and social contexts within the United States,
has given rise to an exclusionary literary canon. The required teaching of
this canon serves to cultivate the continual production of a literary culture
based on Western Eurocentric views. For groups that have lacked power,
their histories, language, and literature have been marginalized to the
status of "supplemental" to the literary canon. Henry Giroux's (1987a)

interpretation of this phenomenon in school literacy programs is worth quoting at length:

> [S]chools are not merely instructional sites designed to transmit knowledge; they are also cultural sites. As cultural sites, they generate and embody support for particular forms of culture as evident in the school's support for specific ways of speaking, the legitimating of distinct forms of knowledge, the privileging of certain histories and patterns of authority, and the confirmation of particular ways of experiencing and seeing the world. Schools often give the appearance of transmitting a common culture, but they, in fact, more often than not, legitimate what can be called a dominant culture. (p. 176)

Adopting a critical pedagogy for the training of educators in the United States has its risks. As Freire and Macedo (1995) point out, there is a growing mechanistic approach to the implementation of critical pedagogy. Like Freire and Macedo, I am disturbed by the interpretations of the critical position that give lip-service to a democratic pedagogy but fail to address the history of race, class, and gender oppression as experienced in the United States. Further, there is a tradition in U.S. educational circles of downplaying the importance of race, class, and gender; of minimizing the importance of acknowledging a history of forced servitude; of ignoring the history of legal denial of access to literacy; and of ignoring the history and role of privilege. Beneath the surface of the rhetoric and methodological rigidity lies the refusal to deal with the ideological positions that have supported and maintained race, class, and gender oppression. Whether educators are unwilling or unable to make explicit the role of oppression is unclear. I believe the reluctance to acknowledge a history of oppression in the United States may be due to the realization that such an acknowledgment would impose an obligation to adopt alternative ideologies and instructional practices.

Critical pedagogues are not without their critics. Especially vocal are those who believe that Freire's theory acts as an umbrella for all forms of oppression, while not adequately addressing specific forms of oppression, namely, gender and race. In their most recent installment of a decade-long dialogue of critical pedagogy, Freire and Macedo (1995) directly address some of their harshest critics. The critics have raised questions in an effort to understand how Freire's theory can account for the varying forms of oppression. In *Pedagogy of the Oppressed*, Freire (1970) focuses on social-class differences and political barriers to literacy attainment. Freire's (1994) response situates his early work within the historic and social contexts in which it was written. He states that "readers have some responsibility to place my work within its historical and cultural context. . . . I believe that what one needs to do is to appreciate the contribution of the work within its historical context" (p. 109).

By situating Freire's work within the historical and social contexts in which it was written, his critics can see how his original work cannot account for contemporary concerns of racial and gender oppression. Moreover, current application and translation of critical pedagogy should identify the unique ideological, historical, and social contexts in which it is used. Macedo (1994) also responds to critics by adding that "what we need to do is to understand the fact that the different historical locations of oppression necessitate a specific analysis with a different and unique focus that calls for a different pedagogy" (p. 110). While I strongly support Freire and Macedo's (1995) call for a review of specific histories, situated in the contexts that gave rise to them, I believe that it is also important to understand the forms of ideology that were present and remain as part of ongoing oppression. When reading specific histories, as in multicultural literature—told from the historical perspective of the oppressed (not through a marginalized view written by the oppressor)— we read the product of a cultural artifact.

Expressly and plainly addressing the history of class, racial, and gender oppression in the United States—in their varying forms—appears to be a risk-taking position for those seeking to adopt a critical pedagogy. The failure to acknowledge a history of oppression may have impeded the progress of education in the United States for oppressed groups. For example, the ideological, historical, and social burden of racial oppression in American society is poorly admitted in education. In a recent work, Ladson-Billings (1994) argues that "while it is recognized that African-Americans make up a distinct racial group, the acknowledgment that this racial group has a distinct culture is still not recognized. It is presumed that African-American children are exactly like white children but just need a little extra help" (p. 9). Importantly, ideological positions that gave rise to oppression and the ideologies that have sustained them, when examined in light of their specific historical and social contexts, illustrate how intimately power and knowledge have worked together to limit access to literacy in the United States.

My use of a critical literacy approach to the teaching of multicultural literature emphasizes the various forms of ideologies as part of the contexts that underlie the relationship between power and knowledge in the United States. I believe that it is important that future teachers understand these relationships historically as well as currently. Teachers' understanding of the contexts that supported the writing of oppressed people will help them better inform their students and make wise decisions on instructional and evaluative materials. Reading the text, in the mechanical sense, is not a problem for the majority of secondary students. However, gaining an understanding and appreciation of the literature may be difficult for those new to multicultural literature. Freire, among others, suggests that literacy is more than the construction of meaning from print: Literacy must also include the ability to understand oneself and one's relationship to the world. I support his thinking and in my course require a fresh reading of historical and social contexts of oppressed people. That is, I use the voices of the oppressed, as told through their literature, to foreground a study of multicultural literature.

While Freire offers a compelling argument for adopting a critical literacy position as a matter of policy, he does not offer suggestions for its implementation. Adopting a critical literacy stance does not come with a manual. In fact, he is concerned about the translation of "purist" notions into some sort of method. Thus I have relied heavily on the work of Shor, among others, to create a multicultural literature course for preservice teacher educators. In a broad sense the use of multicultural literature as inquiry, even in the exploration of issues of diversity, is not an innovation on my part. Current research in the area of multicultural literature by Harris (1992), Barrera (1992), Spears-Bunton (1992), Bishop (1992), Au (1993), Diamond and Moore (1995), among others, emphasizes the importance of using multicultural literature for understanding cultural differences, building community, and preparing students for the twenty-first century. Multicultural literature, however, should not be limited to use with traditionally underrepresented groups. The use of multicultural literature can be empowering to all children since it offers a more expansive context for students than the traditional literary canon. Moreover, multicultural literature can include differences that arise within race, class, and gender writings.

My course is in a constant state of redesign. With each new class comes a review of the histories underrepresented in most U.S. curriculums and, thus, new challenges. I begin, as Giroux (1987a) suggests, by reinventing the literature curriculum for preservice secondary English majors. My reading of Freire and Macedo (1995) suggests that they would be in agreement with my creation of a critical pedagogy that encourages preservice teachers to adopt a multicultural perspective toward literature. A brief overview of some of the barriers to curriculum reform will prove insightful.

THE MULTICULTURAL LITERATURE CURRICULUM:
BARRIERS TO REFORM

James Banks (1994) suggests that in preparing teachers for increasingly culturally and linguistically diverse student populations teacher educators need "to acquire an understanding of the meaning of cultural and ethnic diversity in complex Western societies, to examine and clarify their racial and ethnic attitudes, and to develop the pedagogical knowledge and skills needed to work effectively with students from diverse cultural and ethnic groups" (p. vi). This is a rather tall order for teacher educators. In the field of English/language arts there are several issues that complicate a smooth transition of multicultural literature from teacher educator to student and from teacher to student: (1) the demographics of teacher educators, (2) the history of English methods courses, (3) the teaching of the canon, and (4) the issue of diversity in literacy education for preservice teachers.

Demographics of Teacher Educators

Most preservice teachers have very limited experiences with diverse populations. As Fuller's (1992) statistics reveal, the majority of the preservice teachers are European American (92%), female (75%), and middle-class (80%), and most grew up in suburbs, small cities, or rural areas (80%). Preparing students to meet diverse school populations will require more than a tourist approach (Sleeter, 1994) to multicultural education. Students will need knowledge, experiences, and skills to effectively conduct classroom dialogues that support democratic values and include the language and literature of increasingly diverse student populations. Multicultural education is needed by all students. It is imperative, in a pluralistic society, to help preservice teachers acquire experiences and skills that will allow them to understand multiple perspectives, multiple voices, and multiple ways of knowing.

A History of English Methods

The training of English educators has a long history of maintaining the status quo. Graff's (1992) findings of the undergraduate English curricula offered nationwide suggest that there has been little substantive change in the literature offered to English majors since 1965. Generally, the literature that dominates college and high school English curricula offers a very narrow view of the world, one that is not part of the cultural schema of every student. Giovanni (1994) declares:

In the universities we have seen white men declare time and time again that they cannot teach women, they cannot teach Blacks, they cannot teach Native Americans, because they do not have any "experience" in this area. Yet we who are Black and women and not white males are expected to teach literature written by them because it is "universal"? I think not. It is called education because it is learned. You do not have to have had an experience in order to sympathize or empathize with the subject. (p. 109)

Research by Bonnie Sustein and Janet Smith (1994) on the use of methods textbooks over a 75-year period indicates that the discussion of the teaching of the literary canon as part of English methods instruction has had a cyclical history. Debates over the selections to include have been waged since the late 1800s. They cite the earliest "standard authors" list, issued by Harvard in 1874, as the beginning of the debate. The debate has considered student choice, minority literature, and gender issues but has not changed significantly. They discuss the difference between English methods courses that reflect the need for change and the lethargic response of publishers to adopt change. Finally, they expose the difficulty encountered by English majors as they try to make sense of opposing forces:

[O]ur preservice teachers arrive in our methods courses not only with institutionalized values about what literature makes them successful in school, but with a treasury of other reading experiences which broadens their personal definition of "literature" and "great books." (p. 53)

This is not the case just in English methods courses. Research by Au (1993) notes that most preservice teacher education courses are dominated by traditional transmission models of literacy instruction that support a mainstream middle-class perspective of literacy and inadequately address the needs of culturally or linguistically diverse students. Preservice teachers need to be taught strategies to help make implicit cultural knowledge explicit for students reading outside of their culture. These strategies need to permeate all teacher training courses.

The Literary Canon

When considering teaching English at the secondary level, there is a tacit assumption that, with varying degrees of competence, all secondary students have mastered the mechanics of reading. What becomes more important at this stage is not teaching students how to read, but helping them understand what they read. Many researchers believe that this begins with helping students make a connection between what they read and their personal lives. No teacher can be assured that all students will always be able to make a connection between the assigned reading and their life experiences; however, continued use of the literary canon assures that the experiences of underrepresented groups will remain unvoiced and marginalized in school settings. Multicultural literature clearly offers a wide range of literature choice for teachers. The selection of literature has been at the heart of the debates in the culture wars. Gates (1992) has pointed out that this is where the debates in the culture wars get messy: Whose values are most important for the succeeding generations to emulate? Gates (1992) argues:

> [T]he teaching of literature *is* the teaching of values; not inherently, no, but contingently, yes; it is—it has become—the teaching of an aesthetic and political order in which no women or people of color were able to discover the reflection or representation of their images, or hear the resonances of their cultural voices. The return of "the" canon, the high canon of Western masterpieces, represents the return of an order in which my people were subjugated, the voiceless, the invisible, the unrepresented, and the unrepresentable. (p. 35)

The most comprehensive look at secondary literature curricula is offered by Arthur Applebee (1993) in his current text *Literature in the Secondary School: Studies of Curriculum and Instruction in the United States*. In this text he examines literature and literature instruction in public and private schools. Applebee notes that literature instruction includes a variety of facets, but none so important as the book-length works used to convey a sense of who and what literature is important to study.

Applebee's (1989, 1992) nationwide survey reports the consistent use of canonical literature in our nation's high schools. He cites the continual use of works by Shakespeare, Steinbeck, Dickens, and Twain, yet few works by women and minority authors. (Similar traditional approaches to high school literature had been observed by Tanner [in Applebee, 1989] and Anderson [in Applebee, 1989]). Further analysis by Applebee of his findings reveals only one European American female author and two African American authors (one female, one male) among the top 50 listed authors. Applebee (1992) draws several important conclusions from his study:

1. A comparison of the studies reveals little change in the nature of the selections in the 25-year period.
2. There have been only marginal increases in titles by women and diverse authors.

3. Few book-length works by women and diverse authors have entered the canon.

If Applebee's conclusions about the importance of book-length works is correct, students are receiving a very narrow view of what literature, values, and people are important. As Applebee (1991) puts it, "Whether intentional or not, schools have chosen to ignore diversity and assimilate everyone to the classical culture that found its way into schools before the turn of the century" (p. 235). He goes on to state that "we are failing in a fundamental way to open the gates of literacy to the majority of the students we teach" (p. 235). Applebee's conclusions suggest that the literature used in classrooms today does not offer the best possible link with the children who are required to read it daily. His conclusions are supported in the research of Barrera (1992) and Diamond and Moore (1995), among others. Applebee offers suggestions for change that include the challenge of expanding the canon to be more reflective of the history, life experiences, culture, and literature of all Americans. Applebee argues that the expansion of the canon begin with preservice programs that require students to read and discuss book-length works written by authors of underrepresented groups. Moreover, Applebee suggests that preservice English courses may help students develop a repertoire of effective teaching strategies to use when teaching the literature. Although I support Applebee's suggestions for an updated canon that is more inclusive and the improved training of preservice English teachers, I believe his argument can be strengthened by offering a framework in which preservice teachers can be educated.

Additionally, Applebee's suggestion for canon expansion does not acknowledge the need for increased understanding of the complex issues surrounding the ideological, historical, and social contexts of multicultural literature. Such expansion without sufficient understanding of the contexts will give preservice teachers inadequate knowledge with which to instruct students. Expansion of the literary canon should be accompanied by a rearticulated theory that includes an understanding of the ideological, historical, and social contexts. If we as a nation are committed to the democratic values we espouse and to the development of a more just society, teacher training can be a starting point for change.

Substantiating Applebee's findings, Karen Peterson (1994) reports on a recent College Board survey citing the following 20 books and plays as those most frequently recommended for high school seniors and college freshmen: *The Scarlet Letter, Huckleberry Finn, The Great Gatsby, Lord of the Flies, Great Expectations, Hamlet, To Kill a Mockingbird, The Grapes of Wrath, The Odyssey, Wuthering Heights, The Catcher in the Rye, The Crucible, Gulliv-*

er's *Travels*, *Julius Caesar*, *Of Mice and Men*, *The Old Man and the Sea*, *Pride and Prejudice*, *The Red Badge of Courage*, *Romeo and Juliet*, and *Death of a Salesman*. According to spokesman Fred Moreno, The College Board examined curriculum guides, private school reading lists, research surveys, federal reports, and other sources in conducting the survey. A review of the titles shows that the list favors the literature of European or European American males and includes only three titles by women authors. The list does not include any works by authors from historically underrepresented groups. The marginalization of the works by women and people of color even prompted the well-known traditionalist E. D. Hirsch to observe that "this is a very traditional list that doesn't reflect new thinking. . . . It is clearly defective in not including books such as *Black Boy* (Richard Wright), *Song of Solomon* (Toni Morrison) and *I Know Why the Caged Bird Sings* (Maya Angelou)" (quoted in Peterson, 1994, p. 17). He later predicted that it may take another decade before the list is more representative. It is not clear from the article what has prompted Hirsch to alter his position on the use of multicultural literature.

ADDRESSING ISSUES OF DIVERSITY IN THE TRAINING OF PRESERVICE TEACHERS

Research in the area of literacy by Delpit (1988), Barrera (1992), and Reyes (1992), among others, has suggested that teacher education courses may offer the best opportunity to make significant inroads into how literacy is redefined and taught. Barrera (1992) argues that there is a desperate need to fill in what she refers to as a "cultural knowledge gap" (p. 227). Barrera argues that teachers need to improve their understanding of culture in three specific domains: cultural knowledge, cross-cultural knowledge, and multicultural knowledge. This cultural knowledge is needed by teachers to meet the literacy needs of all students, but most especially those of culturally and linguistically diverse children. Barrera's argument finds support in recent research by Reyes (1992) that indicates the importance of not assuming that theories of literacy designed with a homogeneous cultural group somehow magically meet needs of diverse cultural groups. Diamond and Moore's (1995) longitudinal study of multicultural literacy issues, the most complete to date, suggests that "teachers need additional cultural and social knowledge as they work with increasing numbers of students from varied cultural and linguistic backgrounds" (p. ix). The call for increased cultural and social knowledge can be met during preservice teacher training.

As stated earlier, my response to meeting the needs of preparing teachers for future generations of learners has been the development of a multicultural literature course that sees literature as an artifact of cultural production. To better understand this viewpoint, let us begin with a definition of multicultural literature. Harris (1992) defines multicultural literature as literature that focuses on people of color (such as African Americans, Asian Americans, Hispanic Americans, and Native Americans), on religious minorities (such as the Amish or Jews), on regional cultures (such as Appalachian and Cajun), on the disabled, and on the aged. This definition fits well with my notions for developing a better understanding of the historical, ideological, and social contexts of oppressed groups. Moreover, the definition is broad enough to include variance in the broad categories of race and class. Gender issues are not defined separately but are subsumed under race and class. The definition also includes forms of difference (religious, regional, etc.) that are often unmentioned.

I am fortunate to work at a university that respects and honors attempts to work collaboratively among departments. I teach what is known, informally, as the "combined course." The course is so called because it combines high school literature and reading methods for grades 9–12. The English Department agreed to permit me to teach the course if I would agree not to delete all the dead white men (their words) from the reading list. I actually found this quite funny, but in all fairness, the concerns of select members of the English Department are quite valid. There has been constant, often heated, debate in the professional and public literature over the literary canon. I had no intention of excluding the works of these men; however, I did not intend to make their works the center of my attention or concern. I do not take an either/or position on the canon debate. It seems to me that there is enough literature for expanded notions of the canon to include both "Western classics" and multicultural literature.

CREATING A MULTICULTURAL LITERATURE COURSE FOR PROSPECTIVE ENGLISH TEACHERS

How I translate critical pedagogy and the recent research on the instruction and use of multicultural literature to preservice teachers is the subject of this section. How is a teacher to know which literature to select? How is it that certain works of literature are valued more than others? If literature reflects the language, life experiences, values, interests, and beliefs we hold dear, whose values are celebrated and learned? Whose values are not? In a pluralistic society, should we recognize, read, and learn about the multiple voices that represent literary contributions? Or is there one set of readings that form American literature? The question of what becomes part of the curriculum, then, becomes what Giroux (1987b) calls "a battleground over whose forms of knowledge, history, visions, language and culture, and authority will prevail as a legitimate object of learning and analysis" (pp. 19–20). In my course students are offered an alternative to the traditional course on literature for the high school in that they are required to read multicultural literature.

Questions may arise as to the willingness of high school and college students to read multicultural literature. Research by Beach (1994; Chapter 3, this volume), among others, suggests that white high school and college students often have negative reactions to multicultural literature. However, Spears-Bunton's (1992) study of the use of multicultural literature with African American and European American students proposes that literacy lessons can be used to alter students' negative responses to multicultural literature. Her research found that some European American students were forced to rethink some of their previously held stereotypical notions of African Americans as a result of reading and discussing literature written by African Americans. Importantly, Spears-Bunton's study reveals that the responses of African American students to literature written by African Americans improved their self-esteem, involvement, and performance. She states that African American students "personally identified with the language, theme, characterization and world view of the text" (p. 394). From her study, Spears-Bunton concludes that there are "multiple ways in which the students took ownership of the process and products of their reading and the ways in which they used their reading of the text in combination of their reading of the world to construct meaning" (p. 400). The willingness of all students to read and respond to multicultural literature may be a product of the classroom environment, the instructional strategies used, students' option to enroll in the course, the specific works included, and students' educational background (Beach, 1994).

The need for a multicultural pedagogy that is transforming is perhaps best captured by bell hooks (1993). She articulates the need in this manner:

> Despite the contemporary focus on multiculturalism in our society, particularly in education, there is not nearly enough practical discussion of ways classroom settings can be transformed so that the learning experience is inclusive. If the effort to respect and honor the social reality and experiences of groups in this society who are non-White is to be reflected in a pedagogical

process, then as teachers on all levels, from elementary to university settings, we must acknowledge that our styles of teaching may need to change. (p. 91)

An Alternative Approach to English Methods

New holistic approaches to literacy have influenced the ways in which literature and language arts courses are taught in preservice teacher education. Reading and writing workshops, journal writing, reading logs, literature circles, reader responses, and portfolios are becoming commonplace. Yet the actual literature required has changed little (Applebee, 1989; Graff, 1992). Despite an increase in the number of books written and published by authors from groups that have been historically underrepresented in the canon, multicultural literature still does not have a permanent place in high school or college curriculums. I submit that to continue to maintain the literary canon means to ignore the needs of culturally and linguistically diverse students and to ignore the literary contributions of their forefathers and foremothers. Soon this will mean ignoring the needs of the majority of the students in our classrooms. Maintenance of the literary canon also suggests that teacher-training institutions are ill preparing a future teaching force to adapt to the changes in student populations.

An excellent reference for developing instructional strategies, grounded in Freirean theory, is Ira Shor's (1987) *Freire for the Classroom*. I have adopted and adapted several instructional strategies described in the text for my course. A number of activities that students engage in on the first day of class sets the tone for participation and dialogue for the remainder of the semester. My goal throughout the course is to model practice that is worthy of emulation. For example, the first day of class begins with oral self-introductions and oral responses to six questions requiring a sharing of personal preferences (e.g., what is your favorite color, animal, etc.). Each student is expected to participate and does so naturally. I, too, participate as a member of the class. Use of this introductory technique creates an early impression and atmosphere for the participatory nature of the course. Responses offered by the students are recorded and used throughout the course for small-group assignments.

Next, students are asked to list every book they have ever read that was written by a person of color. Responses to this activity vary with each student's tastes in academic and pleasure reading. Their responses reveal that, as English majors, my students are familiar with canonical literature but less familiar with multicultural literature. The first day ends with students responding to the following question: "How does your cultural perspective affect the students you teach?" (Hansen-Krening, 1992, p. 125; permission to use this question was granted in a personal communication with Nancy Hansen-Krening). Written responses to this activity also vary in length and completeness. However, generally all students try to give a response they believe answers the questions. A few responses will help to illustrate my point:

STUDENT A

I have so often heard people say that they are not biased, or prejudiced, and are completely open-minded to everyone and their perspectives. I suppose we'd all like to believe that we are without fault and values that maybe aren't so liberating. The truth is that we all contain within ourselves a very unique set of values and perspectives that have developed largely from what we have experienced in our lives.

STUDENT B

My own cultural perspective, because it shapes who I am in the classroom, will affect my students. I am a mixed-blood Central American Indian, Mexican, and Western European. . . . I do have a cultural point of view; despite working at being open-minded, my beliefs and values may conflict with [my] students values.

STUDENT C

I believe that your cultural perspective has a significant impact on the students that you teach. As a teacher you will interact daily with students from various cultural backgrounds who have various ideas and beliefs. It is important for a teacher to not only respect each student and his or her background but also to have some understanding of the students' cultures and the personalities that accompany their cultural perspective.

I repeat this final activity on the last day of class. Content analysis of the students' precourse/postcourse responses reveals how their thinking and attitudes have changed over the course of the semester as they have explored multicultural issues and multicultural literature.

Students are also required to write two autobiographies. In the first autobiographic sketch they are to trace their families' cultural and linguistic heritage back four or five generations. This activity is always quite revealing to students, since most young people know little of their family history beyond their maternal and paternal grandparents. Each year I am amazed as students discover who they really are as a person from long-distance calls around the country to parents and relatives. An example helps to illustrate this point. In a concluding paragraph, a female student observed:

> It is often asked what we second-generation "Korean Americans" consider ourselves as Korean or American. It's a difficult question to answer because our "Korean-ness" and our "American-ness" are in conflict. We cannot consider ourselves as fully Korean because we were born and raised in America. At the same time, however, it is also difficult to say we are fully "American" for a number of reasons. First, the families, cultures, customs, traditions, and lifestyles are not typically "American." They are, in fact, very different from some of the traditional American customs people have held since the beginning of American history. Secondly, our outward appearance must confuse people into thinking that we are foreigners to the American way of life. Lastly, it is just plain difficult to define what "American" really is, especially now, in the X-generation and the politically correct wave of thought.

The discovery of our varied cultural backgrounds is shared in small groups. Volunteers may share with the whole class any portion of their autobiographic sketch. I also share my autobiographic sketch with the class. While I appear to be an African American female, most of my students are also surprised to learn that my lineage includes English and French slave owners who fathered my grandparents. Moreover, they are amazed to learn that I have an Irish great-grandfather who married his African slave and a great-grandmother who was a Cherokee Indian (full-blooded). After sharing our autobiographic information, students are more aware of the variety of histories, languages, cultural values, and culturally mediated traditions that each of us brings to the classroom.

Students are also asked to write autobiographies of their school literacy experiences. Britzman (1986) describes the experiences that preservice teachers bring with them as "their implicit institutional biographies—the cumulative experience of school lives—which, in turn, informs [sic] their knowledge of the student's world, school structure, and of curriculum" (p. 443). Students have shared memories that include learning to read and write, their favorite childhood books, and experiences in junior and senior high school language arts classes. The most hurtful memories tend to be those associated with being placed in a low reading group or being asked to read aloud in class. For most students, it is their college experiences that have provided the most diverse settings for literacy instruction.

An Alternative to the Canon

The literature selected for my course centers on the literature produced by groups who have historically been underrepresented in the canon and also includes literature produced by European American males and females. I have created a technique I call *freedom within structure* in selecting the titles to be reviewed and chosen for class readings. Each year I update a list of multicultural titles by following an adapted version of guidelines for the selection of multicultural titles offered by Rudine Sims Bishop (1992). I also read widely, ask for recommendations from colleagues and local high school English teachers, browse in bookstores, and scan lists of award-winning books for young adults. While it is impossible to have read every book written, it is necessary to make some decisions about what the students are asked to read. Furthermore, in an effort to support my notion of literature as an artifact of cultural production, I offer my students a list of titles that I believe can be used to uncover the ideological, historical, and social contexts of oppression. Hence students have the *freedom* to select which titles to read, yet I have supplied a *structure* that supports my pedagogical position. With these parameters in mind, below is a sample of the title list I distribute. This is by no means an exhaustive listing of all the available multicultural titles. Please note that on this abbreviated list I have included European and European American authors as well as works by women in each cultural group.

EUROPEAN AND EUROPEAN AMERICAN TEXTS

Growing Up, Russell Baker
The Great Gatsby, F. Scott Fitzgerald
The Outsiders, S. E. Hinton
Death of a Salesman, Arthur Miller
The Optimist's Daughter, Eudora Welty

AFRICAN AMERICAN TEXTS

I Know Why the Caged Bird Sings, Maya Angelou
Narrative of the Life of an American Slave, Frederick Douglass
The Autobiography of Malcolm X, Malcolm X with Alex Haley
Their Eyes Were Watching God, Zora Neale Hurston
The Darkside of Hopkinsville, Ted Poston with Kathleen Hauke

ASIAN AMERICAN TEXTS

Donald Duk, Frank Chin
The Year of Impossible Good-byes, Sook Nyul Choi
The Floating World, Cynthia Kadohata
The Joy Luck Club, Amy Tan
Farwell to Manzanar, Jeanne Wakatsuki Houston and James D. Houston

LATINO/A TEXTS

Bless Me, Ultima, Rudolfo Anaya
The Last of the Menu Girls, Denise Chavez
Chronicle of a Death Foretold, Gabriel Garcia-Marquez
Silent Dancing: A Partial Remembrance of a Puerto Rican Childhood,
    Judith Ortiz Cofer
Days of Obligation, Richard Rodriguez

NATIVE AMERICAN TEXTS

Ceremony, Leslie Silko
Two Old Women, Velma Wallis
House Made of Dawn, N. Scott Momaday
Winter in the Blood, James Welch
The Education of Little Tree, Forrest Carter

My students receive a longer and more contemporary list than can be included in this chapter. The list includes literature that has been written by insiders (members of a minority group) and outsiders (people from outside the minority group about which they write); literature that offers a balanced representation of specific cultures and literature that does not; and literature that is appropriate for grades 9–12 and literature that is not. The literature that is not appropriate for grades 9–12 (usually adult novels or novels that are stereotypical or written by those outside the culture) is generally unknown to the students. I have "planted" the literature in the list so that the students can discover areas of concern. My goal is to have them read carefully enough to be concerned about the inclusion of multicultural literature that may be seen as problematic when used in school settings. When questions arise in class, out of discovery and concern, we have some very lively discussions.

Course readings begin with European and European American novels. Situating the ideological, historical, and social contexts of the novels is easiest at this point. For the most part, the contexts are familiar to the students, since these works have been the meat of their literature and history courses to date. However, as we begin to venture into the other groups, students bring far less understanding and knowledge about the history and literature of underrepresented cultural groups as a whole. Moreover, they lack information and understanding of the groups as part of U.S. history. Having students supply the ideological, historical, and social contexts for discussions of the novels is important for their understanding of the literature.

Cultural Production of African American Literature

A history of the genesis of African American literature offers an excellent example of literature as an artifact of cultural production. It is imperative that members of each new generation know and understand these roots before approaching the task of teaching them to the next generation. Many of the early Africans brought to the New World were kidnapped from the shores of western Africa. It is difficult to pinpoint one dominant language of the people from this region, for many languages were spoken. Although diverse languages and cultures existed among various African clans, there were also commonalities. There were, however, few written languages. Because these were predominantly oral societies, the literature and history of each tribe of west Africa was also oral. Franklin and Moss (1994), two respected experts on the history of African Americans, declare that "the oral literature was composed of supernatural tales, moral tales, proverbs, epic poems, satires, love songs, funeral marches, and comic tales" (p. 23). The oral literature that grew from their everyday activities served many functions in the African way of life, such as to educate, govern, and entertain. Bell (1987) suggests that the varying forms of verbal art used helped to

> transmit knowledge, value, and attitudes from one generation to another, enforce conformity to social norms, validate social institutions and religious rituals, and provide psychological release from the restrictions of society. (p. 16)

As men, women, and children were kidnapped, sold, transmitted, and resold to colonists in the New World, old folkways, languages, rituals, and beliefs gave way to acculturation to a new language and way of life.

Initially African slaves were brought as indentured servants who could work to earn or purchase their freedom, as many of them did. They also bought property and initially lived as other groups did, even enjoying some political rights. However, as the economic demand for increased labor mounted and more African slaves were brought to the colonies, the more stringent laws became in forcing people of African descent into servitude. The rights, land, and property of the "free" African Americans were not protected by the laws of the colonies—nor was their freedom. Any slave owner could, in effect, rescind any promise of freedom, land, or property. An analysis of class, or of economic social constructions, cannot account for the continued racial oppression endured by the African Americans.

There is a long and unfaltering history of legal barriers to literacy acquisition—from the enactment of Virginia slave codes in 1636 to the 1990 court battles over Africentric schools in major U.S. cities with large African American school populations. Using one of the earliest slave codes as an example will help to illustrate this point. One of the laws in the slave codes called for maintaining control over the travel of slaves in order to limit the number runaways and to prevent revolts. Slaves were required to have written permission to travel away from the master's property. It was reasoned that since slaves could not read or write they could not produce written travel documents, and thus slave owners were assured of maintaining control. Further, it was reasoned that if slaves became literate they would no longer submit to the inhumane treatment of slavery. Barksdale and Kinnamon (1972) suggest that it is important to understand the circumstances of America's "peculiar institution" in situating African American literature. They note that "slavery had the negative effect of divesting Africans of a substantial portion of their own culture [and] denied Blacks the opportunity and the occasion to create written literature" (p. 2). There were, of course, exceptions to the enforced illiteracy of slaves. There were some "benevolent" slave owners who allowed their slaves to acquire literacy skills. Most common among this group of slaves were the children of the slave owner and a slave woman.

An analysis of the early writings of people of African descent after their capture and arrival in the New World notes how Africans adapted the language, style, and genres of European American writings with their own interpretations. The early writings also depict a longing for freedom and their homeland in the midst of their inescapable lives as slaves. One of the most important genres of African American literature began during the eighteenth century with the publication of fugitive slave narratives. These were most similar to autobiographies which were popular during this period. Stepto (1984) has called the slave narrative the beginning of "the creation of an Afro-American fiction based upon the conventions of slave narratives" (p. 178). Two popular themes in slave narratives were the need for self-actualization through literacy and the call for literacy to help stay the hand of the oppressor. Thus literacy was linked to the fight for individual and group liberation from the ideology of a slave-owning society. The fugitive slave Frederick Douglass best captures the sentiment of slave holders' perception of the threat of liberation through literacy acquisition. In his autobiography, Douglass (1845/1968) quotes the objection of one of his masters, Mr. Auld, to his being taught to read:

> A nigger should know nothing but to obey his master—to do what he is told to do. Learning would soil the best nigger in the world. "Now," said he, "if you teach that nigger (speaking of myself) how to read would be no keeping him. It would forever unfit him to be a slave. He would at once become unmanageable, and of no value to his master." (p. 49)

Douglass's literacy acquisition is pivotal to his understanding of freedom in two important ways. Literacy freed Douglass intellectually and allowed him to use the language of the oppressor to state his case (Smith, 1987). Smith observes another important issue unveiled in Douglass's narrative. She writes that "Frederick Douglass' narrative participates in one of the major ideological controversies of his day, the dispute over the question of Negro humanity and equality" (p. 21). The ideological controversy continues in the misunderstanding of the role of ideology in shaping the social and political constructs of race and how they are actualized in U.S. society. I have used this short historical perspective to make explicit the role of race in the cultural production of literacy.

It is my belief that there is no escaping the centrality of race and class as key factors in the politics of literacy acquisition and in the production of a unique literature as a cultural artifact in the United States. W. E. B. DuBois (1903/1989) prophetically declared:

> This history of the American Negro is the history of this strife,—this longing to attain self-conscious manhood, to merge his double self into a better and truer self. In this merging he wishes neither of the older selves to be lost. He would not Africanize America, for America has too much to teach the world and Africa. He would not bleach his Negro soul in a flood of white Americanism, for he knows that Negro blood has a message for the world. He simply wishes to make it possible for a man to be both a Negro and an American. (p. 3)

Although the above description is helpful in the understanding of the racial and class oppression of the African American male, it does not reveal the special case of oppression that can be made for African American women. In contextualizing their oppression it would be necessary to include the sexual exploitation to which many women were subjected. The only accounts available that tell of the ideological position of a society that would tolerate forced concubinage, of the privilege of white women and their children over the black family of the slave owner, and of the breakup of families—sold to other slaveowners—can be found in the writings of slave women. The few fugitive slave writings by African American women (*Our Nig,* by Harriet E. Wilson, and *Incidents in the Life of a Slave Girl,* by Harriet Jacobs) are not included on traditional lists. Yet they, too, tell a story of oppression—one that crosses race, class, and gender lines. Similar historical, social, ideological, and cultural contextualizing is done by the students for each novel they read.

As students share their written responses to the novels and their investigations into the ideological, historical, and social contexts of the novels, it often becomes clear that they are working from a narrow understanding of the history of oppression in the United States. Moreover, their written responses reveal that, for most of them, their college lives, both academically and socially, are the most diverse settings they have ever experienced. It is in discussions of the contexts of multicultural literature that unvoiced assumptions about culture, class, and power begin to be recognized and addressed. Many students seem unaware of the ideological, historical, and social privilege they have experienced in an educational system designed to support Eurocentric views of history, norms, and values. It is difficult for the students to examine the ideological, historical, social, and institutional structures that have aided their success. McIntosh (1989) argues that "absence of a racial discourse on whiteness reinforces the widely accepted myth that whiteness is morally neutral, normal, and average, and also ideal" (p. 2).

King (1991) suggests that some preservice teachers may unknowingly bring with them dysconscious racism. She defines dysconscious racism as

> a form of racism that tacitly accepts dominant White norms and privileges. It is not the *absence* of consciousness (that is, not unconsciousness) but an *impaired* consciousness or distorted way of thinking about race as compared to, for example, critical consciousness. (p. 135)

Many students have not considered their whiteness. One student writes:

> I have always considered myself to be very open-minded, not racist. Now I realize that I can, or do, carry around certain stereotypes even though I have good friends from many cultures. It is a hard thing to admit . . . white racism is hard for people to talk about because racism is usually hushed up. People do not like to claim responsibility for some of their ideas. I do not choose to carry around some of mine—they were handed down to me, not necessarily by parents but by [the] environment. By sharing these misconceptions

aloud and acknowledging them for what they are, it may be easier to dispel them.

I believe it is important for students to begin to assess their personal responses to their newfound knowledge of the larger ideological, historical, and social contexts that are part of a history of oppression in the United States. Moreover, it is important for students to reflect upon their responses to multicultural literature as they anticipate teaching others. As an artifact of the process of cultural production, multicultural literature can be the heart or source for rearticulating literacy.

The class has been challenged and required to consider the relationship among notions of ideology, culture, and history through their explorations of multicultural literature as an artifact of cultural production. Student voice, whether written or oral, continues throughout the semester, as on the first day, to be an important and welcome facet of the course. From the first day's sharing of personal preferences to later sharing of students' responses to text (both oral and written) during discussions, we have grown. The students have not come to the course as tabulae rasae, nor should they expect to leave without gaining some knowledge. Acknowledgment of the history, attitudes, and sometimes baggage we bring to class helps to move us toward change. This acknowledgment also allows us to deconstruct the past and build toward a shared understanding of the present as we plan for the future. Therefore it is necessary to include students' cumulative social experience—as they understand and analyze it—as part of the content of the classroom discussion (Britzman, 1986; Florio-Ruane, 1994; Giroux, 1987a). In small-group discussions and in small working groups based on responses given the first day of class, students begin to negotiate the meaning of multicultural literature, often extending their knowledge and understandings to personal and work situations. Small groups learn to work and cooperate as they select novels to read and write individual response during the semester. Small-group discussions follow the reading of each novel and the sharing of written responses. It is during the small-group discussions that students reveal their lack of historical, ideological, and cultural awareness. As a facilitator I often supply this information, but students who are more knowledgeable are encouraged to supply documentation of alternative views of history. For example, after a student wrote a response, she proudly shared it with her group. The response reflected her thinking (and later she explained her background). She was surprised to learn that in her small group, her response was in the minority. She sought to make others understand her point of view, citing historical references. They listen patiently and told her they understood but did not agree with her viewpoint. They shared their interpretations of the text and offered historical, political, and ideological data to support their claims. As a group they were required to summarize the text for the class. The student with the dissenting voice asked if she could reconsider her position. During the course of the class, she became an active listener to the opinions of others and more sensitive in her responses to text. Thus in small-group discussions students become aware of the multiple interpretations of text and the need to negotiate among themselves about the meaning of the text. After the small-group meetings we reconvene and share our readings, responses, and reflections with the class.

A CONTINUING PROCESS

The course I have described is based on a theory of critical literacy that views multicultural literature as an artifact of cultural production. The instruction and use of multicultural literature is designed to address the specific ideological, historical, and social contexts of the novels read. Using multicultural literature, I believe, offers preservice teachers some direct experiences in gaining knowledge about different ethnic and cultural perspectives. My hope is that the experiences will motivate preservice teachers to sensitively consider the decisions they make about the school literacy experiences they design and plan for their students.

I would like to continue this research by tracking former students through their student teaching experience and into the first year or two of teaching. It occurs to me that Giroux (1987b) is correct in assuming that schools are sites "where dominant and subordinate cultures collide and where teachers, students, and school administration often differ as to how schools' experiences and practices are to be defined" (p. 17). I would like to know of the support or resistance teachers face when they bring a critical literacy approach to the instruction and use of multicultural literature in the classroom. Several students have managed to stay in contact with me through their early careers. Recently a former student who uses many of the methods and materials from class wrote:

> I am teaching at West Somewhere High School. The school is 75% EuroAmerican and 25% Latino/a. Kids are the same in this small community as they are in a bigger one. I have an outside reading requirement of 3,000 pages over the course of the year, and students must select one book each quarter written by one of the authors that we used in your class. These kids are beginning to see outside of their own little world and get a look at situations that have not

been distorted by television. Many of the girls are "hooked" on the list of authors that I provided. One girl actually told me that I was the first teacher who had introduced any Hispanic authors to her and said I was the first teacher she has ever had who made her proud to be Hispanic, instead of ashamed of it.

Wouldn't it be grand if every child could be similarly influenced?

NOTE

My sincerest thanks to Ed Buendia, Eunice Greer, Robert Jimenez, Cameron McCarthy, and Shuiab Mechem, who read and critiqued earlier drafts of this chapter.

REFERENCES

Applebee, A. N. (1989). *A study of book-length works taught in high school English courses* (Report No. 1.2). Albany, NY: Center for the Learning and Teaching of Literature.

Applebee, A. N. (1991). Literature: Whose heritage? In E. Hiebert (Ed.), *Literacy for a diverse society: Perspectives, practices, and policies* (pp. 228–236). New York: Teachers College Press.

Applebee, A. N. (1992). Stability and change in the high school canon. *English Journal, 81*(5), 27–32.

Applebee, A. N. (1993). *Literature in the secondary school: Studies of curriculum and instruction in the United States.* Urbana, IL: National Council of Teachers of English.

Au, K. (1993). *Literacy instruction in multicultural settings.* Fort Worth, TX: Harcourt Brace.

Banks, J. (1994). *An introduction to multicultural education.* Boston: Allyn & Bacon.

Barksdale, R., & Kinnamon, K. (1972). *Black writers of America: A comprehensive anthology.* New York: Prentice-Hall.

Barrera, R. (1992). The cultural gap in literature-based literacy instruction. *Education and Urban Society, 24*(2), 227–243.

Beach, R. (1994, April). *Research on readers' response to multicultural literature.* Paper presented at the Annual Meeting of the American Educational Research Association, New Orleans.

Bell, B. (1987). *The Afro-American novel and its tradition.* Amherst: University of Massachusetts Press.

Bishop, R. (1992). Multicultural literature for children: Making informed choices. In V. Harris (Ed.), *Teaching multicultural literature in grades K–8* (pp. 37–54). Norwood, MA: Christopher-Gordon.

Britzman, D. (1986). Cultural myths in the making of a teacher: Biography and social structure in teacher education. *Harvard Educational Review, 56* (4), 442–456.

Delpit, L. (1988). The silenced dialogue: Power and pedagogy in educating other people's children. *Harvard Educational Review, 58,* 280–298.

Diamond, B., & Moore, M. (1995). *Multicultural literacy: Mirroring the reality of the classroom.* White Plains, NY: Longman.

Douglass, F. (1968). *Narrative of the life of Frederick Douglass: An American slave, written by himself.* New York, NY: Penguin Books. (Original work published 1845)

Du Bois, W. E. B. (1989). *The souls of black folks.* New York: Bantam. (Original work published 1903)

Florio-Ruane, S. (1994). The future teachers' autobiography club: Preparing educators to support literacy learning in culturally diverse classrooms. *English Education, 26,* 52–66.

Franklin, J., & Moss, A. (1994). *From slavery to freedom: A history of African Americans. Seventh Ed.* New York: McGraw-Hill.

Freire, P. (1970). *Pedagogy of the oppressed.* New York: Continuum.

Freire, P. (1994). Foreword to Macedo, D., *Literacies of power: What Americans are not allowed to know.* Boulder, CO: Westview.

Freire, P., & Macedo, D. (1995). A dialogue: Culture, language, and race. *Harvard Educational Review, 65*(3), 377–402.

Freire, P., & Macedo, D. (1987). *Literacy: Reading the word and the world.* Westport, CT: Bergin & Garvey.

Fuller, D. (1992). Monocultural teachers and multicultural students: A demographic clash. *Teaching Education, 4*(2), 87–93.

Gates, H. (1992). *Loose canons: Notes on the culture wars.* New York: Oxford University Press.

Giovanni, N. (1994). *Racism 101.* New York: Morrow.

Giroux, H. (1987a). Critical literacy and student experience: Donald Graves' approach to literacy. *Language Arts, 64,* 175–181.

Giroux, H. (1987b). Introduction. In P. Freire & D. Macedo (Eds.), *Literacy: Reading the word and the world* (pp. 1–27). Westport: CT: Bergin & Garvey.

Graff, G. (1992). *Beyond the culture wars: How teaching the conflicts can revitalize American education.* New York: W. W. Norton.

Hansen-Krening, N. (1992). Authors of color: A multicultural perspective. *Journal of Reading, 36*(2), 124–129.

Harris, V. (Ed.). (1992). *Teaching multicultural literature in grades K–8.* Norwood, MA: Christopher-Gordon.

hooks, b. (1993). Transformative pedagogy and multiculturalism. In T. Perry & J. Fraser (Eds.), *Freedom's plow: Teaching in the multicultural classrooms* (pp. 91–97). New York: Routledge.

King, J. (1991). Dysconscius racism: Ideology, identity, and the miseducation of teachers. *Journal of Negro Education, 60*(2), 133–146.

Ladson-Billings, G. (1994). *The dreamkeepers: Successful teachers of African American children.* San Francisco: Jossey-Bass.

Macedo, D. (1994). *Literacies of power: What Americans are not allowed to know.* Boulder, CO: Westview.

McIntosh, P. (1989, July/August). White privilege: Unpacking the invisible knapsack. *Peace and Freedom*, pp. 10–12.

Peterson, K. (1994, December 27). "Scarlet letter has 'A' position on reading lists." *USA Today*, p. 16.

Reyes, M. (1992). Challenging venerable assumptions: Literacy instruction for linguistically different students. *Harvard Educational Review, 62*, 427–446.

Shor, I. (1987). (Ed.). *Freire for the classroom: A sourcebook for liberatory teaching.* Portsmouth, NH: Boynton/Cook.

Sleeter, C. (1994). White racism. *Multicultural Education, 1*, 5–39.

Smith, N. B. (1987). *Self-discovery and authority in Afro-American narrative.* Cambridge, MA: Harvard University Press.

Spears-Bunton, L. (1992). Literature, literacy, and resistance to cultural domination. In C. Kinzer & D. Leu (Eds.), *Yearbook of the National Reading Conference: Vol. 41. Literacy research, theory, and practice: Views from many perspectives.* Alexandria, VA: National Reading Conference.

Stepto, R. (1984). Storytelling in early Afro-American fiction: Frederick Douglass's "The heroic slave." In Henry Louis Gates, Jr. (Ed.), *Black literature and literary theory* (pp. 177–180). New York: Methuen.

Sustein, B., & Smith, J. (1994). Attempting a graceful waltz on a teeter totter: The canon and English methods courses. *English Journal, 83*(8), 47–54.

Willis, A. (1995). Reading the world of school literacy: Contextualizing the experience of a young African-American male. *Harvard Educational Review, 65*(1), 30–49.

CHAPTER 7

Reflections on Cultural Diversity in Literature and in the Classroom

LAURA E. DESAI

Do you feel safe when you visit your husband's family in New Delhi, India? I mean, isn't it dirty, overcrowded and dangerous? Can you talk to the people? Do they accept you?

—Conversation with author

WHILE I HAVE TAKEN some poetic license with the above quote so the reader will understand the context that framed its occurrence, it does capture the essence of a recent conversation. The questions, not meant to be offensive, were asked with a genuine desire for knowledge and understanding. My companion, aware only that India is a third-world country and extremely poor, could not imagine how I could enjoy or appreciate visits to my Indian in-laws. However, hers is not an unusual concern. A fourth-grade teacher, with whom I was speaking about my 10- and 15-year-old Indian nieces, expressed the assumption that once they had the opportunity to visit the United States they would be reluctant to return to India. Again, a comment made without malice—but perhaps also without an understanding of people and places beyond the borders of her own life.

While these incidents might be a reflection of a lack of understanding about a people and a place to some extent removed from the United States, I offer another personal example that has been a recurring experience throughout my life. While I would define myself as a white American woman, I could also add the term *Jewish* to the preceding cultural and ethnic description. However, over the years I have found that this final term can prompt a great deal of consternation for some. Apparently,

I do not look the part nor fit the stereotype that many hold of Jewish Americans. In fact, there have been times when people have vehemently argued that I could not possibility be Jewish. Again, I would suggest that these comments were uniformly made without apparent prejudice—but also without an understanding of someone from a background different from their own.

I have offered these personal anecdotes based on a belief in the importance of narrative. As noted by Connelly and Clandinin (1990), "education and educational research is the construction and reconstruction of personal and social stories; learners, teachers, and researchers are storytellers and characters in their own and other's stories" (p. 2). It is my own story that has prompted my interest in the role that the stories of others might play in the development of our students' multi-ethnic understandings. While there has been a great deal of support (Harris, 1991; Norton, 1985, 1990; Sims, 1982; Sims Bishop, 1990) for the role that literature plays in classroom instruction, and while many have suggested that multicultural literature can provide students with valuable examples of the unique differences among people while also highlighting the universality of the human experience, there has been little consideration of exactly how a child interacts with multicultural texts. How do the stories in the texts impact the stories that comprise the lives of our students? What is the link between multi-ethnic understanding, the classroom, and children's literature?

My choice of topic does not come by accident. It is shaped by who I was, who I am, and those I wish to affect who are in the process of becoming, as a result of their experience with literature. While I believe that literature has the power to enable children to experience more fully what they already know, as well as to be touched by people, situations, and events that they might otherwise never encounter, I am, as yet, uncertain as to how this happens. It is, however, a journey toward understanding on which we must embark. We need to carefully consider the issues that frame the discussion. If, as Rabinowitz (1987) suggests, the writer and reader exist as members of a shared social interpretive community, we need to determine the impact a society with multiple communities has on our interpretations and understanding of text. We need to look at the definitions of terms, the claims made about multicultural literature, and the studies that have framed our understandings. As we look at the role of culture in a reader's response, we must consider the multiple communities that frame our social, cultural, and political context, and we can then begin to consider the role that a teacher and the classroom play in this process.

THE POWER OF THE STORY

Joshua is 9 years old now, but he has been going to visit his grandmother almost every Sabbath since he was 5. These Sabbath visits are a special time, because not only does Joshua have the chance to help his grandma Goldina light the Sabbath candles, he also has the opportunity to hear her remembrances about the past. Through the objects in her remembering box he learns about his grandmother, her life, and their religion, a way of life that frames both their worlds. He also learns about the willow stick that can find water, the ribbons his grandmother placed in her horse Mazel's mane, the money kept in her knippel, and the silver bell that called the people of her childhood village to their Sabbath prayers.

Eth Clifford's (1985) *The Remembering Box* is a story about family love across the generations, but it is also about tradition and about a young boy who comes to realize the value of the past as well as the present. As such, it is a book that has the power to speak to all of us regardless of ethnic background, but I would suggest for those readers who happen to be Jewish, it can bring a smile, a tear, and a feeling of warmth.

How does this happen? What impact does culture have on a reader's response to a text? There are layers of meaning that we need to understand as we consider a reader's "cultured" response to a text. The search for an answer necessitates an understanding of the reading process, the notion of culture, and the nature of response. None of these concepts is simple, nor is there universal agreement regarding definitions of the terms. Consequently, before the question can begin to be answered, the terms must be unpacked and defined.

WHAT ARE CULTURE AND ETHNICITY?

Culture, or ethnicity, as defined here is an adaptive system, or the way of life of a particular human society, which is composed of learned, shared group behavior. Erlich (1990), an anthropologist, notes that anthropologists see culture as a survival mechanism for a way of life created by human groups. The paradox, as suggested by Erlich, is that while on the surface cultures appear to be all different, they are, in reality, all the same. They all represent "adaptations to similar demands of living a group existence" (p. 3) and are all organized around the same set of basic institutions: kinship, legal and political, religious, and economic. Each of these institutions is part of a set of integrated interrelationships, and, as a result, change within one institution will have repercussions in all other parts of the culture. Cultures are, therefore, systems that operate as a whole and that are continually adapting to specific environmental settings.

Banks (1979) defined ethnicity almost exactly as Erlich defined culture. His definition stated that "an ethnic group is an involuntary group which shares a heritage, kinship ties, a sense of identification, political and economic interests, and cultural and linguistic characteristics" (p. 239). On the other hand, he defined culture as consisting of "the behavior patterns, symbols, institutions, values and other human-made components of society" (p. 238). Based on these definitions, Banks suggested that "multi-ethnic education is also a form of multicultural education since an ethnic group is one kind of cultural group" (p. 239).

In *Teaching Strategies for Ethnic Studies,* Banks (1991) has expanded on these definitions and explanations of ethnicity and culture. He suggests that while ethnicity is an important part of American culture, there remains a strong American culture and identity. Using the phrases *microcultural groups, ethnic groups, ethnic minority groups,* and *people of color,* Banks suggests that there are many smaller groups within the American culture. He notes that "these microcultural groups share many characteristics with the common national group but have some distinguishing characteristics that set them apart from other cultural groups" (p. 14). He differentiates between these various group terms by suggesting that while microcultural groups are voluntary groups, an ethnic group is, for the most part, involuntary, although identification with that group may be optional. Ethnic minority groups are also ethnic groups but are groups with "a numerical minority that have minimal economic and political power" (p. 14). He makes one further distinction, which provides an explanation of race by saying that within an ethnic minority group there are people of color who are nonwhite and share unique physical and cultural characteristics. Finally, we exist in a global society in which the American culture is but one of many global cultures.

Given the strength of the American cultural identity as suggested by Banks, how do we incorporate in our classrooms, as well as in society itself, the multiple ethnic minority groups that exist as part of the American culture? At what point do we exist in a shared interpretive community and at what point does our cultural or ethnic affiliation become the lens through which we view our lives and their stories?

A young fifth-grade child sits quietly at her desk on what, even for Texas, is a somewhat warm November day in 1964. Suddenly her teacher asks if anyone in the class is Jewish and would be willing to bring in a menorah to help represent the upcoming Jewish holiday of Hanukkah. Our young student does not immediately raise her hand but considers her options. If the teacher does not know that she is Jewish, why should she admit something that has remained hidden for the past year and a half? On the other hand, what happens if her deception is uncovered? Slowly and extremely reluctantly, she raises her hand. No one in this class of 10-year-olds cares or for that matter really even notices, but a lingering question remains. Of what was I afraid? Why did I think it would matter that my religion or ethnic group differed from that of every other child in the classroom? Could something or someone have made a difference in my reaction?

VALUE OF MULTICULTURAL LITERATURE

"Literature," writes Itty Chan (1984),

> is a literary record of our collective human experience. It introduces us to other human beings, and invites us to share their lives—their thoughts and convictions, feelings, sufferings, and joys. Our outlook on life is broadened, our understanding of it deepened, and our own life takes on added meaning and significance as it is interpreted in the context of other lives. . . .
>
> Minority children too, seeing their own lives and cultures represented in the literature they read, will no longer feel that minority means insignificant or inferior, and will come to cherish their own cultural heritage, and be proud of it. (pp. 19–20)

Esther Jenkins (1973) writes:

> A multi-ethnic literature program which introduces each child to his own heritage along with that of others and which is flexible enough to allow him to sample according to his own needs yet, at times, focuses his attention on the universalities of human experience should add another dimension to current efforts to improve the image of each minority group and could make learning more relevant to all. (p. 694–695)

Donna Norton (1985) suggests that the benefits of sharing multicultural literature are so powerful and persuasive that they are beyond dispute and that they not only shape attitudes but also stimulate children's language and cognitive development. Violet Harris (1991) sees similar benefits from children's interaction with African American literature, and she suggests that this exposure not only increases general knowledge but also supports reading processes, develops visual literacy, increases understanding of literature and how it works, explores critical issues, prompts imagination, inspires the creation of literary and artistic products, and, last but certainly not least, entertains.

However, while these experts suggest that children's literature allows our students to vicariously experience their own culture as well as that of others and to learn about the similarities and differences among the peoples who comprise our world, the research to support this view is just now slowly beginning to emerge. At this point it is not only that the claims outweigh the evidence, but also that the questions being asked do not necessarily reflect the complexity of the issues. Should literature in fact be a vehicle for cultural understanding? Given the multiple communities that frame our world, and frame the stories that we write and read, how are we to make sense of the role that literature plays in determining our cultural understandings? Although I exist as an individual when reading a text, I am a product of numerous interpretive communities. So, too, is the author of the text I read. As Rosenblatt indicates, we are each members of numerous cultures and subcultures. As individuals existing within a culture, we all impact each other. However, all of us are products of numerous ethnic and cultural backgrounds. So in reality we each talk with multiple voices. We need research that considers not only the role of literature but also the role of the multiple communities that comprise the interpretive communities of our classrooms. Such questions add a new level of complexity to what is already a complicated issue.

The research that does currently exist can be found in three areas of work that provide in-roads but often result in more questions than answers. The first two areas look at the impact of literature on children's cultural attitudes and understandings. One is a set of experimental studies looking at the impact of cross-cultural books on children. The first of these studies was done in 1944, but they appeared predominantly in the 1960s and 1970s. The other area includes a set of studies loosely grouped under the category of "reader response." While these began in the late 1970s and were largely experimental at that time, they continue today, using a variety of research methodologies. Their purpose is to study the nature of a reader's response to various pieces of culturally diverse literature. Finally, the third area looks at the nature of a reader's response from the perspective of literary theory. While there is little agreement among literary theorists regarding the nature of interpretation, they share the common goal of seeking to understand what happens when a reader reads a text, or how the interpretation, or accomplishment of meaning, occurs. Although, for the most part, their work has not specifically asked questions regarding the role that culture plays in interpretation, their theories leave much room for speculation regarding the impact that culture might have on the accomplishment of meaning.

RESEARCH ON CULTURALLY DIVERSE LITERATURE

Campbell and Wirtenberg (1980), in their review of the literature, note that the majority of the early experimental studies were comparison studies looking at the effects of what was then termed to be curriculum containing "multicultural" books and curricula said to have more traditional, less equitable materials. For the most part, these studies found that these "multicultural" materials had positive effects on children's attitudes and achievements.

Those studies grouped under the broad umbrella of reader response focus on six basic areas: cultural impact as tied to *schema;* cultural impact on *personal response;* cultural influence and *gender* differences; *race* as a cultural issue; the impact of cultural *views of literacy;* and *literature's* impact on cultural understanding.

By far the largest group of these studies looks at the role of cultural schemata in the comprehension and recall of stories (Kintsch & Greene, 1978; Malik, 1990; Reynolds, Taylor, Steffensen, Shirey, & Anderson, 1982; Rogers-Zegarra and Singer, 1985; Steffensen, Jaog-Dev, & Anderson, 1979). These studies suggest that cultural schemata not only influence how material is read and interpreted but also affect the amount of information retained after reading. The studies show that readers remembered far more, and elaborated and extended their retellings more appropriately, after reading culturally familiar texts than after reading those that were culturally unfamiliar. It seems apparent that current research suggests that culture or ethnic background impacts understanding and response. However, the nature of that impact is still being questioned. Culture is often broadly defined and fails to consider the true "multicultural" nature of any given culture. Therefore, when studies suggest that the cultural content of a story affects understanding (Kintsch & Greene, 1978; Malik, 1990; Pritchard, 1990; Steffensen et al., 1979) and that subjects remember more, provide correct elaborations, and offer fewer distortions when they retell texts taken from their own culture, there is little indication that the complexity of the issues involved in bridging multiple voices has been considered. There is also no indication that a reader's response is linked to "understanding" the text. Readers from different cultures within a culture have arrived at different responses and understandings from reading the same text (Reynolds et al., 1982). Given the current reading-response research, this is worth stating but is not surprising. Interpretation or "understanding" results not only from the text but also from the reader and from the interpretive community of the classroom. As a result, it is important that the multiple voices become part of the research.

The studies (Bunbury & Tabbert, 1989; Ho, 1990; Tobin, 1990) that looked at the relationship between culture and personal response focused on the response of students to characters and settings both familiar and unfamiliar to their own culture and found an ability to appreciate those texts at different levels. Rogers-Zegarra and Singer (1985) found that "since cultures are not homogeneous, even within a nation, groups of individuals can be identified whose perspectives on issues and events will vary considerably" (p. 615). Tobin (1990) also noted that an important component in cultural literary interpretation is access to the interpretive community of the classroom. She suggested that when readers are deprived of interaction with their interpretive community, their understanding of and response to text are missing an important component. Given the perceived importance of the role of an interpretive community in understanding and response, research needs to look more carefully at the nature of that interaction. How do we bridge the multiple voices that are part of the classroom's interpretive community, and what role does literature play in this process?

It is equally important, when involved in cross-cultural research, to look at issues of race as related to issues of culture. Sims Bishop (1983) has looked at the portrayal of African Americans in literature for children and has examined the texts in terms of author, intended audience, and perspective. Spears-Bunton (1990) has looked at the impact that literature might have on students' cultural understandings. In an ethnographic study of one teacher's attempts to include African American literature in the curriculum of her eleventh-grade honors English class, Spears-Bunton found that students were forced to deal, on an individual and on a group basis, with important cultural and ethnic issues. Through case studies, she documented the change and growth of two female students, an African American and a white American, and noted the positive impact the change in curriculum had on both of these students.

A related issue is the acknowledgment and understanding of varying views of literacy held by diverse cultures. The work of Heath (1983) and Fishman (1987) has pointed to the fact that cultural views of literacy learning have a strong influence on the nature of language learning and success in school.

A weakness in studies that have considered culture as a factor in response is that they have only examined the issue from one perspective, the effect that a reader's own culture has on his or her own understanding of text. Few studies have followed Spears-Bunton's (1990) lead and have investigated the role that literature can play in determining our cultural understandings. I would like to suggest that as such our response studies need to carefully consider the roles that the culture or ethnic background of the author, reader, and interpretive community play in the development of our responses. An equally important issue is the role that literature plays in the growth of our cultural and ethnic understandings, and the insight that our responses to that literature might provide. The work of literary theorists provides some interesting possibilities, but again we are left with as many questions as answers.

LITERARY THEORY

At the outset I would like to suggest that it is difficult to answer a question which considers the impact that culture might have on the processes of an individual reader's meaning-making. Response theorists strive to answer the question of where meaning resides: in the reader, the text, the interaction between the reader and the text, or the context. According to Mailloux (1989), all the theorists "share a common assumption: Validity in interpretation is guaranteed by the establishment of norms and principles for explicating texts and such rules are derived from an account of how interpretation works in general" (p. 5). However, there is no single reader-response theory. These "norms" and "rules" are more reflective of a "critic" culture than an "ethnic" one. Rosenblatt (1991) suggests that there is a "spectrum" of response theories, with theorists grouped under reader-oriented theories (Holland, Bleich), text-oriented theories (Culler, Scholes, Fish), reader-plus-text-oriented theories (Iser, Rosenblatt), and feminist, ethnic, and other critical theories (Mailloux). Rogers (Chapter 4, this volume) argues that these views are limited because they fail to consider the society or culture in which the reader or any literary text originates. I would suggest that while each of us is an individual, there is no such thing as an individual reader. We are each a product of our interpretive communities and of our ethnic and cultural backgrounds. By this I do not mean that we do not each have our own personality and beliefs, because we do, but these beliefs did not develop in isolation. Therefore, when we read, we bring our own individuality to what we read, but we also need to consider what it is that framed and continues to frame our personality. I would like to suggest that it is our cultures that frame us and that our interpretive communities are in many ways synonymous with our cultures.

Literary theory reminds us that we do not live in isolation, nor do we read and interpret in isolation. We understand what we read through some combination of ourselves as the readers and the text with which we interact, but this is never free of the multiple contexts that frame us. Contexts have determined our personal identity (Bleich, Holland), the way we transact (Rosenblatt), the gaps we find in the text (Iser), the conventions we use to interpret the text (Culler), and our public shared interpretive strategies (Fish).

Scholes (1989) has suggested that all life is a text and that we read our lives as we read books. He says that we are reading culture. Given the mobility and changes in our lives, perhaps it is more accurate to say that all life may constitute one or more texts, as life is rarely seamless or continuous. I would also argue that our culture reads us, or, as Fish (1980) says, we are writing ourselves as we read. The theorists argue for the importance of the reader in developing an understanding of a text. They all acknowledge the significance of the communities from which the reader emerges and the impact those communities have on the reader. Mailloux (1977) suggests that it is the power of the rhetoric which exists in our communities that frames our interpretations. He also suggests that the context which frames our interpretive conventions is impossible to define. If we cannot define the context, does this mean we cannot define our interpretive communities and cannot define our cultures? How can we judge culture's impact if we cannot define what it is that is influencing our reactions? While, as I indicated earlier, this is a difficult and complex question to answer, I believe that it is important to make the attempt. When we begin to ask questions about culture, we need to consider issues of difference, multiple voices, and multiple communities, and our research must acknowledge this complexity.

Although I exist as an individual when reading a text, I am a product of numerous interpretive communities. So, too, are those with whom I interact. Our strength comes from these voices. Our interpretive community is richer for the multiplicity of voices that exist within it. As individuals we need to listen to the voices, listen to the rhetoric, and arrive at our own ethics of understanding. However, we need to acknowledge the voices and to celebrate their diversity. Therefore, the questions with which we are left are: What voices impact an individual reader's response to a text? How might this response be ethically negotiated within the community of voices that surrounds it?

THE CLASSROOM

What happens in a diverse classroom when children are given the opportunity to respond to literature? How is the response ethically negotiated when multiple communities exist together? What is the shared social interpretive community? How is a teacher to bridge the multiple voices and to celebrate the diversity?

To begin to answer these questions I spent the 1994–95 school year in a fourth-grade classroom as the teacher, Martha Klingshirn, and I collaboratively developed a culturally diverse literature program for her classroom. The site for the study was an urban public school. Ninety-two percent of the school's students receive a free or reduced-price lunch. Through an English as a Second Language (ESL) program, the school serves students from 22 different countries. Many of the neighborhood students attending are from the Appalachian regions of Ohio, West Virginia, and Kentucky. A large proportion of the African American students attending the school are bused in from a nearby housing project. The result is a rich and diverse, albeit economically poor, group of students.

Given the collaborative nature of the study, my focus was to document changes in the grounded theoretical understandings of the need for culturally diverse literature held by the teacher and the researcher, and the resulting change, if any, in the teacher's classroom practice. Seven specific units were taught over the course of the year using culturally diverse literature, and more than 85 culturally diverse picturebooks were shared during read-alouds. Field notes, researcher and teacher journals, videotapes of selected lessons, structured interviews, interviews with focal students, copies of the students' work, and transcribed audiotapes of the teacher's and researcher's conversations regarding the units and the literature used have helped to frame the emerging insights.

The story that emerges from the data documents our concerns and questions as we struggled together to determine how best to bring multicultural literature to the children and how to negotiate ethical issues. As teachers, we believed that we held responsibility for the development of the classroom's shared interpretive community. It is not enough merely to use the literature. As teachers, we need to understand what our purposes are for introducing books to the children, and we must carefully consider the issues that arise through our book discussions. Throughout the study we found that we often had more questions than answers as we struggled with the issues.

In February, we had just finished a unit that focused on Mildred D. Taylor's *Roll of Thunder, Hear My Cry* (1976); *Song of the Trees* (1975); *Mississippi Bridge* (1990); *The Friendship and the Gold Cadillac* (1989); and *The Well* (1995). We were very concerned about how we were negotiating the issue of similarities and differences, particularly as it was tied to issues of racism and discrimination. This became apparent in one of our debriefing conversations.

LAURIE: What do you think the children learned from these books?
MARTHA: I think they learned that at that time in history African

Americans were treated differently and unfairly. Maybe they learned a little bit about prejudice, what it is and what it entails. Maybe, not thinking that it happens now, but what it is.

LAURIE: I don't think they believe it exists today. But I think they learned it was a terrible thing to believe. I think they learned that we're really all alike. I think they've got that concept—that people are alike regardless of their cultural background. I don't think they've got the concept that they're also different.

MARTHA: But I think it's because they don't want it to be. They want it to be that we're all alike. African Americans shouldn't be treated any differently because we're all alike. So they can't separate the *shouldn't be treated any differently* from being different.

LAURIE: OK. That makes sense.

MARTHA: And I think that's why they don't—because they kind of don't want to see that—they don't want to admit differences because they think if they're admitting differences that's treating people differently and they're not separating those two things.

Later in the conversation this dichotomy between similarities and differences arises again:

LAURIE: After finishing these books, what are your opinions about the value of multicultural literature for use in the classroom?

MARTHA: Teaching prejudice and racism. I think the main thing is to value differences. I think that is more important than teaching that people are alike.

LAURIE: To value differences, but all we're teaching is that they're alike.

MARTHA: I know, that's where we need to make the distinction that the kids aren't making and we're not either—that being treated differently and being different are two separate things.

LAURIE: I can do a little bit of talking about that with *The Carp in the Bathtub*. I can talk about how people treated me because I was Jewish. As much as I've talked about being Jewish and liking *Elijah's Angels*, I've never talked about any other stuff. I've never talked about anti-Semitism.

MARTHA: And I don't think they have any idea that that exists.

LAURIE: That goes right into your concern about whether we are introducing something that they don't even know about by talking about it.

MARTHA: Are you saying that's wrong?

LAURIE: That was your concern.

MARTHA: I don't know—stated that way it doesn't sound like . . .

LAURIE: What I heard you say was that it's OK for fourth graders right now to feel that we're all alike.

MARTHA: I'm struggling really hard with this whole thing.

LAURIE: I am, too.

MARTHA: Every time a different situation comes up, I change my mind.

LAURIE: But let's just think about it.

MARTHA: But then when you said what I said before it doesn't jibe. A lot of things that I think we should do and teach don't jibe with what I think is happening.

LAURIE: I think maybe we're not as clear on what to do with the multicultural literature because we haven't decided for ourselves what's appropriate to do yet. You can't talk about Mildred Taylor books without talking about differences between the African American and white people. You just can't, but we're not sure how far to push it. Although, I think your question about "niggers" really pushed . . .

Mildred Taylor often uses texts that contain the word *nigger*. In the rural South, during the Depression, that was often the term used by white people when they spoke about, or to, anyone who was African American. However, Martha noticed that when portions of the text that contained that term were read aloud, many students in the classroom looked uncomfortable. She felt that the feeling "needed to be aired" and that the students needed to "look at where the feeling was coming from." She also wanted the students to know that while the author might write words that are offensive, it is not her saying them but the characters whom she has created. As a result, Martha asked the students to respond, in their reading journal, to the question "What would be your reaction if someone called you a nigger?" After the children responded in their reading journals, they shared and discussed their responses.

While the question was not an easy one to answer, the children's responses give some indication of the thought they put into the question. The question itself and the students' developing insights became integrated into the interpretive community of the classroom. The students, the stories, and Martha and I all brought multiple voices to the ongoing discussions.

AFRICAN AMERICAN GIRL: I really don't like the word *nigger* because when the Simms be calling the Logan family niggers and stuff it makes me feel awful and it makes me feel like I'm a nigger when the white people be calling the black people niggers.

WHITE GIRL: It probably feels as they're calling them a bad word or a wimp. When black people get called a nigger they probably feel that they don't have no pride.

WHITE BOY: If someone called me a nigger I would not show them that they hurt my feelings because if they know that they hurt my feelings then they would keep calling me that. Instead I would just walk away so they would not get any satisfaction out of it.

AFRICAN AMERICAN BOY: I feel like I'm being talked about. I feel like they're putting down my color and it really hurts my feelings. And when someone calls me a black [*nigger* is written and erased] I would say and I'm proud to be a black. And I am very proud that I am a black man.

ASIAN AMERICAN GIRL: It hurts my feelings and it will hurt your feelings, too, if someone called you that. If I was a black African American and they called me names I would just call them back just like Hammer did.

While Martha and I had very real concerns about the issues we chose to present to the students, we often felt that we had a "moral imperative" to present issues that might make us or the students feel uncomfortable. When Martha asked the students to consider how they would feel about being called a "nigger," she did so because she believed the issues were present because of the language of the text yet were not being addressed; as a result, many students were feeling uncomfortable. By making this issue part of the conversations of this community, Martha could share her own discomfort with the term and allow the students the opportunity to deal with a difficult issue.

However, as our conversation indicated, we were not always clear about how to negotiate the issues surrounding our use of culturally diverse literature. We were concerned about what the students were ready to deal with and what they were able to understand. The decisions we were making existed within the social, cultural, and political context of the classroom, but they were framed by who we are and what we believe. My background as a white Jewish American clearly influences my choices, as does Martha's Catholic upbringing in a small, rural town in the Midwest. As suggested earlier, it is our culture that frames us and writes our lives, and our interpretive communities in many ways become, or are synonymous with, our cultures.

MULTIPLE VOICES AND INTERPRETIVE COMMUNITIES

As we consider the role of culture or of the interpretive communities in a reader's response to a text, many questions remain. The search for an understanding of the ethics of response in a society framed by multiple communities is challenging and complex. As literary theory suggests, we understand what we read through some combination or transaction among the reader, the text, and the context. However, given the diversity that exists within our culture, this transaction or creation of a shared interpretive community must be carefully negotiated. This is particularly true of the classroom.

While it seems apparent that literature has the power to open eyes and change lives, it is also apparent that this does not happen merely by reading a piece of culturally diverse literature in a classroom. The multiple voices brought to our interpretive communities makes the use of literature as a vehicle for cultural understanding quite complex. As the work done in Martha Klingshirn's fourth-grade classroom indicates, there are important questions that must be considered. While in some cases these questions are experientially or aesthetically related, there are important ethical issues that must be considered.

If we are to use culturally diverse literature in the classroom, we must be sensitive to the multiple communities that exist as we create a shared social interpretive community of unique and special diverse readers. Our lives, our stories, our cultures are framed by our social and political context. All of us are individuals with our own personalities and beliefs. However, as stated earlier, these beliefs are shaped by the multiple communities that frame us. In bringing our individuality to the stories of our lives that we read and write, we have the potential to create a shared social interpretive community. In so doing, it is hoped that readers will see themselves and others in what they read and will grow to appreciate their own uniqueness as well as the diversity that exists in the stories of their lives.

REFERENCES

Banks, J. A. (1979). Shaping the future of multicultural education. *Journal of Negro Education, 48*(3), 237–252.

Banks, J. A. (1991). *Teaching strategies for ethnic studies* (5th ed.). Needham Heights, MA: Simon & Schuster.

Bunbury, R., & Tabbert, R. (1989). A bicultural study of identification: Readers' responses to the ironic treatment of a national hero. *Children's Literature in Education, 20*(1), 25–35.

Campbell, P. B., & Wirtenberg, J. (1980). How books influence children: What the research shows. *Bulletin, 11*(6), 3–6.

Chan, I. (1984). Folktales in the development of multicultural literature for children. TESL TALK, *15*(1&2), 19–28.

Clifford, E. (1985). *The remembering box.* Boston: Houghton Mifflin.

Connelly, F. M., & Clandinin, D. J. (1990). Stories of experience and narrative inquiry. *Educational Researcher, 19*(4), 2–14.

Erlich, A. S. (1990, November). *Reading the world cross-culturally: An anthropologic view.* Paper presented at Understanding Cultures Through Literature Conference, Moorehead State University, Moorehead, MN.

Fish, S. E. (1980). *Is there a text in this class? The authority of interpretive communities.* Cambridge, MA: Harvard University Press.

Fishman, A. (1987). Literacy and cultural context: A lesson from the Amish. *Language Arts, 64*(8), 842–854.

Harris, V. J. (1991). Multicultural curriculum: African-American children's literature. *Young Children, 46*(2), 37–44.

Heath, S. B. (1983). *Ways with words.* Cambridge, England: Cambridge University Press.

Ho, L. (1990). Singapore readers' responses to U.S. young adult fiction: Cross-cultural differences. *Journal of Reading, 33*(4), 252–258.

Jenkins, E. C. (1973). Multi-ethnic literature: Promise and problems. *Elementary English, 50*(5), 693–699.

Kintsch, W., & Greene, E. (1978). The role of culture-specific schemata in the comprehension and recall of stories. *Discourse Processes, 1,* 1–13.

Mailloux, S. (1977). Reader response criticism? *Genre, 10,* 413–431.

Mailloux, S. (1989). *Rhetorical power.* Ithaca, NY: Cornell University Press.

Malik, A. A. (1990). A psycholinguistic analysis of the reading behavior of EFL-proficient readers using culturally familiar and culturally nonfamiliar expository texts. *American Education Research Journal, 21*(1), 205–223.

Norton, D. E. (1985). Language and cognitive development through multicultural literature. *Childhood Education, 62*(2), 103–108.

Norton, D. E. (1990). Teaching multicultural literature in the reading curriculum. *The Reading Teacher, 44*(1), 28–40.

Pritchard, R. (1990). The effects of cultural schemata on reading processing strategies. *Reading Research Quarterly, 25*(4), 273–295.

Rabinowitz, P. J. (1987). *Before reading: Narrative conventions and the politics of interpretation.* Ithaca, NY: Cornell University Press.

Reynolds, R. E., Taylor, M. A., Steffensen, M. S., Shirey, L. L., & Anderson, R. C. (1982). Cultural schemata and reading comprehension. *Reading Research Quarterly, 17*(3), 353–366.

Rogers-Zegarra, N., & Singer, H. (1985). Anglo and Chicano comprehension of ethnic stories. In H. Singer & R. Ruddell (Eds.), *Theoretical models and processes of reading* (3rd ed.) (pp. 611–617). Newark, DE: International Reading Association.

Rosenblatt, L. M. (1991). Literary theory. In J. Flood (Ed.), *Handbook of research on teaching English language arts* (pp. 57–62). New York: Macmillan.

Scholes, R. (1989). *Protocols of reading.* New Haven, CT: Yale University Press.

Sims, R. (1982). *Shadow and substance.* Urbana, IL: National Council of Teachers of English.

Sims, R. (1983, May). What has happened to the "all white" world of children's books? *Phi Delta Kappan,* pp. 650–653.

Sims Bishop, R. (1990). Walk tall in the world: African-American literature for today's children. *Journal of Negro Education, 59*(4), 566–576.

Spears-Bunton, L. A. (1990). Welcome to my house: African-American and European American students' responses to Virginia Hamilton's *House of Dies Drear. Journal of Negro Education, 59*(4), 566–576.

Steffensen, M. S., Jaog-Dev, C., & Anderson, R. C. (1979). A cross-cultural perspective on reading comprehension. *Reading Research Quarterly, 15*(1), 10–29.

Taylor, M. D. (1975). *Song of the trees.* New York: Dial.

Taylor, M. D. (1976). *Roll of thunder, hear my cry.* New York: Dial.

Taylor, M. D. (1990). *Mississippi bridge.* New York: Dial.

Taylor, M. D. (1989). *The friendship and the gold Cadillac.* New York: Bantam.

Taylor, M. D. (1995). *The well.* New York: Dial.

Tobin, B. (1990, April). *Australian readers' responses to the cross-cultural folklore-based fantasy novels of Patricia Wrightson.* Paper presented at the meeting of the American Educational Research Association, Boston.

CHAPTER 8

Out of the Closet and onto the Bookshelves

Images of Gays and Lesbians in Young Adult Literature

MARI M. McLEAN

IN A LITERATE and multicultural society such as exists in the United States, books are powerful vehicles for conveying images of diversity. Because multicultural education has helped bring about "a heightened sensitivity to the needs of all people in American society" (Norton, 1987, p. 502), and because we are "increasingly recognizing the role of children's literature in shaping attitudes" (Norton, 1985, p. 103), we are seeing an increasing emphasis placed on including multicultural literature for children and young adults in the curriculum. This is because multicultural literature is seen to be both a mirror to validate a group's experiences and knowledge, and a window through which those experiences and knowledge can be viewed—and perhaps understood—by "outsiders" (Cox & Galda, 1990). It provides an invaluable opportunity for teachers and students to glimpse into the lives of the "other," to know for a time what it feels like to be a member of a group that is not in the mainstream. Through literature,

> [The reader] will experience . . . other life styles; he may identify with others or find his own self-identity; he may observe from a different perspectives; . . . [and] feel he belongs to one segment of all humanity (Huck, Hepler, & Hickman, 1987, p. 4).

Yet when I look at multicultural education materials, I usually find that one particular "segment of all humanity"—the 10% of the population that is homosexual—is conspicuously absent.

THE INVISIBLE MINORITY

The hypocrisy of multicultural education in the United States is that while emphasizing the importance of increased awareness and under-standing among people from diverse cultures, it is selective about which groups qualify for its benefits. Multicultural educators such as Banks (1979), Garcia (1982, 1984), and Austin and Jenkins (1983) caution us to avoid hurtful and hateful racial, ethnic, or gender slurs; call for equality of opportunity and fair treatment; and champion the right of all people to live in dignity. However, time and again these educators fail to specifi-cally mention homophobia as a dangerously prejudiced attitude that con-tributes to institutionalized discrimination and even violence against les-bian and gay[1] Americans. For example, homophobia is not included in a list of biases that, Garcia (1984) cautions teachers, can lead to discrimina-tion against individual students and, therefore, must be eradicated from classrooms.

Some might argue that the reason references to homosexuals do not appear in many multicultural materials is that there is no "homosexual culture," because homosexuality has no racial or ethnic basis for exis-tence. In our vastly diverse world, however, color and national origin are rather narrow ways to define which groups of people have a right to have their way of life accepted and to be individually respected as valuable members of society. Culture often transcends the boundaries of race and ethnicity. It may be more broadly defined, wrote the anthropologist Franz Boas, "as the totality of the mental and physical reactions and activities that characterize the behavior of the individuals composing a social group" (cited in Garcia, 1982, p. 23).

Because their uniquely shared ways of thinking and doing make them a "specific 'kind' of people" (Tinney, 1983, p. 4), gays and lesbians can and do form a general cultural group, as well as cultural subgroups, which are independent of and frequently cross groupings based on race or ethnic origin. Like members of racial or ethnic groups, people who are homosexual can point to a history, to cultural artifacts, to famous people, and to a celebration of life that is uniquely their own. Like those who belong to racial or ethnic groups, homosexual women and men are often the victims of stereotyping, prejudice, discrimination, and sometimes vio-lence. Like nonwhites and non-WASPs, gay and lesbian Americans have had to struggle, and continue to struggle, to gain both legal rights and human dignity in a society that lauds individualism while demanding conformity.

The need to conform enough to fit in and be accepted is a very real need for many people, especially adolescents. Aileen Nilsen and Kenneth Donelson (1985) point out that finding one's identity is considered by some psychologists to be "the major challenge of adolescence" (p. 5). Having taught middle school and high school students, I can verify that the search for self is nearly all-encompassing for most young people. The adolescent/young adult years can be a troubling time of questioning, self-doubt, real and imagined humiliations, isolation, and even fear for any young person.

Adolescence is an even more traumatic time for the young person whose "different affectional nature" (Tinney, 1983, p. 4) sets him or her apart as possibly the most despised "other" in American society: a queer, a lezzie, a fag, a dyke. Just how traumatic this time can be is evidenced by the fact that gay and lesbian adolescents commit suicide at a higher rate than do adolescents in general (Walling, 1993). The results of a U.S. Department of Health study of youth suicide completed in 1986 (and suppressed for three years by the Bush administration) showed that suicide was the leading cause of death among gay and lesbian youth, who accounted for approximately 30% of all youth suicides annually (Chandler, 1995).

BECOMING VISIBLE TO OURSELVES AND OTHERS

Advocates of multicultural literature such as Rudine Sims Bishop (1987) and Donna Norton (1987) believe that, in addition to helping us appreciate our common humanity, this kind of literature sensitizes us to the way in which people's lives may be affected by things beyond their control and provides validation of one's self and culture. From a psychological point of view, the right literature can be a means of helping any young reader understand others', as well as to accept his or her own, differences. In fact, according to Michael Angelotti (cited in Gallo, 1984), a therapeutic function is one of the four main functions of young adult literature. For the adolescent who must, because of the social stigma attached to homosexuality, wage a very private struggle to understand and accept his or her sexual orientation, good literature can be invaluable in providing the information, validation, and positive role models so necessary to the development of a healthy self-esteem (Wilson, 1984). "Vicariously experiencing the life of a character in fiction," Rosenblatt (1983) wrote, ". . . may enable the [adolescent] reader to bring into consciousness similar elements in his own nature and emotional life. This may provide the basis for a release from unconscious fears and guilt" (p. 201).

How well young adult literature with gay and lesbian characters and/or themes meets the multicultural goal of validating personal experiences and perspectives is best determined by a literary analysis based on certain reader-response theories. While other poststructuralist theories such as feminist and Marxist theories can also inform such issues, reader-response theories are the most appropriate bases for analysis because, across the spectrum of these theories, the reader's personal experience, knowledge, and perspective in the interpretation of a text is honored to varying degrees (cf. Bleich, 1980; Holland, 1980; Iser, 1980; Rosenblatt, 1978). Especially meaningful for analyzing the multicultural value of a text is the work of psychoanalytic response theorists, such as David Bleich (1980) and Norman Holland (1980), who maintain that the interpretation of a piece of literature is very much tied to the individual's personality. Bleich asserts that "the personal need of the critic-reader for self-understanding is definitely a guiding factor in the search for knowledge" (p. 137), so that an adolescent might be expected to read in order to gain self-enlightenment. According to Holland, "interpretation is a function of identity" (p. 123), and "all of us, as we read, use the literary work to symbolize and finally to replicate ourselves" (p. 124). Clearly, to him, a piece of literature can provide the means of validating the self, of raising one's self-esteem.

Of those literary critics who take a psychologically oriented response perspective, it is the feminist response theorists, rooted in psychosociology (Kennard, 1986), whose work most directly addresses the issues related to the portrayal of gays and lesbians in literature. Just as feminist critics see gender as an all-important consideration of *how* they read (Schweickart, 1986), so might lesbians and gays see their own sexuality as an all-important consideration in their interaction with a text. Responding to Fetterley's (cited in Schweickart, 1986) reference to "the powerlessness which derives from not seeing one's experiences articulated, clarified, and legitimized in art," Schweickart argues that reading texts by and about men "draws her into a process that she uses against herself" (p. 42), causing the woman reader to emphasize the male identity at the expense of her own female identity. The response of the gay and lesbian reader to the predominance of texts by and about heterosexuals is no different.

Whether texts structure the reader's experience or whether the reader's experience structures the text, the fact is that the ignoring or denial of a group's existence in literature invalidates the experience and self-identity of members of that group by rendering them invisible, not only to themselves, but to all other groups in a society. A primary value assigned to multicultural literature is that it mirrors the minority youth's culture and experience in positive ways. Yet, like women, lesbian and gay youth are surrounded by books that are neither by nor about themselves. The precious few mirrors that do exist in young adult literature contain many distortions that fail to project a good, clear image.

The inaccurate portrayals, the misinformed assumptions, the failure to even admit to the existence of gay and lesbian culture in literature is played out in the reality of our schools, says gay activist Eric Rofes (1989), and "[t]he result has been the creation of a population [of gay and lesbian adolescents] within our schools who exhibit significant indications of lack of self-esteem, emotional problems, and substance abuse" (p. 445). If this were any other minority population, educators would not allow the situation to continue unaddressed.

MIRRORS AND WINDOWS:
MEETING THE GOALS OF MULTICULTURAL LITERATURE

There are relatively few young adult novels dealing with lesbian and gay issues. At the time of this writing, I have read 34 such novels (see the selected bibliography at the end of the chapter); however, Jenkins (1993) lists 60 titles published between 1969 and 1992. Of the 30 novels used in this analysis, 10 have been written since 1990. The remainder, with the exception of 2, were written prior to 1984, with 2 of the novels written between 1984 and 1990. The decline in the number of titles published about the gay and lesbian experience since 1983 is attributed, in part, to the ascendancy of neoconservatism, the stridency of the so-called Moral Majority, and the subsequent censorship and book-banning campaigns launched during the Reagan–Bush era. In fact, the same decline can be seen in the number of titles published about *all* minority groups during the 1980s (Sims, 1985), a rather bleak commentary on how very "discriminating" an era that prided itself on restoring American values could be.

From a psychosociological reader-response perspective, I have analyzed most of these novels in order to determine whether or not they meet the stated goals of multicultural literature: providing validation of one's self and culture, and contributing to our understanding of "other." Perhaps more significantly, I have also analyzed this literature from an insider's perspective, which makes me very aware of the presence of stereotypes and misinformation that perpetuate damaging myths about nearly 10% of our population. Such myths not only impair the development of a healthy self-identity among gay and lesbian youth, but they prevent members of the lesbian and gay culture from gaining full acceptance in society. One need only look at the recent furor over the issue of gays and lesbians in the military to understand how lack of information (or an abundance of misinformation) distorts judgment and results in protests against the equity demands of the members of a minority.

Jan Goodman (1983) lists several damaging stereotypes and inaccuracies about lesbians and gays that can distort the judgment of heterosexuals and to which we need to be alert in young adult literature. Among these stereotypes and inaccuracies are that lesbian and gay adolescents (1) have been traumatized into homosexuality, (2) are just going through a phase toward heterosexuality, (3) want to change their sex, (4) can expect a lonely, isolated adulthood characterized by a series of unhappy love relationships, (5) are interested in seducing heterosexuals, particularly younger ones, and (6) will be punished for their sexuality. From my analysis of young adult novels with gay and lesbian characters and themes, I would add that—especially in the older novels—gay and lesbian adolescents are frequently depicted as guilty, ashamed, bitter, desperately unhappy individuals who would give anything to be "normal." Also, among all of the books, the stereotype of the "artistically inclined" homosexual is all too common.

Like other minority-group adolescents, lesbian and gay youth need literature that provides "validation for their feelings and hope for a bright future that involves self-affirmation" (Goodman, 1983, p. 15). Books that promote the above stereotypes and misinformation cannot provide such validation and will only complicate the struggle toward self-identity. Rather, these adolescents need to read about stable, committed, and loving gay and lesbian relationships, and about contented, productive, and quite "normal" lesbian and gay characters.

Several questions were in my mind as I read these young adult novels with lesbian and gay characters and/or themes: (1) Do these novels meet the goals of multicultural literature? (2) What images of gay and lesbian characters and culture are depicted in these novels? (3) What is the overall characterization of gays and lesbians, how are same-sex relationships depicted, and what are the societal and personal consequences of following one's affectional nature? (4) What might be the effects of these images on a homosexual adolescent's self-esteem, or on a heterosexual student's perceptions about alternative lifestyles? To attempt to answer these questions, I will discuss examples from a number of these novels.

YOU CAN ALWAYS SPOT ONE: GAY AND LESBIAN STEREOTYPES

To the credit of the authors of these young adult novels, the physical descriptions of the gays and lesbians are uniformly complimentary—and "normal." This is a relief, considering that we live in a society obsessed with noting physical differences and in which many people erroneously believe that all lesbians are tough and brutish and all gays are mincing and limp-wristed. In *A Boy's Own Story,* the narrator does describe himself as "effeminate" and a "sissy," but this is a semi-autobiographical novel, and, as an insider, Edmund White is allowed some license. The closest any other author comes to perpetuating the idea of a stereotypic appearance is Rosa Guy (*Ruby*), whose character Daphne is 6 feet tall and embraces her lover with "powerful arms." Daphne is redeemed, however, by being very beautiful. In Marilyn Levy's *Rumors and Whispers,* Sarah describes her gay brother as "the beautiful one," but there is no other indication that this could be construed as meaning he is effeminate. In general, however, all of the authors except Holland (*The Man Without a Face*), whose character Justin is unattractive because of a disfiguring scar over half of his face, describe their gay and lesbian characters as either attractive or unremarkable in appearance.

A recurring stereotype that, as an insider, I found annoying was that of the artistically sensitive homosexual. Among the lesbian and gay characters depicted in these novels are four actors, four writers, two singers, one pianist, five artists, and three lovers of poetry or music. While I have no quarrel with artistic sensitivity itself, this quality is sometimes used by heterosexuals to "excuse" or "explain" why a friend or family member is gay or lesbian: "You know, those sensitive people are just *that* way." These books pander to the idea that being gay or lesbian is more likely, more tolerable, perhaps more "understandable" and acceptable if the person has an "artistic temperament."

The books written prior to 1984 generally perpetuate the stereotype that gays and lesbians are ashamed, guilt-ridden, and bitter. Nearly all of the characters in these novels struggle to understand their homoemotional and/or homoerotic feelings, not only bearing their own shame and guilt but also having to deal with that of family and friends. Because the early novels are more interested in the struggle than with the end result of that struggle, they deprive the reader, both homosexual and heterosexual, of an important insight: After the adolescent's struggle for self-acceptance, a happy and well-adjusted lesbian or gay adult usually emerges. Although it might be argued that the intent of the authors is to show how societal pressure is responsible for placing unfair burdens of guilt on individuals, the subtlety of that intent might lead the burdened adolescent to find confirmation that one *should* feel guilt, shame, and bitterness about being gay or lesbian.

For many people, a homosexual encounter or even a relationship can be more easily "accepted" if it is believed to be a temporary aberration. It is therefore no surprise that, stereotypically, the development of a same-sex relationship in young adult literature is frequently linked to some traumatic event(s) in the life of a young person (Goodman, 1983). Since some heterosexuals regard being homosexual as a condition deserving of pity, it is convenient to believe that, like any noncongenital disfigurement, homosexuality is something that results from being in the wrong place at the wrong time. Also, it is known that people who have been traumatized can, with the proper treatment, be returned to a "normal" life. Thus the message from the novels that imply a connection between trauma and the development of a same-sex relationship is that homosexuality, contrary to recent scientific discovery of a "gay gene" (Henry, 1993), does not have to be a permanent condition.

Guy's *Ruby,* Scoppettone's *Happy Endings Are All Alike,* Donovan's *I'll Get There. It Better Be Worth the Trip,* Futch's *Crush,* Holland's *The Man Without a Face,* White's *A Boy's Own Story,* and Winterson's *Oranges Are Not the Only Fruit* all have characters who have to deal with the trauma of loneliness, alienation, and a ruptured or dysfunctional family. Ruby contends with the recent death of her mother, a domineering father, an unsatisfactory relationship with her sister, and a school life that only contributes to her feelings of loneliness and alienation. Peggy, in *Happy Endings,* has also lost her mother and must put up with an inattentive father and a psychologically unbalanced older sister. Lexie, in *Crush,* is left in the care of a guardian by her wealthy, indifferent parents. Davy's parents, in *I'll Get There,* are divorced, and he lives alone with his alcoholic mother. In *The Man Without a Face,* Charles lives with two half-sisters, one of whom continually bullies and torments him, and an indifferent mother. The mothers and fathers in the semi-autobiographical novels are extremely eccentric characters who do not provide anything approaching a "normal" family life for their children. Readers of Hall's *Sticks and Stones* might get the idea that since Ward's first "homosexual involvement" was "with another guy in my [Army] barracks" (p. 183), it resulted from the trauma of separation from family and friends. Whatever "caused" Ward to give in ("I do have these—tendencies," p. 183) is really peripheral to this story, however, since the book is not really as much about homosexuality as it is about the stigma of being accused of it.

As befits the idea that conditions related to life trauma are reversible, Ruby, Charles, and Davy eventually head off into the heterosexual sunset. We suspect that Peggy might opt out of same-sex relationships because she *is* confused about her sexuality: She admits to Janet that "the trouble is I still do care what people think but I have to try not to" and "I can't make you any promises" (p. 201). Only in *A Boy's Own Story*, in *Oranges*, in both of Garden's novels, and in *Rumors and Whispers* do the characters remain true to their sexual identity, belying the myth that homosexuality is a temporary condition, a phase that will eventually pass along with adolescence.

If the implied message from these novels is that same-sex relationships are "one-shot deals" that develop "accidentally" out of the confusion and pain of adversity, then an accompanying implication is that such relationships must be short-lived. This implication is clear in these novels. Among these novels, only one prior to 1980 depicts a loving, long-term same-sex relationship. Norma Klein's 1978 novel, *Breaking Up*, stands out among the early books as offering a positive, upbeat view of a mother's lesbian relationship and its effect on her teenage children and their father. After 1980, however, the depiction begins to change. In Garden's *Annie on My Mind*, two lesbian teachers at Liza's school have lived together for many years. Perhaps more important for young lesbian readers is the fact that the book ends with the strong suggestion that Annie and Liza will, despite the obstacles, reestablish their loving relationship and develop their own long-term commitment. In Garden's later novel, *Lark in the Morning*, Gillian and Suzanne have already made a long-term commitment when the story begins, and nothing occurs to shake that commitment in the course of the novel. In *Rumors and Whispers*, Sarah's brother and his lover live together and are committed to a monogamous relationship.

INCURRING GOD'S WRATH: THE BIBLICAL INFLUENCE ON IMAGES

Perhaps because the Judeo-Christian ethic prevails in American society, there exists the fairly common belief that those who engage in homoerotic relationships will be punished in some way for their "sin." (This notion is so widely accepted that recently an antigay protester in Harlan County, Georgia, could be shown on television daring to display a sign reading "Thank God for AIDS.") True to the belief that homosexuality does or should result in punishment, all of the earlier novels involve some kind of loss (most notably, death) or violence that is either overtly or implicitly linked to a homoerotic act. The loss in Reading's *Bouquets for Brimbal* is relatively minor: A close friendship nearly ends because Macy cannot accept Annie's lesbian relationship with an older woman. In *Happy Endings* and in *Oranges*, parents are faced with loss of prestige in their communities when their daughters' lesbianism becomes public knowledge. In both stories, parents and children become estranged from one another, which is also a theme in one later novel, *Rumors and Whispers.*

Punishment through loss of livelihood occurs in *Annie on My Mind,* in which the lesbian teachers are fired for unwittingly providing a place for 17-year-olds Liza and Annie to make love. Peggy's father, in *Happy Endings,* has his livelihood threatened when a number of his patients desert his medical practice because of his daughter's lesbianism. In *Crush,* both Lexie and Jinx are expelled from their prestigious private school, and Jinx is faced with the possibility that she will not be able to pursue her career choice because her expulsion might affect her college admission. In *Ruby,* the main character is beset by several losses: Ruby's shaky relationship with her father is further damaged by her lesbian relationship with Daphne, Ruby eventually loses Daphne, and then she almost loses her life in a suicide attempt.

In light of the presumed effect of Judeo-Christian ethics on the messages in young adult literature, it is important to note that the only Old Testament injunctions against homosexuality are directed toward males (Leviticus 18:23 and 20:13). It is not surprising, then, that in five novels about gays, a death occurs that the reader might easily link to homosexuality. In Scoppettone's *Trying Hard to Hear You,* Phil is killed while trying to "prove" to himself and others that he is really "straight." Tom, the protagonist in *Sticks and Stones,* is so angered and confused by the gossip that he is a homosexual that he causes an accident in which another boy is killed. A reader influenced by fundamentalist beliefs could see 47-year-old Justin's sudden death by heart attack in *Man Without a Face* as divine punishment for his homoerotic attachment to 14-year-old Charles. Certainly that same fundamentalist reader would see divine retribution in the impending death of the art teacher who is dying of AIDS in *Rumors and Whispers.* We presume that the teacher has contracted the disease as the result of homosexual activity: "He's queer," Jimmy said. "Either that or he's shooting up heroin, and I ain't seen any track marks on his arm" (p. 101).

In both Donovan's and Holland's novels the violent death of a beloved pet is directly linked to a homoerotic act. In *I'll Get There,* Davy's dog is killed when his mother takes him for a walk so that Davy's father can speak to him privately about Davy's relationship with Altshuler. "She took him out because of me," says Davy, "She wanted to leave me alone with my father to talk. Is that why it happened? Yes, God, yes. It's my fault. Because of everything I did" (p. 172). Charles's cat in *The Man Without a Face* is killed because Charles, who has spent the day with Justin, was not home to protect him from his sister's boyfriend, Percy. "Moxie died about an hour later. Percy was telling the truth. It was his boot. But it was as much my fault as his" (p. 138).

If the message to young adult readers is not "If you're gay or lesbian (but especially if you're gay), you'll die," then it is "If you're gay or lesbian, you can get badly hurt." Both of Sandra Scoppettone's novels strongly suggest that being gay or lesbian can drive heterosexuals to commit bodily assault. Even though Scoppettone—an insider—portrays the heterosexual assailant in both books as psychopathic, and even though her sympathies are clearly with the gay and lesbian characters, a naive reader may still see these acts of violence as, at best, a warning or, at worst, justified. In either case, the message is that gays and lesbians can expect to be victims of prey. They can also be the victims of excessive religious piety, as with Winterson's character, who undergoes an exorcism that falls just short of torture.

DIFFERENT IMAGES OF SAME-SEX LOVE

It is interesting to note the different ways in which the authors of these young adult novels treat lesbian and gay sexuality, a difference that reflects the importance society places on males and the unimportance with which females are regarded. Male homosexuality is obviously more offensive than female homosexuality since gays and their pets die because of same-sex relationships, but lesbians do not. Centuries after the Leviticus passages (see above) labeled the male homosexual act "an abomination," authors of young adult literature are still carrying out the sentence on their gay characters: "They shall be put to death; their blood shall be on their own heads." That lesbian characters escape such a fate is undoubtedly linked to the fact that nowhere in the Old Testament is lesbianism even mentioned. Apparently, God did not want Abraham, Isaac, and Jacob to engage in homosexual activity but was not overly concerned about what Sarah, Rebecca, and Rachael might do with each other.

The different treatment of male and female homosexuality is also shown in what the authors tell of the homoerotic act itself. In the lesbian novels, authors have the young women touch or kiss intimately and sometimes even admit to sexual arousal: "Peggy put her hand inside Jaret's blouse" (*Happy Endings*, p. 85); "Her mouth was being kissed, and she responded eagerly to those full, blessedly full, lips" (*Ruby*, p. 55); "I kissed Annie, somehow moved away from her and reached for my clothes" (*Annie on My Mind*, p. 163). In *Crush*, there are several scenes in which Futch describes Jinx's physical and emotional response to the intimacy of being in bed with Lexie. While no intimate lesbian scenes are described in *Bouquets for Brimbal* or *Lark in the Morning*, the characters do refer to themselves as "lovers" or to the act of "making love."

By contrast, with the exception of *A Boy's Own Story* (which, it must be remembered, is semi-autobiographical), sexual intimacy is only hinted at in the gay novels, and arousal is never mentioned. In *The Man Without a Face* the characters are in bed together, but when Justin puts his arms around Charles, it is a comforting, rather than sexual, embrace. The homoerotic act is only alluded to by Charles's statement ("Even so, I didn't know what was happening to me until it had happened" [p. 141]) and by the fact of his changed attitude toward Justin the next morning. Although Jeff and Phil are mercilessly tormented for their relationship in *Trying Hard to Hear You*, the only glimpse the reader gets of homoeroticism in this book is when a third party reports, "We found these two creeps kissing, for godsake" (p. 182). In *Rumors and Whispers,* a hint of sexual activity is given by the mention of a single queen-sized bed in the apartment of Sarah's brother and his lover.

There is no homoerotic act in *I'll Get There,* but there is the damaging accusation of it. In Donovan's novel, Davy playfully gives his friend Altschuler "a dumb kiss" (p. 158), and after drinking whiskey, they fall asleep together on the floor, but only in Davy's mother's mind does anything erotic happen. In *Sticks and Stones* there is no sexual activity between Tom and Ward, although they obviously have a close and loving friendship. As in *I'll Get There*, all the homoeroticism in *Sticks and Stones,* just as in Tolan's lesbian novel, *The Last of Eden,* happens in the minds of other people.

However, as an interesting aside, it should be noted that in neither the gay nor the lesbian novels is any consummation of the sex act described, although some of the novels rather graphically describe heterosexual sex. Perhaps the authors are responding to the sensitivity of many heterosexuals that they not be told what homosexuals actually do in bed! More likely, the authors do not want to be accused of tempting teenagers who are not so inclined into homosexual experiment. Also interesting to note is that heterosexual "immorality" is portrayed by some of the characters themselves as far less serious than corresponding homosexual behavior. Thus, in *The Last of Eden,* students react violently to the idea that a woman teacher might be having an affair with a female student but are indifferent to or condone the fact that the teacher's husband is having an affair with a female student.

Returning to the different treatment of the gay and lesbian homoerotic act in these novels, we may find that the explanation for it is that all women, and what they do, are relatively unimportant in male-dominated societies. Male homosexuality has apparently been far more worrisome and disturbing to these societies than female homosexuality. For example, of the six biblical references to homosexuality, only one (Romans 1:26–27) deals with lesbianism, and that reference is so vague that we cannot even be certain that lesbianism is the "abomination" being mentioned. In the United States, lesbianism per se is not illegal, although it is sometimes prosecuted under widely interpreted sodomy statutes (Scanzoni & Mollenkott, 1978). If lesbian love-making is more openly depicted in young adult literature than is gay love-making, the reason may be that society agrees with Peggy's father in *Happy Endings:*

> "Are you horrified?" she asked tentatively.
>   Was he? Of course not. That was much too strong. Actually, Tom realized, sex between two girls, two women, just didn't seem important to him.
>   "No, I'm not horrified, Peggy. As a matter of fact, I think it's hard for me to take lesbianism very seriously." (p. 187)

Related to the "seriousness" with which American society seems to take male homosexuality but not lesbianism is the message the reader might get from the earlier books that gays are, or should be, more tormented by guilt than are lesbians. None of the gay novels written before 1982 include a character comfortable with his sexuality, although two books written by insiders, Scoppettone's *Trying Hard to Hear You* and White's *A Boy's Own Story,* have characters who seem to have, with great difficulty, come to terms with their sexuality. In contrast, over the past 20 years, a number of lesbian characters seem to have been spared the agonizing struggle to accept their sexuality that besets their male counterparts. Liza, and to some extent Annie, in *Annie On My Mind,* Jaret in *Happy Endings,* Annie and Lola in *Bouquets for Brimbal,* and Gillian and Suzanne in *Lark* all are fairly content and well-adjusted. The narrator in Jeannette Winterson's semi-autobiographical novel even manages to accept her sexuality despite the hellfire and brimstone atmosphere of her fundamentalist home.

Overall, the earlier novels support the stereotype of instability in homosexual relationships: How would the tormented and guilt-ridden characters in Guy's, Donovan's, Holland's, and Hall's books turn out? What future togetherness could Janet have with Peggy, who is committed only for "now"? What happiness could embittered Daphne ever have for herself, or give to anyone else? How could Jinx ever make a commitment to a relationship when her first lesbian relationship was filled with such betrayal and terrible consequences? The outlook for happiness is bleak; the gloomy message might not be so easily shaken off by a gay or lesbian adolescent and is only likely to confirm for outsiders that life in the lesbian and gay culture is either pitiable or contemptible—but certainly *not* acceptable.

BRIGHTER WINDOWS AND MIRRORS: THE MOST RECENT IMAGES

There is cause to hope, however, that authors might be leaving some of those negative messages about gays and lesbians behind: The more recent books, those written since 1990, all have strong homosexual characters who accept themselves and seem quite capable of establishing stable, long-term relationships; dispel some of the myths about homosexuals used as discriminatory excuses; and present a new and very positive picture of families headed by gay or lesbian couples. I think the most striking thing about the most recent novels, from the perspective of an insider, is a change in "tone." Although a reader could point to parts of the novels written since 1990 as contributing to the stereotypes Jan Goodman warns about (e.g., Slim's gay father, Mack, in Nelson's *Earthshine*, dies of AIDS), the overall characterizations are so positive and so "normal" that any possible stereotypic images are stripped of their power. Since most gays and lesbians must remain invisible in order to protect themselves from discrimination and abuse, it is almost impossible to say whether or not this change is because more insiders are writing about the gay or lesbian experience.

As "coming-out" stories, Brett's *S.P. Likes A.D.*, Walker's *Peter*, and Sinclair's *Coffee Will Make You Black* depict the struggle that young people beginning to question their sexuality must go through in a dominantly heterosexual society. Yet these stories all conclude with the young persons working through the imposed guilt and fear to the point where they are accepting of their possible homosexuality and hopeful of their future happiness in a same-sex relationship. It is also significant that in each of these stories, the young person is counseled by a homosexual adult in ways that belie the myth of the predatory gay and lesbian seeking to "recruit." In Walker's novel, Vince fends off the advances of the younger man because he is too young, but his gentle and sensitive counseling, similar to Nurse Horn's in Sinclair's book and to Kate and Mary's in Brett's novel, gives comfort to the younger person that sets him on the path to self-acceptance. In each of these novels, we are left not knowing for certain whether or not the young person will become involved in a homosexual relationship. What is refreshing, though, is that each book ends with the possibility, even the likelihood, that it will happen and that when it does, it will be a positive life experience.

A major change in the tone of the books since 1990 is that despite the centrality of the issue of homosexuality in these books, the treatment of it has a matter-of-factness to it. My hope is that this indicates a subtle shift away from seeing homosexuality as an abnormality to be shunned toward seeing it as one more aspect of human diversity to be understood and accepted. Recent novels are showing, in positive ways, that homosexuality is an unchangeable fact of some people's lives. Garden's *Lark in the Morning* is a wonderful example of the way in which a novel can have a homosexual protagonist without making homosexuality its focus.

Toward this tone of acceptance, we are seeing in these novels a new consciousness-raising phenomenon: the positive portrayal of gay and lesbian family life, complete with children and dogs and cats and casserole dinners and taxes to pay and lawns to be mowed. Even though the father is dying in *Earthshine,* the "normalcy" of the family life cannot be overlooked. The same is true for Salat's *Living in Secret,* even though the lesbian family must adopt new identities and be very secretive about themselves in order to keep the court from removing Amelia from her mother and her lover's home. It is also important for the "recruitment" myth that in both families, neither child sees herself as homosexual, even though she lives in the midst of the lifestyle.

AIDS, which might be considered a topic that lends itself to stereotypic images, is receiving the kind of treatment in these more recent books that can help to change readers' perspectives. In an older novel (*Night Kites,* published in 1986), M. E. Kerr gave the first really sympathetic and sensitive portrayal of a young man dying of a dread disease and of his family's struggle to come to terms with it. Although it might be argued that Kerr has bought into the idea of God's punishment of male homosexuals, it must be noted that the author's central message is that by its ostracism of those who are different, society pushes people into a self-hate that often leads to self-destructive behavior. By his own admission, Eric's brother, Pete, says that contracting AIDS was the result of his sexual promiscuity. But why did he think he had been promiscuous? He tells Eric:

> I think relationships scared the hell out of me. I guess it was because if one lasted, I'd have to face a lot of shit I didn't want to. I'd be seen with one guy all the time. How could I explain that to the family . . . ? I've always had a problem with being openly gay. . . . That's probably why I couldn't get used to being with just one person. . . . (pp. 178–179)

In Durant's *When Heroes Die* and in *Earthshine,* AIDS is viewed in an entirely different way. How the disease might have been contracted is simply not an issue. The focus of both of these more recent novels is on the way in which a loving family comforts and supports both the dying loved one and each other. Neither book looks to blame or excuse whatever behaviors might have led to the illness, but rather strongly suggests that in a plague time, loving care and seeking a cure are the things that really matter.

Gay and lesbian activism in demanding the search for treatments and cure of AIDS is well-documented. *Earthshine*'s protagonist, Slim, learns the importance of activism, of doing something positive in the face of disaster, in the course of the novel. In fact, the authors of recent novels are portraying gay and lesbian activism in sympathetic ways, and they are also sending the message to readers that activism for social justice issues takes great courage and commitment from individuals. One of the many redeeming messages of Bette Greene's otherwise depressing and horrifying novel of homophobia, *The Drowning of Stephan Jones,* is the positive portrayal of those organizations fighting for the civil rights of gays and lesbians. Their Ghandian response to the cruelty and violence of the Christian Right makes them heroic and belies the myth of the wimpish, cowardly homosexual. The appearance of such organizations in young adult literature also provides assurance to the reader that there are certainly a great many more homosexuals around than the invisibility of the culture allows people to realize.

Finally, along the lines of "invisibility," I want to return to the stereotype of appearances. These recent novels are showing evidence, by the ways in which characters are physically portrayed, that we have progressed to a point where we can accept the full spectrum of differences among homosexuals. It is a fact that most gays and lesbians are invisible because they do not fit the physical stereotypes that still dominate many people's thinking. However, stereotypes frequently embody some truth, and another fact is that some gays and lesbians do fit those stereotypic images: There are effeminate gays and mannish lesbians. The genre has progressed to the point where an author can now honestly and sympathetically tell the story of a character who some years ago would only have represented a bad example. M. E. Kerr has refreshingly and sympathetically portrayed butch lesbians in *Deliver Us from Evie.* In this novel, very butch Evie is the seduced rather than the seducer, and her seducer is a very feminine stereotype herself. The novel not only admits to the reality of some stereotypes but dispels the myth of the butch predator as well as the myth that such stereotypic people will never find happiness. Evie and Patsy are mutually loving and clearly destined for a long-term relationship. As Evie explains to her mother:

Some of us *look* it, Mom! I know you so-called normal people would like it better if we looked as much like all of you as possible, but some of us don't, can't, and never will! And some others of us go for the ones who don't, can't, and never will. (p. 86)

In a sense, we have come almost full circle, but that circle appears to be ending on a more positive note than the one on which it began.

BREAKING THE SILENCE

Multicultural literature for young adults is a promising vehicle for developing awareness, understanding, and acceptance among cultural groups. It is also a potentially valuable took for validating one's own knowledge and experience. In doing so, it may help the reader discover him- or herself and build self-esteem. But for this to happen, the reader must be able to find familiar, friendly images in the literature. As the feminist critics point out, reading the androcentric canon is destructive to women's self-images because they are always reading against themselves. Likewise, because literature, whether of the canon or not, is predominantly heterosexual, gays and lesbians are always reading against themselves, since they never see themselves reflected. How unfortunate, especially for gay youth, that when a book that seems to mirror readers finally turns up, it presents such an unattractive distortion that readers find that they are reading against themselves once more.

Those students who are gay or lesbian are looking for respectable role models and for validation of their feelings and experiences as surely as African American, Hispanic, Asian American, Native American, or heterosexual female students are. Because there is still considerable misunderstanding, fear, and hostility actively directed toward homosexuals, lesbian and gay youth can rarely speak or ask openly about their concerns. There are virtually no role models (allowed into the curriculum) for them to look to, and their gay and lesbian teachers must suffer with and for them silently out of fear of losing their jobs. Along with the psychosociological damage, the increasing physical threat of AIDS makes the continuation of such enforced silence immoral. Under these repressive circumstances, there is an even greater need for these students to have literature that offers positive images of people like themselves, gives an honest portrayal of the gay and lesbian culture, and helps them develop into emotionally healthy and happy adults.

Unfortunately, there is not enough young adult literature about the gay and lesbian culture, and a number of the older books convey some troubling messages. But even if there were an abundance of "good" literature, it would not be enough in and of itself. Heterosexual teachers need to deal with their own homophobia before they can help heterosexual students deal with theirs, and certainly before they can help build the self-esteem of their gay and lesbian students. Ideally, these young people would benefit if lesbian and gay adults, especially teachers, were free enough to become advocates for them. Sadly, as Rofes (1989) points out, that is unlikely to happen as long as homosexual teachers continue to be victims of "witch hunts" and as long as local laws continue to be passed that "forbid *positive* discussion of homosexuality in public school classrooms" (p. 451; emphasis added).

The best hope for combating homophobia in our schools and our society is *not*, however, through multicultural education or with multicultural literature, but through the recognition by various racial/ethnic and cultural groups of their common oppression. Only when such groups realize that they "belong to each other [and] suffer at the hands of the same oppressor . . . [can they] attain liberation by jointly beating down the door to those whose fortunes are due to [their] misfortunes" (Tinney, 1983, p. 5). Any minority group that demands liberation for its members in the name of equity and justice is morally bound to demand liberation for all. If they do not, then they need to change their particular demand to what it really is, favoritism and the right to become oppressors themselves.

If multicultural education is sincere in its goals of countering discrimination, fostering cross-cultural respect and understanding, and assuring equal opportunity for all Americans, then it must be morally committed to eradicating *any* oppression that is based on diversity, including oppression directed at gay and lesbian Americans. If the goals of multicultural education are partly achieved through literature that "permits children whose lives are mirrored to know that their ways of living, believing and valuing are important, legitimate, and to be valued . . . , [and] also permits them to reflect on the human condition" (Sims, 1984, p. 155), then we need to take a close look at the accuracy of the portrayal of *all* minority and oppressed cultures: We cannot behave as if the eradication of one oppression is more "worthy" than another. As Audre Lorde (1983) wrote, "Among those of us who share the goals of liberation and a workable future for our children, *there can be no hierarchies of oppression* [emphasis added]" (p. 9). The oppression of lesbians and gays "is usually the last oppression to be mentioned, the last to be taken seriously, and the last to go. But it is extremely serious, sometimes to the point of being fatal" (Smith, 1983, p. 7).

NOTE

1. The term *gay* is sometimes used to refer to all homosexual people, male and female. It is increasingly being used, as in this chapter, to refer only to homosexual males.

REFERENCES

Austin, M. C., & Jenkins, E. (1983). *Promoting world understanding through literature.* Littleton, CO: Libraries Unlimited.

Banks, J. A. (1979). Shaping the future of multicultural education. *Journal of Negro Education, 68,* 237–252.

Bleich, D. (1980). Epistemological assumptions in the study of response. In J. P. Tompkins (Ed.), *Reader-response criticism: From formalism to post-structuralism* (pp. 134–163). Baltimore: Johns Hopkins University Press.

Chandler, K. (1995). *Passages of pride: Lesbian and gay youth come of age.* New York: Random House.

Cox, S., & Galda, L. (1990, April). Multicultural literature: Mirrors and windows on a global community. *The Reading Teacher,* pp. 582–588.

Gallo, D. (1984, November). What should teachers know about YA lit for 2004? *English Journal,* pp. 31–34.

Garcia, R. (1982). *Teaching in a pluralistic society.* New York: Harper & Row.

Garcia, R. (1984). Countering classroom discrimination. *Theory Into Practice, 23,* 104–109.

Goodman, J. (1983). Out of the closet, but paying the price: Lesbian and gay characters in children's literature. *Interracial Books for Children Bulletin, 14,* 13–15.

Henry, W. A. (1993, July 26). Born gay?: Studies of family trees and DNA make the case that male homosexuality is in the genes. *Time,* pp. 36–39.

Holland, N. N. (1980). Unity identity text self. In J. P. Tompkins (Ed.), *Reader-response criticism: From formalism to post-structuralism* (pp. 118–133). Baltimore: Johns Hopkins University Press.

Huck, C. S., Hepler, S., & Hickman, J. (1987). *Children's literature in the elementary school* (4th ed.). New York: Holt, Rinehart & Winston.

Iser, W. (1980). The reading process: A phenomenological approach. In J. P. Tompkins (Ed.), *Reader-response criticism: From formalism to post-structuralism* (pp. 50–69). Baltimore: Johns Hopkins University Press.

Jenkins, C. A. (1993). Young adult novels with gay/lesbian characters and themes 1969–92: A historical reading of content, gender, and narrative distance. *Journal of Youth Services in Libraries, 7*(1), 43–55.

Kennard, J. E. (1986). Ourself behind ourself: A theory for lesbian readers. In E. A. Flynn & P. P. Schweickart (Eds.), *Gender and reading: Essays on readers, texts, and contexts* (pp. 63–80). Baltimore: Johns Hopkins University Press.

Lorde, A. (1983). There is no hierarchy of oppressions. *Interracial Books for Children Bulletin, 14,* 9.

Nilsen, A. P., & Donelson, K. L. (1985). *Literature for today's young adults* (2nd ed.). Glenville, IL: Scott, Foresman.

Norton, D. E. (1985). Language and cognitive development through multicultural literature. *Childhood Education, 62,* 103–107.

Norton, D. E. (1987). *Through children's eyes.* Columbus, OH: Merrill.

Rofes, E. (1989). Opening up the classroom closet: Responding to the educational needs of gay and lesbian youth. *Harvard Educational Review, 59,* 444–453.

Rosenblatt, L. (1978). *The reader, the text, the poem: The transactional theory of the literary work.* Carbondale: Southern Illinois University Press.

Rosenblatt, L. (1983). *Literature as exploration* (4th ed.). New York: Modern Language Association.

Scanzoni, L., & Mollenkott, V. R. (1978). *Is the homosexual my neighbor?: Another Christian view.* San Francisco: Harper & Row.

Schweickart, P. P. (1986). Reading ourselves: Toward a feminist theory of reading. In E. A. Flynn & P. P. Schweickart (Eds.), *Gender and reading: Essays on readers, texts, and contexts* (pp. 31–62). Baltimore: Johns Hopkins University Press.

Sims, R. (1984). A question of perspective. *The Advocate, 3,* 145–156.

Sims, R. (1985). Children's books about blacks: A mid-eighties report. *Children's Literature Review, 8,* 9–14.

Sims Bishop, R. (1987). Extending multicultural understanding through children's books. In B. E. Cullinan (Ed.), *Children's literature in the reading program* (pp. 60–67). Newark, DE: International Reading Association.

Smith, B. (1983). Homophobia: Why bring it up? *Interracial Books for Children Bulletin, 14,* 7–8.

Tinney, J. A. (1983). Interconnections. *Interracial Books for Children Bulletin, 14,* 4–6 and 27.

Walling, D. R. (1993). *Gay teens at risk.* Bloomington, IN: Phi Delta Kappa Educational Foundation.

Wilson, D. E. (1984, November). The open library: YA books for gay teens. *English Journal,* pp. 60–63.

SELECTED BIBLIOGRAPHY:
YOUNG ADULT NOVELS DEALING WITH LESBIAN AND GAY ISSUES

Barger, Gary W. *What Happened to Mr. Forster?* New York: Clarion, 1981.

Brett, Catherine. *S. P. Likes A. D.* East Haven, CT: Inland Press, 1990.

Chambers, Aidan. *Dance on My Grave.* New York: Harper & Row, 1982.

Donovan, John. *I'll Get There. It Better Be Worth the Trip.* New York: Harper & Row, 1969.

Durant, Panny Raife. *When Heroes Die.* New York: Antheum, 1992.

Ecker, B. A. *Independence Day.* New York: Avon, 1983.

Forster, E. M. *Maurice.* New York: Norton, Inc., 1971.

Futcher, Jane. *Crush.* New York: Little, Brown, 1981.

Garden, Nancy. *Annie on My Mind.* New York: Farrar, Straus & Giroux, 1982.

Garden, Nancy. *Lark in the Morning*. New York: Farrar, Straus & Giroux, 1991.

Greene, Bette. *The Drowning of Stephan Jones*. New York: Bantam, 1991.

Guy, Rosa. *Ruby*. New York: Viking, 1976.

Hall, Lynn. *Sticks and Stones*. Chicago: Follett, 1972.

Hautzig, Deborah. *Hey, Dollface*. New York: Bantam, 1978.

Holland, Isabelle. *The Man Without a Face*. New York: Bantam, 1972.

Homes, A. M. *Jack*. New York: Macmillan, 1989.

Kerr, M. E. *Deliver Us from Evie*. New York: HarperCollins, 1994.

Kerr, M. E. *I'll Love You When You're More Like Me*. New York: Harper & Row, 1977.

Kerr, M. E. *Night Kites*. New York: HarperCollins, 1986.

Klein, Norma. *Breaking Up*. New York: Pantheon, 1978.

Levy, Elizabeth. *Come Out Smiling*. New York: Delacorte, 1981.

Levy, Marilyn. *Rumors and Whispers*. New York: Fawcett Juniper, 1990.

Mosca, Frank. *All-American Boys*. Boston: Alyson, 1983.

Nelson, Theresa. *Earthshine*. New York: Orchard, 1994.

Reading, J. P. *Bouquets for Brimbal*. New York: Harper & Row, 1980.

Salat, Cristina. *Living in Secret*. New York: Bantam, 1993.

Scoppettone, Sandra. *Happy Endings Are All Alike*. New York: Harper & Row, 1978.

Scoppettone, Sandra. *Trying Hard to Hear You*. New York: Harper & Row, 1974.

Sinclair, April. *Coffee Will Make You Black*. New York: Avon, 1994.

Snyder, Anne and Pelletier, Louis. *The Truth About Alex*. New York: Bantam, 1981.

Tolan, Stephanie S. *The Last of Eden*. New York: Bantam, 1980.

Walker, Kate. *Peter*. Boston: Houghton Mifflin, 1993.

White, Edmund. *A Boy's Own Story*. New York: Dutton, 1982.

Winterson, Jeanette. *Oranges Are Not the Only Fruit*. New York: Atlantic Monthly Press, 1985.

CHAPTER 9

Reader-Response Theory and the Politics of Multicultural Literature

MINGSHUI CAI

IN RECENT DISCUSSIONS of multicultural children's literature, critics and educators often debate an author's responsibility for creating culturally authentic works. Contrary to belief in the "death of the author" or the banishment of the author from the interpretation of the text, many hold that the author's perspective has tremendous impact on the outcome of the literary creation and that the author's cultural identity, in turn, has great bearing on his or her perspective (e.g., Harris, 1992; Huck, Helper, & Hickman, 1993; Silvey, 1993; Sims, 1982; [Sims] Bishop, 1992; Yokota, 1993). At present, the "battle about books" is still very much a "battle about author . . . as a social constituency" (Gullory, cited in Gates, 1991, p. 26).

Who should write multicultural books for children? Should an "outsider" write about the experiences of another culture? Can an "outsider" succeed in creating authentic representations of an alien culture? These are some of the major questions raised about the authorship of multicultural literature. As Anita Silvey (1993) of *The Horn Book* magazine observes:

> On the one hand there are those who fight for artistic freedom and license. No one should prescribe what a writer or illustrator attempts, and creative genius allows individuals to stretch far beyond a single life and to write about lives never lived or experienced. On the other side are those who argue with equal conviction that only those from a particular culture can write about that culture or can write valid books about it. (p. 132)

The focus of the debate over multicultural literature is whether the author's or illustrator's cultural identity and perspective have any significant impact on the outcome of their artistic creation. This debate entails many complicated issues, such as the relationship between imagination and experience (Cai, 1995), authors' social responsibilities (Noll, 1995), and censorship. It is beyond the scope of this chapter to deal with all these issues adequately. Here I attempt to justify the concern with the author's cultural identity and perspective in terms of reader-response theory.

The current concern with the author's influence on the text of multicultural literature seems to run counter to the assumptions of reader-response theory, which has shifted the focus of literary criticism from the author and the text to the reader. The author's intention is no longer the locus of meaning. To some critics, emphasis on the author's identity and perspective appears to be outmoded, perhaps even a kind of atavism. In "'Authenticity,' or the Lesson of Little Tree," the noted African American critic Henry Louis Gates, Jr. (1991), argued against preoccupation with authenticity and the author's identity, lamenting that the "assumptions" that "ethnic or national identity finds unique expression in literary forms hold sway even after we think we have discarded them" (p. 26). He went on to say, "After the much-ballyhooed 'death of the author' pronounced by two decades of literary theory, the author is very much alive" (p. 26).

Is the concern with the author's or illustrator's identity and perspective, then, a legitimate one? Does it violate the principles of the presently prevailing reader-response theory? I try to answer these questions by first examining the basic principles of reader-response theory regarding the role of the text and author and then, in the light of these principles, justifying the concern with the author's cultural identity and background.

THE ROLE OF THE AUTHOR IN READER-RESPONSE THEORY

The role of the author in literature is played out through the text he or she creates. From the reader-response perspective, "the communication with the author becomes in fact a relationship through the text" (Rosenblatt, 1978, p. 76). An overview of the position on the status of text taken by various reader-response theorists will shed light on the extent to which they accept the author's role in the process of reading.

It should be noted that reader-response criticism "is not a conceptually unified critical position, but a term that has come to be associated with the work of critics who use the words 'reader,' 'reading process,' and 'response' to mark out an area for investigation" (Tompkins, 1980, p. ix). Varied as they are, all brands of reader-response theories recognize the reader's contribution to the making of meaning. The controversy centers around the status of text and the role of its creator—the author—

in the process of meaning-making. While emphasizing the reader's role, most reader-response theories, to varying degrees, also acknowledge the role of the text and author.

UNIACTION, INTERACTION, AND TRANSACTION

Positions on the relation between the reader and text, in my view, can be classified into three categories: uniactional, interactional, and transactional. The root *action* in the three terms can be operationally defined as the contribution of the agent (reader or text) to the making of meaning. The extreme uniactional view admits only the action of one of the two co-ordinates or elements in literature, namely, either the text or the reader alone has a role to play in the making of meaning.

E. D. Hirsch's (1967) theory of validity is a variant of reader-response theory in the sense that it accepts the fact of the text's openness, that the text can have different significations. Yet his theory is uniactional because it rejects the notion that there can be more than one valid interpretation for a text. For him, the only acceptable meaning of a text is the meaning the author encoded in it. What an individual reader reads into the text is not meaning, but "significance." Therefore, a text can have a constant "meaning" intended by the author but shifting "significances" decoded by the reader.

Stanley Fish's (1980) theory, which claims that all the meaning is supplied by the reader, is uniactional at the other extreme; it is actually a theory of "reader action" instead of reader response. Fish claims that "the interpreters do not decode poems; they make them." The epistemological assumption beneath this assertion is: "It is not that the presence of poetic qualities compels a certain kind of attention but that the paying of a certain kind of attention results in the emergence of poetic qualities" (p. 326). As the author's text has become a nonentity, literature exists only in the reader, whose interpretive strategies can mold the text, like plasticine, into any desired shape. From this theoretical perspective the author is driven totally out of the scene.

David Bleich's (1978) "subjective criticism" is also a uniactional model of reading. He considers the text as a series of symbols, the meaning of which depends entirely upon the reader's mental activity in constructing it. The reader becomes the independent self and the sole agent in the reading process. He rejects the active nature of the text—the guidance and constraints built into the text that the author can give to the reader.

Holland's (1968) psychoanalytical approach borders on uniactional theory. He sees the relationship between reader and text as the self and the "other." He admits that the text as the "other" exists prior to the reader's experience of it and puts constraints on the reader's interpretation. However, his main concern and interest centers on the function of the reader's identity. He later defined interpretation as "a function of identity" (1980, p. 123). Reading becomes a process of re-creating the text in terms of the reader's personal identity.

In contrast to the uniactional theories are the interactional and transactional theories, which incorporate both the reader and text as significant contributors to the reading experience but do not assign a central intended meaning to the text as the universal criterion for validity of interpretation. Both interactional and transactional theorists view the reading process as a reciprocal one, rather than a uniactional one in which a passive reader is acted on by the text or a passive text is acted on by the reader. However, the transactional theory (Rosenblatt, 1937, 1978) collapses the traditional subject/object dichotomy. The transaction between the reader and text is not a process of the subject (reader) responding to the stimuli of the object. It is a "highly complex ongoing process of selection and organization" (1978, p. 49) that results in the evocation of the literary work as distinguished from the text, the sequence of verbal symbols. Rosenblatt does not exalt the reader's creativity. As she notes, "the view that the reader in re-creating the work reenacts the author's creative role superficially seems more reasonable" (1978, p. 49). Nor does she deny the text's constraints on the reader's re-creation.

Robert Scholes's (1985) dialectic view of the relation between reader and text is compatible with Rosenblatt's. He believes that the reader is engaged in three kinds of activity: "reading, interpretation, and criticism. In reading, we produce text within text; in interpretation we produce text upon text; and in criticizing we produce text against text" (p. 24).

Iser's (1974, 1978) phenomenological theory carries some similar assumptions. Like Rosenblatt, who sees meaning-making as experiential, Iser holds that "meaning is no longer an object to be defined, but is an effect to be experienced" by the reader (1978, p. 10). A literary text does not formulate the meanings itself but "initiates performances of meaning" (1978, p. 27). It is this nature of indeterminacy that brings about the text–reader interaction. While the text contains "gaps" (i.e., what is only implied) that stimulate the reader to "concretize" (1978, p. 21) them with their projections so as to synthesize an aesthetic object, it also provides instructions and conditions for the production of that object.

Jonathan Culler's (1975) structuralist reading theory is primarily concerned with literary conventions, the knowledge of which enables a reader to understand literature. The literary conventions are a system of rules governing the operation of literary discourse, like the grammar of a language. Both author and reader have internalized this "grammar of literature" (p. 114) that makes literature intelligible. Reading, metaphorically, is a rule-governed game played by both the author and reader in the court of the text.

Rosenblatt's transactional theory and the interactional theories of Iser, Scholes, Culler, and others acknowledge the constraint and guidance of the text to the reader. These theories justify the investigation of the "textual power" (Scholes, 1985) of literature and the role of the author who infuses the text with that power. Rosenblatt admits the author into the scene of literary experience in this way: "He [the reader] will be conscious always that the words of the author are guiding him; he will have a sense of achieved communication, sometimes, indeed, with the author" (1978, p. 50). In some works, the author intrudes into the text with open comments; in others the author withdraws behind the characters. The author–reader relationship has evolved down through literary history. Yet, whether in the traditional "closed" texts or more modern "open" texts (in Barthes's [1974] terms, "readerly" or "writerly" texts), the author is always there. In children's literature, especially, the author's voice always speaks out loud, conveying attitudes, values, and assumptions that serve to shape the younger reader's mind and heart, even though it is no longer as openly didactic as in the past.

Fish's and Bleich's uniactional and Holland's near-uniactional theories not only put the reader at center stage in literary criticism but have also eliminated the role of the author and text. Their theories constitute the most subjectivist trend in the reader-response movement. In terms of influence, however, their theories by no means represent the mainstream of the movement; the critic most often quoted in educational research is Rosenblatt, not Fish or Bleich. These widely accepted reader-response theories have not banished the author from the criticism of literature.

In reading, as Terry Eagleton (1983) suggests, readers do not merely engage textual objects but also involve themselves in "forms of activity inseparable from the wider social relations between writers and readers" (p. 206). While it is an outdated notion to view the author's intention as the objective of reading, the dynamic of reading certainly lies in the interaction between the author and the reader. This occurs through the latter's reaction to the text, especially when there are discrepancies between the author's and reader's beliefs, assumptions, and values (as frequently happens in reading multicultural literature). According to one feminist view of reader response (Schweickart, 1986), "literature—the activities of reading and writing—[is] an important arena of political struggle" (p. 39). In the case of a female reader reading a male text, she asserts herself against the control of the text, "reading the text as it was not meant to be read, in fact, reading against itself" (p. 50). The reader then becomes a "resisting reader" (Fetterley, cited in Schweickart, 1986, p. 42). If the author were dead and his voice silent, there would be nothing to resist.

Just as female readers resist male-chauvinistic texts, readers from nonwhite cultures have been resisting literature showing racial bias and prejudice. The well-known author Milton Meltzer's (1987) response to the stereotyping of Jews in many literary masterpieces by major writers in history, such as Scott's *Ivanhoe*, Dickens's *Oliver Twist*, and Shakespeare's *The Merchant of Venice*, offers a typical example of reader's resistance to authorial sensibilities. Although he liked these works in his early years, he "tried to ignore everything in the novel that nourished anti-Semitism" (p. 493) and was "anxious to get on to passages less painful to me as a Jewish child" (p. 494). Meltzer speaks for all those who feel strongly about racial bias and prejudice encountered in literature.

These authors of classic literature—many of them were great humanitarians—might not have been aware of the anti-Semitic prejudices in their works. As their perspectives were shaped and conditioned by their times, they might have unconsciously reflected in their works the prevalent prejudices of their times. The prejudices might have been implied rather than intended. This is still the case with some authors of multicultural literature of our times. In whatever age, authors do not live in a social vacuum; their consciousness is determined by their social existence. In short, authors are social beings. If we accept the notion that "the author is dead," we would do nothing less than excuse the authors from their social and ethical responsibilities. A more realistic view is that authors live on, although their authority is reduced, their intention no longer wholly determining the meaning of their texts. We cannot deny the social nature of writing and reading; fiction and other forms of literature are "a contract designed by an intending author who invites his or her audience to adopt certain paradigms for understanding reality" (Foley cited in Rabinowitz, 1987, p. 23). It is up to the readers to decide whether they will accept the author's contract. Meltzer found the author's invitation to view Jews disparagingly in the classics unacceptable and rejected the contract.

THE REAL AUTHOR AND THE IMPLIED AUTHOR

Some reader-response theories not only acknowledge the author's role in reading but also provide new terms to deal with it, such as "implied reader" (Iser, 1974), "authorial audience" (Rabinowitz, 1987), and "implied author" (Booth, 1961). All these terms point to the author's presence in the text and acknowledge his or her role in the event of reading.

While reader-response theories reject the author's intended meaning as the objective of interpretation, as Rabinowitz (1987) observes, reading the author's intended meaning, or "authorial reading," provides a basis for critical reading from "some perspective other than the one called for by the author" (p. 32). Rabinowitz's theory dovetails with Scholes's theory of "producing text against text."

The author's intention may not be realized by the text he or she creates. There may exist a discrepancy between the actual author and his or her implied image in the text. Booth's concept of implied author addresses this discrepancy. Booth is not generally regarded as a representative reader-response theorist, but his concept of implied author is endorsed by Wolfgang Iser, one of the leading reader-response theorists. Iser (1974) states that "we should distinguish, as Wayne Booth does in his *Rhetoric of Fiction*, between the man who writes the book (author) and the man whose attitudes shape the book (implied author)" (p. 103).

According to Booth (1961), the author's presence is implied in his or her artistic creation. Different from the real author who writes the book, the implied author is the real author's "second self." A real author has "various official versions of himself" in different works he or she creates:

> Just as one's personal letters imply different versions of oneself, depending on the differing relationships with each correspondent and the purpose of each letter, so the writer sets himself out with different air depending on the needs of particular works. (p. 71)

The implied author is not to be identified with the speaker in the work, often referred to as "persona," "mask," or "narrator" (p. 73), who is only one of the elements created by the implied author. The narrator could be a dramatized character in the work, but the implied author can not. "The 'implied author' chooses, consciously or unconsciously, what we read . . . he is the sum of his own choices" (pp. 74–75). In fiction, some aspects of the implied author may be inferred from the style and tone of the work, "but his major qualities will depend also on the hard facts of action and character in the tale that is told" (p. 74).

The implied author's attitudes that shape the book are equivalent to what Iser (1978) termed "schematized views" in a literary work. The "schematized views" are not plainly stated but are hinted at by various perspectives offered by the text. In the novel, for example, "there are four main perspectives: those of the narrator, the characters, the plot, and the fictitious reader [the intended reader]" (p. 35). As the reader tries to use these perspectives to relate the "schematized views" to one another, he or she brings the text to life, and their meeting place, which the reader finds at the end, is his or her experienced meaning of the text. Different readers may find different meeting places. However, the network of perspectives predisposes the reader to read in certain ways.

Iser's (1978) term for the series of perspectives, the "network of response-inviting structures," is "implied reader" (p. 34). The term seems to be opposite to Booth's implied author, but in fact they refer to essentially the same thing from different perspectives. Both are theoretical constructs formulated to designate the conditioning force that the real author builds into the text when he or she creates the literary work. Both denote the "perspective view of the world put together by (though not necessarily typical of) the author" (Iser, 1978, p. 35). The relationship of the two concepts is footnoted by these remarks of Booth's: "The author creates, in short, an image of himself and another image of his reader; he makes his reader, as he makes his second self" (1961, p. 138).

An example may help to make these terms less abstract. In 1984, there was a debate between Rudine Sims (1984) and Belinda Hurmence (1982), author of *A Girl Called Boy*, in *The Advocate*. According to Sims, Hurmence's book presents a white perspective that perpetuates stereotypes of African Americans although it is a well-intended attempt to depict their experiences. She bases her argument on the sum of choices the author made consciously or unconsciously in the novel—choices of details to include, of words in the descriptions of things and people, of what to emphasize or deemphasize. For example, while mentioning the cruelties of the slave system throughout the book, according to Sims, the author also emphasizes the benevolence of some slave owners and the slaves' ambivalent attitude toward them. Implied in her literary choices is the author's perspective, or, in Iser's terms, "schematized views" on the reality presented in the book. The reader, such as Sims, would create from the author's choices the implied author—the image the real author created of herself when she created the book. According to Sims's reading, the implied author is a person who is sympathetic to black Americans but is not yet able to look at the world through their perspective. One may argue that Sims's inference about the implied author in the text is inaccurate and that one may then create from the text another very different implied author. Different inferences of the implied author are possible and natural, which explains why there is controversy over a multicultural literary work. In a sense the implied author may also be termed the *inferred author*. The implied author, as its name indicates, is not portrayed by the author in definite terms; it has to be inferred by the reader from the literary choices the author makes. The reader's inference, however, is a "struc-

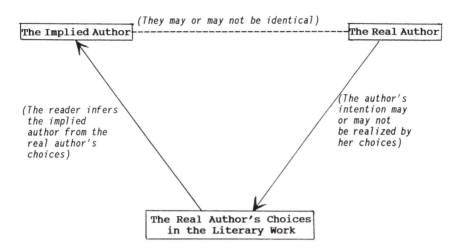

Figure 9.1. The Real Author, the Implied Author, and the Reader

tured act" (Iser, 1978, p. 35), not a random guess. The literary choices the author makes sketch a contour of his or her image in the text. The reader fills in the blanks with shade and color to form a clear picture of the implied author. Figure 9.1 illustrates the relationship among the actual author, the implied author, and the reader.

Despite her good intention to contribute to the representation of black experience in children's literature, the author of *A Girl Called Boy* implies in her choices an author whose perspective is not acceptable to some black readers.

This tension between the reader's and the implied author's perspectives is always present in any process of reading, but it is particularly conspicuous in reader response to "cross-cultural literature," because, conditioned by cultural differences, the gap between the reader's and the implied author's perspectives is often wide. When the implied author and the real author are different, the perspective of the world presented in the text, as Iser notes, is not necessarily typical of the real author. An author who writes about a culture other than his or her own may take on the alien beliefs and values of that culture. The author may give an authentic presentation of the culture in his or her works. The implied author, or the second self the real author creates, may be accepted by readers from that culture.

A typical example of the gap between real author and implied author is the novel by Forrest Carter (1976), *The Education of Little Tree*. This book is about the life of a Native American orphan who learned the ways of his culture from his Cherokee grandparents in Tennessee. When recently reprinted, it was an instant success and was well accepted by some Native American reviewers. Then suddenly it became a cause of controversy, an embarrassment to those who praised it, when the author's true identity was revealed. Forrest Carter turned out to be a pseudonym for a late racist. If a racist can write an authentic book about a minority, then one may ask, do we need to concern ourselves with the real author's perspectives and ethnic identity?

We may counter the question with another question: How many racists have written books like *The Education of Little Tree?* It is only rarely that a racist is willing and able to write an authentic book about the experiences of an ethnic minority group. While some authors may be able to build into their works an implied author that is completely different from themselves, others may not. This is especially true in multicultural literature. In many cases, the implied author and the real author are not two utterly different persons. In creating a literary world, the real author cannot put the complete reality into it but has to choose what to include. The choices the author makes often consciously or unconsciously reflect his or her experiences and perspectives of the real world. It is not easy, as Staples puts it, "to be under somebody else skin" (cited in Swayer & Swayer, 1993, p. 166) or, as Yep states (1987), to become an "invisible man" erasing all the features on your own face, "a blank mirror reflecting other people's hopes and fears" (p. 485). For authors of multicultural literature, this is a remarkable achievement, because they are not only aware of cultural differences but also are able to fill in the cultural gaps in their literary creation.

The distinction between the real author and the implied author makes it possible to explain the existence of such books as *The Education of Little Tree.* The relation between the real author's identity and his or her literary creation is not one of determinism (Gates, 1991). It is possible for authors of the mainstream culture to write authentic books about minority experiences. Minority authors can also write successful works about the mainstream culture. Among the numerous works of cross-cultural literature, there are well-written ones. Outsiders are not doomed to failure when they write about cultures other than their own. The lesson—if there is one—we may draw from *The Education of Little Tree* is not that the author's cultural identity is no longer significant, but rather that, while emphasizing the influence of an author's cultural background on his or her works about another culture, we should not claim an absolute causal relationship between the two. How can we if Forrest Carter, "a Ku Klux Klan terrorist," succeeds in creating a "second self" "who captures the unique vision of Native American culture" (Gates, 1991, p. 26)?

The author's experiences (direct and indirect) and imagination may help him or her surmount cultural barriers and create an implied author acceptable to the reader from a specific culture, but the gaps are not as easy to cross as one might imagine. What Rabinowitz (1987) calls "brute facts" impose great constraints and limitations on the author's imagination. Writing about another culture is comparable to writing about a historical period. Many "brute facts" are independent of the author's imaginations. Careful research is needed before the author can grasp the reality beyond his or her own world. Relying on imagination alone may result in making a laughing stock rather than a respectable self-image of the author (Cai, 1995). There is no lack of examples in the past or present. In a popular picture book *Tikki Tikki Tembo* (Mosel, 1968), the architectural style of the houses, the dresses and hairdos of the characters, and other details are Japanese, but the story is presented as a Chinese story. In a more recent picture book, *The Dwarf Giant* (Lobel, 1991), which is set in Japan, food is served in a manner only appropriate for offering it on the family altar and characters wear kimonos in a manner in which only deceased people would be dressed (Yokota, 1993). To a knowledgeable reader, these ludicrous misrepresentations show the authors and/or illustrators as culturally ignorant.

From the standpoint of ethical criticism, Booth (1988) holds that the actual writer should create for his or her work an implied author that represents a wise ethos. This often means "giving up a beloved fault or taking on an alien virtue" (p. 128). We can apply Booth's notion of an implied author representing wise ethos to multicultural literature. In doing so, we suggest that the actual writer should create in his or her work an implied author that represents the attitudes, beliefs, and values—in short, the perspective—of the culture he or she tries to portray and is thus identified with the readers from that culture. An outstanding example of such an author is Paul Goble, a non–American Indian who has created many pictures that authentically reflect American Indian culture. His works are highly acclaimed for their authenticity and distinct style. His success has been attributed to his long-term relationship with American Indian cultures (Noll, 1995).

THE AUTHOR'S CULTURAL IDENTITY IN MULTICULTURAL LITERATURE

Reader-response theory shifts the focus of critical attention from the text as the sole locus of meaning to the reader as an important constituent of meaning. This shift does not entail the death of the author. While uniactional theories deny the role of the text in literary interpretation, interactional and transactional theories recognize the text as a constraining and guiding force and admit the author's participation in the reading event. These theories justify the concern with an author's cultural identity and perspective as reflected in the text of multicultural literature. The concept of implied author in particular defines the author's presence in the text: The literary choices the actual author makes combine to form an image of the author or his or her second self. This concept also explains possible discrepancies between the author and his or her "second self," between the author's intention and the actual effects of his or her literary creation. This has two significant implications, among others, for the creation of multicultural literature.

First, an author can write about a different culture and create a "second self" that shares the perspectives of the people from that culture, even though he or she has not become one of its members. While we emphasize the influence of an author's cultural background on his or her works about another culture, we should not hold a deterministic view that claims an absolute causal relationship between the two.

Second, a well-intended author may create a literary work about an ethnic culture unacceptable to the people of that culture. The author's cultural identity and background may adversely influence his or her literary choices without the author's knowing it. From the perspective of social progress, multicultural literature is intended to inform people about other cultures, to liberate them from the bondage of stereotypes (Howard, 1991), to foster respect for one's own cultural heritage as well as others, and to promote cross-cultural understanding. Many authors who write multicultural literature for children may be motivated by these lofty purposes, but good intention does not guarantee that the implied author in their books will achieve the desired effects. Instead of insisting on good intentions, authors would be better off turning an eager ear to readers' responses to their works and taking responsibility for the social effects their works may have produced. As promoters and gatekeepers, publishers share some of this responsibility with authors.

The battle over the role of the author will continue in the political arena of multicultural literature. The mainstream reader-response theories are on the side of those who uphold the relevance of the author's cultural identity and perspective regarding the creation of multicultural literature.

REFERENCES

Barthes, R. (1974). *S/Z*. (R. Miller, Trans.). New York: Hill and Wang.
Bishop, R. S. (1992). Multicultural literature for children: Making informed choice.

In V. J. Harris (Ed.), *Teaching multicultural literature in grades k–8* (pp. 37–54). Norwood, MA: Christopher-Gordon.

Bleich, D. (1978). *Subjective criticism*. Baltimore: Johns Hopkins University Press.

Booth, W. C. (1961). *The rhetoric of fiction*. Chicago: University of Chicago Press.

Booth, W. C. (1988). *The company we keep: An ethics of fiction*. Berkeley: University of California Press.

Cai, M. (1995). Can we fly across cultural gaps on the wings of imagination? Ethnicity, experience, and cultural identity. *The New Advocate, 8*(1), 1–17.

Carter, F. (1976). *The education of Little Tree*. New York: Delacorte.

Culler, J. (1975). *Structuralist poetics: Structuralism, linguistics and the study of literature*. Ithaca, NY: Cornell University Press.

Eagleton, T. (1983). *Literary theory: An introduction*. Minneapolis: University of Minnesota Press.

Fish, S. (1980). *Is there a text in this class?* Cambridge, MA: Harvard University Press.

Gates, H. L., Jr. (1991, November 24). "Authenticity," or the lesson of Little Tree. *The York Times Book Review*, November 24, pp. 1, 26–30.

Goble, P. (1988). *Her seven brothers*. New York: Bradbury.

Harris, V. J. (Ed.). (1992). *Teaching multicultural literature in grades k–8*. Norwood, MA: Christopher-Gordon.

Hirsch, E. D., Jr. (1967). *Validity in interpretation*. New Haven, CT: Yale University Press.

Holland, N. N. (1968). *The dynamics of literary response*. New York: Oxford University Press.

Holland, N. N. (1980). Unity identity text self. In J. Tompkins (Ed.), *Reader-response criticism: From formalism to post-structuralism* (pp. 118–134). Baltimore: Johns Hopkins University Press.

Howard, E. F. (1991). Authentic multicultural literature for children: An author's perspective. In M. Lindgren (Ed.), *The multicolored mirror: Cultural substance in literature for children and young adults* (pp. 90–94). Fort Atkinson, WI: Highsmith.

Huck, C. S., Helper, S., & Hickman, J. (1993). *Children's literature in the elementary school*. New York: Holt, Rinehart & Winston.

Hurmence, B. (1982). *A girl called boy*. New York: Clarion.

Iser, W. (1974). *The implied reader: Patterns in communication in prose fiction from Bunyan to Beckett*. Baltimore: Johns Hopkins University Press.

Iser, W. (1978). *The act of reading: A theory of aesthetic response*. Baltimore: Johns Hopkins University Press.

Lobel, A. (1991). *The dwarf giant*. New York: Holiday House.

Meltzer, M. (1987). A common humanity. In B. Harrison & G. Maguire (Eds.), *Innocence and experience* (pp. 490–497). New York: Lothrop.

Mosel, A. (1968). *Tikki Tikki Tembo*. Illustrated by B. Lent. New York: Holt.

Noll, E. (1995). Accuracy and authenticity in American Indian children's literature: The social responsibility of authors and illustrators. *The New Advocate, 8*(1), 29–43.

Rabinowitz, P. J. (1987). *Before reading: Narrative convention and the politics of interpretation*. Ithaca, NY: Cornell University Press.

Rosenblatt, L. M. (1937). *Literature as exploration*. New York: Appleton-Century-Crofts.

Rosenblatt, L. M. (1978). *The reader, the text, the poem: Transactional theory of the literary work*. Carbondale: Southern Illinois University Press.

Scholes, R. (1985). *Textual power: Literary theory and the teaching of English*. New Haven, CT: Yale University Press.

Schweickart, P. P. (1986). Reading ourselves: Toward a feminist theory of reading. In E. B. Flynn & P. P. Schweickart (Eds.), *Gender and reading* (pp. 31–62). Baltimore: Johns Hopkins University Press.

Silvey, A. (1993). Varied carols. *The Horn Book Magazine, 69*(2), 132–133.

Sims, R. (1982). *Shadow and substance*. Urbana, IL: National Council of Teachers of English.

Sims, R. (1984). A question of perspective. *The Advocate, 3*, 145–156.

Swayer, W., & Swayer, J. (1993). A discussion with Suzanne Fisher Staples: The author as writer and cultural observer. *The New Advocate, 6*(3), 159–171.

Tompkins, J. (Ed.). (1980). *Reader-response criticism: From formalism to post-structuralism*. Baltimore: Johns Hopkins University Press.

Yep, L. (1987). A Chinese sense of reality. In B. Harrison & G. Maguire (Eds.), *Verbal icon* (pp. 485–489). New York: Lothrop.

Yokota, J. (1993). Issues in selecting multicultural literature. *Language Arts, 70*(3), 156–167.

CHAPTER 10

Reading Literature of Other Cultures

Some Issues in Critical Interpretation

ANNA O. SOTER

Hence, people enjoy looking at images, because as they contemplate they understand and infer each element (e.g., that this is such-and-such a person). Since, if one lacks familiarity with the subject, the artifact will not give pleasure qua mimetic representation but because of its craftsmanship, color, or for some other such reason.
—Aristotle, Poetics

The perspective of cross-cultural literatures has given explicit confirmation to the perception that genres cannot be described by essential characteristics, but by an interweaving of features, a "family resemblance" which denies the possibility either of essentialism or limitation.
—Bill Ashcroft, Gareth Griffiths, and Helen Tiffin,
The Empire Writes Back

IN ALDOUS HUXLEY'S *Brave New World*, the Savage, an outcast in that utopian society, stumbles across Shakespeare's *The Tempest* and is transformed through its offering of another world that to him is wondrous in all its possibilities until he discovers that it is not what it seems to be (Huxley, 1933; Shakespeare, 1611/1964). In Australia, a young child in the outback enters the world of the English romantic poets, dreaming of "verdant lands" in the midst of a rocky, red-dirt landscape.

Questions of what constitutes "literature" and, related to this, questions of truth, values, knowledge, and culture have always been with us even in our study of the classics as incorporated in high school and college curricula in the past century. We could argue that a student living and studying Jane Austen's *Emma* (Austen, 1816/1969) or Shakespeare's *The Tempest* in the Australian outback is nearly as far removed from the contexts that created both of those works as are current students in American urban and suburban school settings. Yet the power of literature to transport readers into other worlds has never been doubted by those who, despite their own sometimes narrow worlds, have been captured by writers no matter how different the culture they inhabit. Certainly, we could also argue that an understanding of the political context in Czechoslovakia would enable us to better understand and appreciate ironies in Milan Kundera's *The Book of Laughter and Forgetting* (Kundera, 1986). Or, if we were familiar with the sociocultural and political character of contemporary Israel, we might make much more of A. B. Yehoshua's *A Late Divorce* (Yehoshua, 1984) than we are able to as outsiders. However, it would be utterly inaccurate to suggest that lacking such knowledge always precludes both enjoyment and even critical appreciation of such literature. In addition, much of our reading would be severely curtailed.

Yet not all readers in our schools will so readily connect with Bloom's (1994) claim of the "autonomy of imaginative literature," although they may well agree with the "sovereignty of the solitary soul," even if not in the way Bloom intended (p. 10). To understand and appreciate the significance of the arguments put forth by many scholars for the necessity of including literature of other cultures, and not necessarily canonical texts within those cultures, we must, I believe, return to the beginnings of the literary history of our diverse, individual students. If we do not, we assume a literary sophistication and experience that more resembles our own, with frequently disappointing consequences.

LITERATURE OF OTHER CULTURES IN THE CLASSROOM

To date, the focus of much discussion on the use of literature representative of other cultures—whether within or outside of the United States—has been on *the content* of that literature. Our concern with using that literature in classrooms has centered, and rightly so, on the following: the relevance to readers in school (Chisunka, 1991); the appropriateness to students at different ages and levels (Applebee, 1990; Diamond & Moore, 1995); issues related to negative stereotyping (Ramirez, 1992; Viehmann, 1994); questions of accessibility (Perkins, 1992); and questions related to the range of selections (Applebee, 1991; Harwood, 1993). We are now at a point at which the notion of using literature representative of other cultures (within and outside the United States) is well established in the professional literature and is increasingly accepted in schools, which suggests that at least some progress has been made in addressing the concerns described above. My concern in this chapter, as in much of this book, is to address the question of what we *do* with these books once they are in the classroom. I am particularly interested in exploring the notion of aesthetic restriction in terms of how it influences us as readers of often quite unfamiliar content found in the literature of other cultures, and what we as teachers can do about this.

AESTHETIC RESTRICTION IN THE FACE OF THE UNFAMILIAR

While educators may readily admit that reading books by writers of other cultures provides us with a rich and immensely enjoyable literary experience, as well as some understanding of those cultures, our starting point for engagement *and* interpretation will be different from that of "insiders." Therefore we are faced with new critical challenges if we intend to use literature representative of different cultures in our classrooms. Dasenbrook (1992), however, suggests that this need not be an insurmountable obstacle, for "the informed position," he asserts, "is not always the position for the richest or most powerful experience of a work of art. And this becomes even more true when crossing cultural barriers" (p. 39).

I was recently reminded of these and other insights when discussing with a class the concluding chapter of Katherine Susannah Prichard's novel *Coonardoo,* first published in Australia in 1925 and since reprinted in a variety of editions (Prichard, 1925/1994). The novel is about, among other things, the unacknowledged love between a white man and an Aboriginal woman. Unacknowledged love (and more frequently, sex) between white men and Aboriginal women was not entirely uncommon in the outback of Australia. However, it did not do to speak about the subject. Nor is it, even now, a subject many want to address.

Drusilla Modjeska, in her introduction to the recent edition, observed that, in an rather unusual step, Prichard had originally explained this particular work of fiction in the following way:

> Life in the north-west of Western Australia . . . is almost as little known in Australia as in England or America. It seems necessary to say, therefore, that the story was written in the country through which it moves. Facts, characters, incidents, have been collected, related, interwoven. That is all. (1994 edition, p. v)

Given both the critical acclaim and the public outrage following the novel's original publication, Prichard seems to have been gifted with special insight in presenting her justification of the work for its "imaginative, historical and social accuracy" (1994 edition, p. v).

I was interested in seeing how a group of American graduate students in a large midwestern university would respond to the novel. Reluctance to declare "outrage" was evident in my class, although it is also likely that none was felt. Only one person in the class wished to talk about it in depth. However, others felt the power of the novel, which in its concluding stages approaches the scope of grand tragedy. Nevertheless, there was strong reluctance to talk about it, for, seemingly, the following reasons: Students felt they did not know enough about the context to comment on the events and characters; the setting and events seemed so far-fetched in the midwestern American context that a starting point for discussion was difficult to find, despite the empathy that everyone felt for the Aboriginal woman, the main character; and the mixture of fact and fiction also made students feel that they lacked "background knowledge" that they admittedly did not have. Unlike me, my students had not grown up in Australia, let alone the outback. None had any previous contact with Australian Aboriginals. Unlike me, they could only connect with the relationship between Hugh (the white man) and Coonardoo (the Aboriginal woman) through urban and suburban eyes, in a markedly different context. I had known of such relationships in a firsthand experience—one of my close childhood friends was the son of a white man and an Aboriginal woman. I had also known of white men and Aboriginal women whose relationship went beyond sex to the similarly unacknowledged emotional bond the novel describes between Hugh and Coonardoo.

The begged question became: What is the starting point for this and other similarly "foreign" works? Where does a teacher begin to help students make the connections at the personal level and at the aesthetic level that establish the ground to engage in interpretive criticism, to evaluate the novel as a work of art, and to commence what Geertz (1979) described as "entering into a kind of conversation" with these "depicted lives of other peoples" (p. 226). In *Coonardoo*, as in other works, readers might also have to overcome aesthetic restriction (my term) brought about by ethical and, possibly, religious repugnance (Gunn, 1987). At the same time, it is worth noting that an uncritical acceptance may also occur simply because the context and its representation in the literary object are unfamiliar. I find myself in this quandary when reading a collection such as Fauzia Rafiq's *Aurat Durbar* or Masha Gessen's anthology, *Half a Revolution: Contemporary Fiction by Russian Women* (Rafiq, 1995; Gessen, 1995).

Similarly, what adjustments must I—a well-seasoned reader—make when confronted with the following excerpt, powerful as it is in its effect, from Marina Palei's "The Bloody Women's Ward"?

> Razmetalsky delivers his lectures only when he has temporarily set aside his razor blade, sat himself down in the abortion theater with a martyred air and is bearing his cross in the form of a pair of uplifted female legs. Then, with Darya Petrovna lovingly maneuvering the surgical basin into which the bloody tatters are to slop, Razmetalsky delivers his lecture in his dull monotonous voice, and seems to the woman the lord of all creation. (Palei, 1992, p. 75)

The widely experienced reader will more readily accord this and other "different" literature sufficient distance from the reading "self" in order to grant it literary merit. In general, as I read, I am already contextualizing the literary text. If it is by a writer from another culture, I am prepared for "difference"; if it is a novel, I more readily suspend my judgments, disbeliefs, resistances because I must read further than a few pages to give the book a chance to "work" on me; if it is a contemporary work, I must be prepared for a greater degree of directness, bluntness, perhaps even shock-effect; and so on. Most, if not all, readers who are naturally drawn to a rich and varied literary diet will not have great difficulty in accepting the initial strangeness sometimes experienced when reading literature representative of different cultures. However, the inexperienced or young reader is, as a rule, not so readily accommodating. The reader inexperienced in reading literature outside of his or her cultural context may have considerable difficulty in finding "fits," in making space so that the unfamiliar, the potentially shocking, will not create aesthetic shut-down. This aesthetic shut-down is the core of my earlier use of the phrase "aesthetic restriction."

Aesthetic restriction is not, I think, the same as the notion of "aesthetic distance" described by Jauss (1982), although the concepts are related. Jauss's use of the concept of aesthetic distance implies the possibility of the acceptance of a literary work because the readership is *receptive* to it. He argues that the "sum total of reactions, prejudgments, and verbal and other behavior that greet a work upon its appearance" is capable of being altered (cited in Godzich, 1994, p. 40) such that there can be acceptance. Jauss acknowledges that resistance, implied in distance, may also result in the rejection of the work until such time that a "horizon of expectation" for that work is "forged" (Godzich, 1994, p. 41). My notion of aesthetic restriction, on the other hand, dismisses the work out of hand *because* of elements in the text that the reader finds unacceptable, and it is often as much because of *content* as of form that the rejection occurs. Thus the literary text cannot "work on the reader"—it is at the level of personal response related to values, tastes, life experiences, predilections, openness to possibilities of other lives and values that the work is untenable for the reader. The distance necessary for the values to be held in suspension, allowing for a dispassionate evaluation of its other possible merits, cannot occur with this kind of reading.

I also do not see the notion of aesthetic restriction operating in the same way as Fetterley's (1978) notion of "the resisting reader," for in my use of the term, "restriction" is primarily an unconscious act, and in Fetterley's case it is proposed as a conscious act:

> Clearly then, the first act of the feminist critic must be to become a resisting rather than assenting reader and, by this refusal to assent, to begin the process of exorcising the male mind that has been implanted in us. (p. xxii)

Let me explore how the notion of aesthetic restriction might work when applied to a story written by a writer from a different literary tradition. The author, Alifa Rifaat (1989), draws much of her material from her experience of living in the Egyptian countryside, according to the editor of the collection in which her story is found. We are moved into the story, "Another Evening at the Club," somewhat innocuously as a woman waits for her husband:

> In a state of tension, she awaited the return of her husband. At a loss to predict what would happen between them, she moved herself back and forth in the rocking chair on the wide wooden veranda that ran along the bank and occupied part of the river itself, its supports being fixed in the river bed, while around it grew grasses and trees. (p. 148)

The long, multi-embedded sentence winds its way into our minds but also suspends the action and, in doing so, suspends us, too—we seem to be caught in the seemingly breathless moment before action. Rifaat maintains the suspense as she describes, in great detail, the setting for the main event, the loss of an emerald ring given to the woman by her husband as part of her betrothal package. The story is told in retrospect as the woman recalls her husband coming to her parents' house to meet her for the first time. The emerald ring is subsequently bought by her husband-to-be as a birthday present. We move through her memories to her marriage, when on her wedding night, her husband instructs her that she must pretend that she comes from a well-known Barakat family and that her father is a judge. He then gently pats her cheeks "in a fatherly,

reassuring gesture that he was often to repeat during their times together" (p. 150).

From that point we move quickly to the critical event—the loss of the
emerald ring—a result of a somewhat tipsy evening prior to the telling
of the story when the woman accidentally drops the ring and falls asleep
to awaken next morning and discover the ring gone. She alerts her husband, who interrogates the maid, who, in turn, is interrogated by the
police, who have "their ways and means" to make people talk (p. 152).
The following day the woman finds the ring, which had slipped between
the legs of the table and the wall. She informs her husband, who does
nothing, because to inform the police would mean a loss of face in having
to admit that his wife had been tipsy the night before. He then asks her
to give him the ring. He will sell it when he next goes to Cairo to get
something else in its place. In the face of her surprisingly uncharacteris-
tic protest,

> he gently patted her on the cheeks . . . the gesture telling her more eloquently
> than any words that he was the man, she the woman, he the one who carried
> the responsibilities, made the decisions, she the one whose role it was to be
> beautiful, happy, carefree. Now, for the first time in their life together the
> gesture came like a slap in the face. (p. 154)

The situation described in the story is not totally unfamiliar even for
a Western female reader. However, this is a story set in modern Egypt,
by a modern Egyptian writer. That is, it is not a story set in a contemporary U.S. context. In reading this tale, we know almost nothing about the
author, almost nothing about the tradition of Egyptian modern writing;
therefore we must start, in effect, with what is in the story. As modern
readers in a culture where the rights of women are a "given" and where
women expect to be equal to men in all respects (at least, rhetorically),
what aesthetic resistance to the story itself will result from the passage
quoted above?

Furthermore, both the husband's and wife's nonchalance concerning
the potential fate of the maid is very disturbing. At no point is any concern expressed for her treatment by the police. Can we assume an implied
author who *is* concerned for the maid? Can we read the husband's and
wife's indifference as a critique of that indifference? Although we *can* read
the foregoing extracts as a critique of a culture that imposes a dependent
status on women, issues of class or economic status remain unsolved.

Will this reading result in Jauss's (1982) "aesthetic distance," which,
in turn, may result in the rejection of the work? Or will it do what Jauss
suggests as the alternative effect, that is, make the public (reader) alter

its horizons so that the work is accepted? (Godzich, 1994). How is the teacher to deal with the personal resistance to the content that may, in turn, result in what I have termed "aesthetic restriction"? In effect, the reader is unable to enter the domain of the story from the perspective of the woman. We could, after all, argue that the writer is critical of the context in which a woman has to "put on the right face" in order to "get on" with the rest of her family and with her community. Is the subtext really about acquiescence, or is it a clever way of raising the issue, of critiquing the accepted status of women who must deny their knowledge of truth? At one level, the story is quite a powerful statement about the status of women in the culture inhabited by the writer. But it is very differently expressed than writing that is more familiar to us, as I think this excerpt from Doris Lessing's short story, "Two Old Women and a Young One," will illustrate:

> The Modigliani girl answered her, and her voice was just as much in a local pattern as the American's. . . . For often and everywhere is to be found this voice. . . . a little breathy high voice that comes from a circumscribed part of the women who use it, not more than two square inches of the upper chest, certainly not a chest cavity or resonating around a head. . . . Oh dear, poor little me, they lisp their appeals to the unkind world; these tough, often ruthless young women who use every bit of advantage they can. (Lessing, 1992, p. 177)

The portrait is not a charming one but it *is* recognizable; and we, as Western women, know exactly what is meant and acknowledge the quest for power implicit in the depiction of the use of womanly wiles, even while not necessarily liking it—it is, after all, an unflattering portrait. But as readers situated in a shared cultural context, we do not have to work hard to *overcome initial alienation*. Indeed, we want to know more: How does this story evolve; what happens to the use of the female wiles; is the author addressing us tongue-in-cheek? In contrast, we may resist wanting to know more about the Rifaat story—it has greater potential to cut us out because of its content, making it more difficult for us to pursue at other levels.

Although I have argued that the Rifaat story may bring about aesthetic restriction because of its content, I would hastily add that distinctions between form and content cannot, as a rule, be so neatly made. Even as we read the Rifaat story, we could be influenced (in terms of the content) by the subtle juxtaposition of a serene, luxurious setting described in the opening lines with the jarring indifference of the couple toward the maid and the undercurrent of the wife's warring emotions, which are *not* expressed in her surface features and behavior. That is, *how* something is said will influence *what* is perceived by the reader. As Scott Walker (1989) notes in his introduction to the collection containing Rifaat's story:

> As in other forms of friendship, in order to understand and appreciate, one must meet the other a bit more than halfway. . . . [We] open ourselves to a different aesthetic model. If we perceive and are put off by stiffness in the plot, a static character, or clumsy language, we may entirely miss the music of these tales. . . . It can be a struggle for a reader unaccustomed to reading the myths and stories of another culture to overcome *resistance and predisposition* [emphasis added]. (p. xii)

One way out of the thicket of critical difficulty implied in the previous pages is to define our goals as teachers of literature representative of diverse cultures in terms of creating a literary dialectic, a conversation that prepares the ground for the movement from "uncritical" response (which may include aesthetic restriction) to "critical" appreciation, that is, to evaluative interpretation. Bogden (1992) describes the full literary response as a "dialectic that legitimizes and capitalizes on the responses of partial form by building on whatever emotional and intellectual raw material presents itself at the precritical level in such a way that response can be deepened, refined, and enriched through aesthetic distance" (p. 119). The way in which this kind of distance is accomplished is through perceiving the literary object as a "separate reality," or, as Frye says, as an "alien structure of the imagination" (cited in Bogden, p. 120). The teacher's role, then, becomes one of creating spaces to allow for the transmutation from the real to the imaginative, from similarities with to differences from the real versus the imagined, and to ground the responses more firmly in the world of the text, *having begun them* in the world(s) of the reader.

AESTHETIC RESTRICTION AND AESTHETIC EVALUATION

In my experience, the teacher of literature of other cultures, no matter how liberal, must be prepared to encounter and deal with readers' puzzlement and negative reactions to content so that "initial responses can be deepened, refined, and enriched through aesthetic distance" (Bogden, 1992, p. 119). An exploration of how aesthetic restriction can influence subsequent engagement and evaluation of literary works follows, with a description of responses to Ding Xiaoqi's (1994) collection of short stories, *Maidenhome*, used in a recent summer institute on the teaching of global literature. No easy solution appeared in terms of how to prepare readers for the unfamiliar literature they encountered. All of the participants had volunteered to take the institute, all were eager to experience literature representing diverse cultures and wished to use the information in their own classrooms. In many respects, the institute was an ideal starting point for our exploration of unfamiliar territory, given that its participants had a high level of motivation, were all skilled and experienced readers who loved literature, and were open and tolerant of new experiences.

A reading journal was utilized to help the participants connect with the texts and to aid the process of articulating responses. It also provided participants with the opportunity to reflect on how they responded to the selections. Some background information was provided for each of the cultures represented in the course by cultural informants who responded to questions from the participants. Brief historical and cultural background information was also provided to contextualize the literature used in the selections.

The following excerpts from responses to Ding Xiaoqi's stories illustrate how difficult even these experienced and eager readers found it to accept literature that, while gripping and fascinating, was "foreign" to them. At the same time, they also reveal much that teachers can work with, using the initial responses as a foundation for further exploration. One explicit reaction to the contents of the story is the following:

> The thought of parents selling children/young adults [14-/17-years-old] was shocking. She didn't even know she was being sold—just like in the short story, "Maidenhome," in which the girl did not know she was joining the military the day her father signed her up. . . . The lack of information and discussion of the child's future in what seems a family-centered culture is surprising. . . . I was shocked to read "Killing Mom" and I started thinking about other pieces of literature that deal with insanity—"The Yellow Wallpaper" and "The Tell Tale Heart."

This member of the institute attempted to connect (and, therefore, make sense of) some of the *Maidenhome* stories with stories about insanity. Another reader sought to find an "explanation" for what was difficult for him to articulate in the possibility that the author was a cultural anomaly:

> The book of short stories, *Maidenhome*, was fascinating but I wonder whether the stories are very typical. Perhaps the very fact that this author found translators into English and a publisher makes her unusual.

Some members of the institute attempted to give the book its "due" rather than dismiss what they found difficult to accept:

> I am still trying to come to terms with the sterile concept of love of Party above all else. I think I would surely have gone mad under such a regime. Perhaps that is the impetus which drives artists and revolutionaries to acts of courage and risk. Death as the better alternative.

Some were more explicit in their response to individual stories but explained the effect in terms of contextual (in this case, cultural) differences:

> *Maidenhome* was excellent. It was disturbing to think about women in those roles. Actually, it was quite depressing. Love and marriage are not perfect in the United States but at least we have the freedom to make our own choices. I cannot imagine being in a situation like the daughter-in-law in "Indica, Indica." It made me think about how sex is discussed in the United States. Many people feel that it is in the media too much, but I think more people know about it as a result.

Most striking in all the responses was a tension between shock and repulsion at the events described and fascination *because* those events were described—among them, subtle rape (not known until it was over), teenage brides, killing a mother, government control, and breakups in relationships. As some members of the institute noted, some events were universal but many were not. One member observed that the collection of stories "really helped destroy my stereotypical conceptions of what it means to be Chinese, especially a Chinese woman. I thought this book would contain stories about demure, obedient, well-behaved women who suffered at the hands of men. I couldn't believe the women in these stories." Paradoxically, however, the collection does show stories of women who "suffer at the hands of men" and who, on the surface, are "demure, obedient women." The rage, the revenge, the passion is *internal* rather than *external*.

Participants in the institute were required to read the selections prior to its commencement. Many observed that it was not until the presentation by the Chinese cultural informant, who talked of the power and influence of the Cultural Revolution, that they began to understand *Maidenhome*, written as it was after the Cultural Revolution by an author who left China as a refugee in the early 1990s.

These examples are representative of responses made by all of the institute's participants. They are meaningful in terms of my earlier discussion because they illustrate in several ways some of the challenges we face when using literature of other cultures. First, the session on Chinese literature provided participants with cultural and literary information and participants appeared to find this valuable, although they did not use the information directly in "interpreting" the literature. Second, each reader was at a very different "place" relative to background information needed to move beyond very superficial readings of the texts. We found that we had difficulties in assuming shared understandings of meaning and intention in the literature being read. Third, while participants engaged with and interpreted the literature selections from the perspective of their own cultural frames, they nevertheless also approached them as individuals, with quite varying responses (the responses were always written *prior to* discussions). Fourth, content in the literature must be taken into account, especially when considering why readers connect the way they do (as illustrated in some of the responses to the *Maidenhome* stories).

Indeed, the institute substantiated Jauss's claim that "we never come to cognitive situations empty but carry with us a whole world of familiar beliefs and expectations. The hermeneutic phenomenon encompasses both the alien world we suddenly encounter and the familiar one we carry" (cited in Godzich, 1994, p. 41). Like Godzich (1994) we were forced to recognize that readers "are awash in the tradition that has given rise to the object of his or her reading" (p. 41) *only if* the literature being read is representative of the culture that the reader also inhabits. Otherwise, our conceptions of reading and what readers bring to the experience of reading are often in conflict. Such contradiction must also include questions of what we see as aesthetically satisfying to us and, at times, even as aesthetically recognizable.

A Vignette

The time frame and purpose of the institute did not allow for in-depth explorations of how we can assist students in overcoming aesthetic restriction to the works read. However, the following example (discussed in greater detail in Soter, 1996) may help to illustrate how we can guide readers to Jauss's "altered horizons . . . leading to an acceptance of the work which was previously rejected" (cited in Godzich, 1994, p. 44). Students in a college young adult literature course found the novel *Where the Lilies Bloom* (Cleaver & Cleaver, 1960) implausible for several reasons but primarily because they had little familiarity with the lifestyle and values of the Appalachian community that is depicted in the novel. They were unable to accept that the heroine, 14-year-old Mary Call, could be as competent and mature as she appears to be. For example, students found her wildcrafting expertise difficult to accept; they found her clever ruses in covering up her father's death absurd; they could not accept her inability to see her older sister (Devola) as anything but "cloud-headed"; and they were reluctant to believe that Mary Call could outwit her apparent adversary, 30-year-old Kiser Pease. Despite evidence later in the novel, Mary Call was perceived as "too good to be true."

Given that authenticity was an issue in the reading of the novel, one would have thought that discussions centering on the book as an authentic rendering of the lifestyle of an Appalachian community might soften the students' resistance. This was not the case. Having encountered similar responses in past uses of the novel, I chose to have students examine it structurally—from the perspective of point of view. I wanted them to see that Mary Call was indeed "flawed" and, at the same time, authentically represented. The focus on first-person point of view developed into a discussion of reliable and unreliable narrators and, subsequently, to a consideration of how Cleaver and Cleaver maintained their control over their narrative. The students came to see that as Mary Call developed insight into the *actual* capabilities of other characters, so did they. As the narrative developed, they came to perceive her as an unreliable narrator prior to her maturing understanding and thus, paradoxically, found her more plausible than had been the case in their first readings of the novel. To help the students understand how significantly a particular point of view influences the reader's perspective of the characters and events in a novel, they were also asked to rewrite the opening chapter from another perspective—some chose an omniscient third-person narrator close to the action; others chose to introduce the narrative from a first-person perspective using one of the other characters. As a result of these approaches, the earlier resistance ("aesthetic restriction" apparently influenced by the students' limited understanding of the role of narrative perspective on our perceptions) gave way to an acceptance that the main character *could* indeed have been authentically cast. More significantly, I think, these approaches resulted in richer readings of a novel that, while deceptively simple, is remarkably complex in its narrative structure.

JOURNEYING THROUGH THE IMAGINATION

To deny that behind this book lies an agenda would be a denial of the obvious: There is a pedagogical agenda, apparent in several ways. First, such obvious phenomena as the title of the book, titles of individual chapters, and, perhaps, the reputations and previous works of many of the authors all indicate that we favor multiple perspectives in the teaching of literature, that we favor sensitivity on the part of teachers toward ethnic and gender diversity, and that we favor the return of authors—not just texts and readers—to discussions of the reading act. Second, we all believe, although to differing degrees, that readers, writers, and texts are culturally situated and bound. Third, as educators, we all believe in the value of teaching literature from such a cultural perspective. Yet, if we argue that teachers already have enough on their hands teaching nineteenth- and twentieth-century American and British literature to classrooms filled with students who find many of these literary experiences irrelevant and difficult because of lack of background knowledge and experience, how can we argue for the inclusion of literature that seems even more removed from them and for which there is relatively little accessible critical material available?

In response to these and other challenging questions raised in this chapter, we could consider the literary journey as comparable to the physical one we take when venturing to another country and culture. No matter how much we may prepare ourselves, arm ourselves with information about the unfamiliar culture, we can be sure of encountering the unpredictable; we can be sure of our own surprise expressed perhaps in terms of "But it wasn't in the guidebook!" We can also be overprepared. Armed with too much preliminary information, we may seek to find what will confirm our "prior knowledge" (albeit limited). Such information may function as a frame or a lens through which the actual is then perceived. We may, therefore, be so preoccupied with confirming what "the guidebook" said that we miss the opportunity for the experience to speak directly to us and not see that:

> This is where the artist begins to work: with the consequences of acts, not with the acts themselves. Or the events. The event is important only as it affects your life and the lives of those around you. The reverberations you might say, the overtones: that is where the artist works. (Hellman, 1989, p. 128)

Similarly, Scholes (1989) brings us back to the *artistry*, to the *imaginative dimension* that is a characteristic of all good literature by which we find ourselves affected. This suggests that we might also give more play to the capacity of humans to *imagine outside their present or immediate realms and experiences* than we frequently do in our discussions of literature and its teaching. Granted, "artistry" and "imaginative dimensions" are culturally loaded terms, accompanied as they are with concepts such as taste, experience, and value. Nevertheless, if we were always to be limited by these, we could not find ourselves moved, despite them, to "enter . . . passing through the looking glass and seeing ourselves in the other" (Scholes, 1989, p. 27). Thus, while I cannot pretend to have shared the space, time, and experience of Ding Xhiao as represented in *Maidenhome*, I can "pass through the looking glass" as much because of her capacity to invite me there as mine to put aside disbelief and resistance. Perhaps we have fallen too far into the trap of thinking first of the text, then of the reader; we may find it provocative in our discussions to consider again the artistry, the power to move, of the writer.

In suggesting that readers are capable of receiving the "reverberations" of artistic works, I am also suggesting that, given the appropriate contexts and approaches for the cross-cultural literary experience, the inclusion of literature of other cultures can provide us with opportunities for widening "our own narrow cultural horizons" (Dasenbrook, 1992, p. 45). The greatest challenge, perhaps, is that in teaching literature representative of other cultures, the teacher, as often as his or her students, must also be prepared to not know, to learn how to experience the unknown afresh, and thus to accept that "the meaning" of the text in hand will no longer function as his or her safe haven when students wander off on uncharted trails.

NOTE

I am very grateful to the following colleagues and friends for their very valuable contributions in helping this chapter become a reality: Mary Ellen Tyus, Denise Wollett, Heather Lewis, Barbara Epstein, Stephanie Connell, Alan Purves and James Phelan.

REFERENCES

Applebee, A. N. (1990). *A study of book-length works taught in high school English courses.* Albany, NY: Center for the Learning and Teaching of Literature.

Applebee, A. N. (1991). *A study of high school literature anthologies* (Report Series 1.5). Albany, NY: Center for the Learning and Teaching of Literature.

Austen, Jane. (1969). *Emma.* New York: Harper & Row. (Original work published 1816)

Bloom, H. (1994). *The Western canon: The books and school of the ages.* NY: Harcourt Brace.

Bogden, D. (1992). *Re-educating the imagination: Toward a poetic, politics, and pedagogy of literary engagement.* Portsmouth, NH: Boynton Cook/Heinemann.

Chisunka, C. (1991). The impact of cultural background and worldview on the literary responses of American and African college students. *Dissertation Abstracts International, 53,* 744A. (University Microfilms No. 92–22, 247)

Cleaver, V., & Cleaver, B. (1960). *Where the lilies bloom.* New York: HarperKeypoint.

Dasenbrook, R. W. (1992). Teaching multicultural literature. In J. Trimmer & T. Warnock (Eds.), *Understanding others: Cultural and cross-cultural studies and the teaching of literature* (pp. 35–46). Urbana, IL: National Council of Teachers of English.

Diamond, B. J., & Moore, M. A. (1995). *Multicultural literacy: Mirroring the reality of the classroom.* NY: Longman.

Ding Xiaoqi. (1994). *Maidenhome* (C. Berry & C. Silber, Trans.). San Francisco: Aunt Lute Books.

Fetterley, J. (1978). *The resisting reader: A feminist approach to American fiction.* Bloomington: Indiana University Press.

Geertz, C. (1979). From the native's point of view: On the nature of anthropological understanding. In P. Rabinow & W. Sullivan (Eds.), *Interpretive science: A reader* (pp. 225–242). Berkeley, CA: University of California Press.

Gessen, M. (1995). *Half a revolution: Contemporary fiction by Russian women.* Pittsburgh: Cleis.

Godzich, W. (1994). *The culture of literacy.* Cambridge, MA: Harvard University Press.

Gunn, G. (1987). *The culture of criticism and the criticism of culture.* Oxford: Oxford University Press.

Harwood, J. D. T. (1993). A content analysis of high school American literature anthology textbooks. *Dissertation Abstracts International, 54,* 932A. (University Microfilms No. 93–20, 207)

Hellman, L. (1989). Interview. In G. Plimpton (Ed.), *Women Writers at Work* (pp. 122–146). London: Penguin.

Huxley, A. (1933). *Brave new world.* New York: Harper & Brothers.

Jauss, R. (1982). *Towards an aesthetics of reception* (T. Bahti, Trans.). Minneapolis: University of Minnesota Press.

Kundera, M. (1986). *The book of laughter and forgetting* (M. H. Heim, Trans.). New York: Penguin.

Lessing, D. (1992). Two old women and a young one. In D. Lessing, *The real thing: Stories and sketches* (pp. 169–179). New York: HarperCollins.

Palei, M. (1992). The bloody women's ward. In N. Perova & A. Bromfield (Eds.), *New Russian writing: Women's view* (pp. 74–93). Moscow: Glas Publishers.

Perkins, E. D. (1992). Response patterns of third-grade African-Americans to culturally conscious literature. *Dissertation Abstracts International, 53,* 2667–2668A. (University Microfilms No. 92–38, 791)

Prichard, K. S. (1994). *Coonardoo.* Sydney, Australia: Angus & Robertson Publications. (Original work published 1925)

Rafiq, F. (Ed.). (1995). *Aurat Durbar.* Toronto: Second Story Press.

Ramirez, G. (1992). The effects of Hispanic children's literature on the self-esteem of lower socio-economic Mexican-American kindergarten children. *Dissertation Abstracts International, 52,* 07A. (University Microfilms No. 91–29, 388)

Rifaat, A. (1989). Another evening at the club. In S. Walker (Ed.), *Stories from the rest of the world* (pp. 148–155). St. Paul, MN: Graywolf.

Scholes, R. (1989). *Protocols of reading.* New Haven, CT: Yale University Press.

Shakespeare, W. (1964). *The tempest.* New York: Signet Classics. (Original work published 1611)

Soter, A. O. (1996). Applying critical perspectives to *My Brother Sam Is Dead* and *Where the Lilies Bloom. Focus: Teaching English Language Arts, 22*(1), 59–68.

Viehmann, M. L. (1994). Writing across the cultural divide: Images of Indians in the lives and works of Native and European Americans. *Dissertation Abstracts International, 55,* 1265. (University Microfilms No. 94–26, 211)

Walker, S. (1989). Introduction to S. Walker (Ed.), *Stories from the rest of the world.* St. Paul, MN: Graywolf Press.

Yehoshua, A. B. (1984). *A late divorce.* New York: Doubleday.

About the Editors and the Contributors

Theresa Rogers is an associate professor of language, literacy, and culture at Ohio State University. Her specializations include response to literature, literacy instruction in urban settings, and drama and literary response. She previously taught English and reading in middle and high schools in Boston, Massachusetts. She is the co-author (with A. C. Purves and A. Soter) of *How Porcupines Make Love II* and *How Porcupines Make Love III* (1990, 1995). Other publications include articles in the *English Journal, Journal of Literacy Research,* and *Urban Review.* She is also co-editor of the *Ohio Journal of English Language Arts.*

Anna O. Soter is an associate professor of English education at Ohio State University. Her specializations include comparative rhetoric, writing instruction and assessment, ESL and writing instruction, applications of critical theories to young adult literature, and teacher learning. She has taught English in Australian secondary schools, taught courses in children's and young adult literature, and, with James Phelan, co-taught two NEH seminars on rhetorical approaches to literature teaching. Since 1994, she has co-edited the *Ohio Journal of the English Language Arts.* She is the co-author (with A. C. Purves and T. Rogers) of *How Porcupines Make Love II* and *How Porcupines Make Love III* (1990, 1995), the co-editor (with G. Hawisher) of *On Literacy and Its Teaching* (1990), and the author of several chapters in edited volumes and articles in various journals.

◖◗

Richard Beach is a professor of English education at the University of Minnesota. He is the author of *A Teacher's Introduction to Reader Response Theories* (1993), co-author (with J. Marshall) of *Teaching Literature in the Secondary School* (1991), co-author (with C. Anson) of *Journals in the Classroom: Writing to Learn* (1995), co-editor (with S. Hynds) of *Developing Discourse Practices in Adolescence and Adulthood* (1990), and co-editor (with J. Green, M. Kamil, and T. Shanahan) of *Multidisciplinary Perspectives on Literacy Research* (1992). He has published numerous book chapters and journal articles on teaching literature and composition and has served as President of the National Conference on Research in English and Chair of the Board of Trustees of the NCTE Research Foundation.

Mingshui Cai is an assistant professor in the Department of Curriculum and Instruction at the University of Northern Iowa. He received his Ph.D. from Ohio State University. His areas of research interest are reader response, multicultural literature, and children's literature. He has published several articles in *The New Advocate, Children's Literature in Education,* and other journals.

Laura E. Desai is a doctoral candidate at Ohio State University. Her research interests include alternative assessment, urban teaching, and the use of multicultural literature for children. She is the co-author (with R. Tierney and M. Carter) of *Portfolio Assessment in the Reading-Writing Classroom* (1991).

Patricia E. Encisco is an assistant professor at the University of Wisconsin–Madison, where she teaches courses in reading and children's literature and graduate courses in culture, reading, and response to literature. She is currently studying preservice teachers' interpretations of those books that are recipients of the Americas Award, a new award recognizing Latino/a children's literature. Recent publications include an article in *Language Arts* and a forthcoming book chapter.

Mary Beth Hines directs the English education program of the School of Education, Indiana University. She received her Ph.D. from the University of Iowa. Her current research focuses on social justice inquiry in literature classrooms. Her recent publications include an article in *English Education* and several chapters in edited volumes.

George Kamberelis is an assistant professor in the departments of Speech Communication and Curriculum & Instruction at the University of Illinois at Urbana-Champaign. He teaches courses and conducts research on sociocultural dimensions of children's reading and writing development, discourse and identity, and multicultural literacy pedagogy. His recent publications include articles in the *Journal of Contemporary Legal Issues, Linguistics and Education,* and *Research in the Teaching of English.*

Daniel Madigan is an associate professor of English at Bowling Green State University, where he is the director of the Center for Teaching, Learning, and Technology. He has published articles in *Language Arts,* the *Journal of Children's Literature,* and the *National Reading Conference Yearbook,* and is the co-author (with V. Rybicki) of a forthcoming book focusing on the overlapping narratives that impact on and contribute to the stories that children tell and eventually write about.

Timothy Mahoney is a doctoral student at the University of Colorado in the School of Education. His research interests include the cultural and historical foundations of literacy, critical theory, and qualitative research methods. In his dissertation, he is exploring the school- and home-based literacy practices of Mexican immigrants in a small rural community.

William McGinley is an assistant professor of English and literacy in the School of Education at the University of Colorado. His research focuses on the role of humanities and the visual arts in public education, literature education, critical literacy, and narrative theory. His recent publications include articles in *Research in the Teaching of English* and in *Statement.*

Mari M. McLean is a high school reading and English teacher in the Columbus, Ohio, public schools. She is also an adjunct assistant professor in the College of Education of Ohio State University, where she coordinates a program that prepares teachers for urban settings.

Jeff Oliver teaches 10- and 11-year-old children at University Elementary School in Boulder, Colorado. He also teaches undergraduate courses in literacy education at the University of Colorado. He is interested in how children's imaginative engagement with stories and literature provides them opportunities for understanding themselves and their worlds.

Victoria Rybicki has been an elementary school teacher in Detroit, Michigan, for 31 years. She is interested in creating a curriculum for her 9- and 10-year-old students that provides them with opportunities to experience some of the imaginative and humanizing possibilities that are associated with learning to read and write. She is presently a doctoral student in literacy education at the University of Michigan. Her dissertation is an autobiographical exploration of her own literacy teaching practices and experiences, and a forthcoming book (co-authored with Daniel Madigan) examines overlapping narratives in stories children tell.

Arlette Ingram Willis is an assistant professor at the University of Illinois, where she teaches courses in secondary reading methods, multicultural literature for grades 6–12, and trends and issues in reading research. Her research interests focus on the history of reading research in the United States from a critical perspective and on teaching and using multicultural literature for preservice teacher educators. Her publications include articles in the *Harvard Educational Review* and *Discourse.*

General Index

Index of Literary Works for Children and Young Adults